CHRISTIANITY AND THE STRANGER

South Florida-Rochester-Saint Louis
Studies on Religion and the Social Order
EDITED BY

Jacob Neusner   William Scott Green   William M. Shea

CHRISTIANITY AND THE STRANGER
edited by
Francis W. Nichols

CHRISTIANITY AND THE STRANGER

Historical Essays

edited by
Francis W. Nichols

Scholars Press
Atlanta, Georgia

CHRISTIANITY AND THE STRANGER

edited by
Francis W. Nichols

Published by Scholars Press
for the University of South Florida, University of Rochester,
and Saint Louis University

Funds for the publication of this volume were provided by

The Tyson and Naomi Midkiff Fund for Exellence
of the Department of Religious Studies at the University of South Florida

The Max Richter Foundation of Rhode Island

and

The Tisch Family Foundation of New York City

Library of Congress Cataloging in Publication Data

Christianity and the stranger / edited by Francis W. Nichols.
       p.   cm. — (South Florida-Rochester-Saint Louis studies on
religion and the social order ; v. 12)
   Includes bibliographical references and index.
   ISBN 0-7885-0125-9 (cloth : alk. paper)
   1. Strangers—Religious aspects—Christianity—History of
doctrines. 2. Strangers in the Bible. 3. Alienation (Theology)—
Case studies. I. Nichols, Francis W. II. Series.
BR115.S73C48 1995
261.8'34—dc20   95-17647
                                 CIP

Printed in the United States of America
on acid-free paper

"How gracious is my adored Master

who gives

even to the countenance of the Stranger

the look of kindness and pity."

Elizabeth Seton

Italian Journal, November 30, 1803

Contents

1

INTRODUCTION

Christianity and the Stranger

Francis W. Nichols

"I was a stranger and you welcomed me" (Mt 25:35). Thus the Son of Man addresses those at his right hand on the awesome day of judgment scene near the end of Matthew's gospel. The righteous will be identified on that day as those who had received God himself in the person of the stranger. For Christians this is a dreadful challenge, because in the long history of the Christian Church, in spite of all its noble examples of care and succor of the stranger, the outcast, the other, there have also been all too many occasions when not just individual Christians but even the institutional Church itself failed to welcome the stranger: the heretic, the other Christian, the Muslim, the Jew, the sinner.

God often comes to us in the guise of the stranger. In fact, for Christians, Jesus himself comes to the world as the ultimate stranger. "He was in the world, and the world came into being through him; yet the world did not know him" (Jn 1:10). Matthew pictures Jesus at his birth being received by strangers, wise men from the East; Luke has shepherds, the outcasts of Israelite society, welcome Jesus into the world—not the religious and social elite. In one of Luke's Easter stories Jesus joins two disciples on the road to Emmaus. "Are you the only stranger in Jerusalem who does not know the things that have taken place there in these days?" they ask (Lk 24:18). Only when the disciples see this stranger with the eyes of faith, here in a eucharistic setting, "Then their eyes were opened, and they recognized him" (Lk 24:31). For Christian faith Jesus is the incarnation of the Wholly Other, so God appears on earth as both very familiar and very strange. Hence, the theme of stranger and recognition in so many of the New Testament resurrection stories. God comes among us as in some ways familiar and in others strange.

In fact, Jesus himself is the model for welcoming strangers. He associated with the outcasts of society, not just with the high and the mighty, the pure and the good. "Why does your teacher eat with tax collectors and sinners?" (Mt 9:11). When Jesus was approached by the centurion whose servant he would heal, Jesus exclaims that "many will come from east and west and will eat with Abraham and Isaac and Jacob in the kingdom of heaven" (Mt 8:11) and not just those who, to all appearances, belong to that kingdom already. And when Jesus presents an example of someone who was neighbor to a person in need, he tells the story of the Good Samaritan (Lk 10:30-37). A stranger within the strange. Samaritans were for Jesus' contemporaries especially alien, and here we have a Samaritan stranger caring for a stranger who fell among thieves.

Christians, then, are called by God to recognize his presence in the person of the stranger. But it was not an easy lesson for the first Christians, any more than it has been easy for Christians who came later, or for Christians today. One of the most dramatic passages in the Acts of the Apostles is the story of the reception of the first gentile into the Christian community. In Acts 10 and 11 Peter was confronted with a most elaborate vision and summoned to accept something that his whole being was inclined to reject. The gentile stranger was presented to him in the form of unclean food which Peter was commanded to eat. "God has shown me that I should not call anyone profane or unclean" (Acts 10:28). Behind this story was doubtless the painful struggle within the earliest Christian community around the decision to welcome the stranger, the gentile, into the Christian faith. "I truly understand that God shows no partiality" (Acts 10:34), Peter concludes. This openness to strangers eventually came to be understood as one of the marks of authentic Christian life, however imperfectly it was sometimes observed. "Extend hospitality to strangers" (Rm 12:13), Paul instructed the Romans. And in Hebrews the author warned, "Do not neglect to show hospitality to strangers, for by doing that some have entertained angels without knowing it" (13:2). This passage, of course, refers to the story of how "the Lord appeared to Abraham by the oaks of Mamre" in the form of three strangers (Gen 18:1).

Abraham welcoming the three strangers—offering them a calf, "tender and good" (Gen 18:7), as well as curds and milk, all set before them under the tree—three strangers who turn out to be the Lord, summons up all the elaborate biblical legislation for the reception and protection of foreigners. This tradition of the Jewish scriptures, as well as the person and example of Jesus, was behind the long Christian tradition of caring for strangers. Instructions about the welcoming of strangers appeared as early as the *Didachē* (chapters 10-11). The historian Sozomen told the story of the founding of the hospital of Edessa in Syria by the hermit Ephraem, who in 370 "ordered about three hundred beds to be fitted up in the public porches" for "all those suffering from the effects of the famine—strangers and inhabitants alike."[1] Other early Christian hospitals are reported as established by bishops elsewhere in the East. The Council of Chalcedon (451) recommended them. In the West welcoming strangers took the form of hospitals intended for invalids and hospices attached to monasteries to shelter travellers. There was practically no monastery in the Middle Ages without its *xenodochium* (inn for travellers), and many had a *nosocomium* (for the treatment of acute illness) as well. The hospice of the Great St. Bernard on the St. Gothard pass between Italy, France and Switzerland with its famous dogs and their legendary whiskey kegs still existed at the beginning of the nineteenth century.[2]

Of course the mysterious, ambivalent and sometimes sacred character of the stranger is buried deep in the human psyche. We can sense this vacillation in the Latin word *hostis* which has both the meaning of foreigner, stranger, enemy, but also guest, visitor.[3]

In his famous sociological analysis of the phenomenon of the stranger, Georg Simmel pointed out the tensions in the concept. "The stranger is an element of the group itself...an element whose inherent position and membership involve both an exterior and an opposite." It involves "mutually repulsive and opposing elements...[in] a form of a joint and interacting unity."[4] That is, strangers, originally and typically

[1]Sozomen *H.E.* 3.16.

[2]G. Bonet-Maury, "Hospitality (Christian)," in *Encyclopedia of Religion and Ethics*, ed. James Hastings 6 (1913) 804-08.

[3]E. Fascher ("Fremder," in *Reallexikon für Antike und Christentum* 8 [1972] 308) maintains that this double meaning is an illusion because, he says, *hostis* originally meant guest-friend and only took on the meaning "enemy" when *hospes* took over the meaning guest-friend. The affinity remains, however, and the fact that guest can so easily also come to mean enemy needs explanation.

[4]Georg Simmel, "The Sociological Significance of the 'Stranger,'" in *Introduction to the Science of Sociology*, 3rd ed., eds. Robert E. Park and Ernest

traders, appear as different, as foreigners, as aliens, who belong to other cultures, but who are also perceived as in some ways desirable because they bring valuable things from afar. Consequently, though these strangers are recognized as strange, they are at the same time accepted into the group without losing their distance. Furthermore, strangers "experience and deal with the relation of nearness as though from a bird's-eye view," consequently, these strangers bear "all sorts of dangerous possibilities. From the beginnings of things, in revolutions of all sorts, the attacked party has claimed that there has been incitement from without, through foreign emissaries and agitators."[5] Strangers both belong and they don't; they are at once familiar and strange; they are both welcome and dangerous. From this sociological perspective, it is easy to understand the continuity between ancient suspicion of Christians, heretic hunting, Jew baiting, anti-Muslim crusades, witch hunts, and contemporary Red scares. In all these cases there is at once a sense of a certain closeness—fellow humans, Christians even if of another sort, sharers of the same biblical roots, worshippers of the same God and devotees of the same holy places, witnesses of the same spirit world, engaged in the same struggle for social justice—but also a clear difference. Consequently strangers are perceived as threats to the regnant world view, the familiar culture, the sacred home. The instinctive impulse is to reject these foreigners, but, at a more profound level, there is also an awareness that the stranger bears certain values, truths, goods that the home culture needs; a feeling that the stranger understands something about the familiar world which that world cannot or will not recognize; a sense that the stranger brings a vital message from beyond.

Not only modern sociology but also the history of religion shows how the figure of the stranger often bears mysterious weight. In many religious traditions the gods come to their devotees in the form of the stranger. Teigo Yoshida discusses the "belief [in rural Japanese tradition] that a stranger unexpectedly appearing in a village in fact may be a god in human guise."[6] Or, to take an example from the other

---

W. Burgess (Chicago: U of Chicago P, 1969) 322; the original essay by Simmel appeared in *Sociologie* (Leipzig: Duncker und Humblot, 1908) 685-91.
    [5]Ibid. 324.
    [6]"The Stranger as God: The Place of the Outsider in Japanese Folk Religion," *Ethnology* 20 (1981) 87.

end of the cultural spectrum, Homer in the *Odyssey* says, "Aye, and the gods in the guise of strangers from afar put on all manners of shapes, and visit the cities, beholding the violence and the hospitable treatment of men."[7] It is not just the Bible that pictures God approaching in alien forms. In fact the religious significance of the stranger is a universal human trait.[8] The fascination and the fear that the stranger elicit are another example of the *mysterium tremendum et fascinans* that Rudolf Otto claims belongs to the essence of the experience of the holy.[9]

These religious and anthropological insights are the remote background for this collection of historical essays. But in addition to the intrinsic interest connected with the theme of religion and its relationships with the stranger, there is also an urgent need today for religious scholars to reflect on the ways in which religious traditions have come to terms with the stranger, with the other, especially with the religiously other—and how religions have failed to do so. At one time it may have seemed possible for religious groups to live isolated from others, possible to pretend that the others did not really exist. Today, however, universal media coverage, international politics, immigration, movements of refugees, trade and travel mean that all religions exist in each others' faces to an extent hardly possible before. Furthermore, the inhabitants of many nations are becoming more and more culturally and religiously complex, above all in North America, but also in other places in the world, for example in Europe where Middle Eastern, African, and Asian groups, with their assorted religious affiliations, are now present in historically Christian countries in significant numbers, occasioning rising social and religious tensions. Finally, and above all, the Holocaust, the Nazi attempt to annihilate European Jewry, and the long Christian story of hostility toward Jews which nourished modern anti-Semitism, summon Christians to reflect on their own history and on its failures to imitate Jesus' attitude

[7]*Homer: The Odyssey*, trans. A.T. Murray (Cambridge, MA: Harvard UP, 1980) 17.485-88.

[8]See P.J. Hamilton-Grierson, "Strangers," in *Encyclopedia of Religion and Ethics* 11 (1920) 883-96; Jan de Vries, "Fremde," in *Die Religion in Geschichte und Gegenwart* 2 (1958) 1124-25; "Fremdenrecht," in *Paulys Real-Encyclopädie der classichen Altertumswissenschaft* 4 (1924) 511-16.

[9]Rudolf Otto, *The Idea of the Holy* (New York: Oxford UP, 1958), especially chapters IV and VI.

toward the stranger.

The obligation to open one's heart to the stranger is a responsibility of the individual Christian, of course, but it is also a task for the corporate Christian community as well. Imitating Jesus, Peter, Abraham, is incumbent upon the Church itself, not just on individuals. Religious societies must ask themselves how they relate to those outside, to apparent outsiders within, and even to the experience of otherness within their own hearts. Popes and bishops, Church councils and religious authorities of all kinds have this responsibility. At the Second Vatican Council (1962-65) the Catholic Church made great progress in facing the question of how it ought to relate to strangers. About other religious groups it said that "the Catholic Church rejects nothing which is true and holy in these religions" (*Nostra aetate*, no. 2).[10] It also recognized that the divisions among Christians themselves are due to "developments for which, at times, men of both sides were to blame" (*Unitatis reintegratio*, no. 3). Though the Council insisted on respect for religious freedom on the basis of Christian principles (*Dignitatis humanae*, nos. 9-15), it failed to recognize how important the contribution of non-believers, the Enlightenment in general, had been to the promulgation of those rights in modern times. Still, the Church embraced those human values which two hundred years of official teaching had rejected as untenable by Christians. In short, the Council attempted to enter into honest dialogue with strangers of all sorts, implying that they too had values which the Catholic Church could not only respect but at times even welcome into its own life. "This Council can provide no more eloquent proof of its solidarity with the entire human family with which it is bound up...than by engaging with it in conversation" (*Gaudium et spes*, no. 3).

Changes in Church policies do not happen in a vacuum, nor are they executed automatically. Changes like these new openings to the stranger require changes in corporate consciousness, in community self-understanding. The Second Vatican Council struck many Catholics and more outsiders as an amazing transformation. Indeed, many of the Council's pronouncements and consequences have been startling. But those who were aware of developments in Catholic theology during the previous quarter century or so found nothing in the content of these

[10]Council citations are from Walter M. Abbott, ed., *The Documents of Vatican II* (New York: America P, 1966).

decrees surprising. Of course the will of Church leaders to embrace these developments was striking since many ideas proclaimed by the Council were originally proposed by theologians who for many years had lived under an official cloud. But it was these very theologians who had educated bishops and stimulated the whole Church by their writings, however unwelcome in some circles; and it was these same theologians who wrote the documents eventually approved by the Second Vatican Council. Now in the years after the council theologians have the task of trying to work out the implications of these decisions. If non-believers, if other religious groups, if other Christians are worthy of respect, if they call for honest conversation, if they are deemed capable of bearing important truths for the Catholic community, what then? What then about missionary movements? What about the relationship between Catholics and all these other groups? How should Catholics understand themselves today as sojourners along with so many apparent strangers?

These are questions that systematic theology has been actively pursuing within all Christian communities in recent years. It is far from clear what the final answer will be, but the questions remain urgent for all the social and cultural reasons already mentioned, as well as for the inner life of Christianity itself. But systematic analysis is not the only theological task at hand. It is equally important for the Christian Churches, and especially so for a Church as historically self-conscious as the Catholic Church is, to examine the historical roots of the problem Christianity has had with the stranger. Christianity must come to terms with its past if it is to have the resources to face its future. It must recall the times it has closed itself to the stranger and the times it has opened up. The Church must try to understand what enabled it to grow in dialogue with the other, and how its hostility to strangers has stifled its own life. This entry into the fertile resources and bad baggage, the roads not taken and the dead ends, of Christianity's past is the task of the historical theologian. The Christian community is an historical reality, and ultimately its truths, as all truths, are fixed in history. Consequently, there is no way to understand religious truths except within their concrete historical matrices. As Karl Rahner put it, "The history of faith-consciousness is not at its end, and its future will always be brought about *in company with* reflection on what has gone before."[11]

It is especially the responsibility of the university, above all the Catholic university, to take on this task of historical self-examination. On the intellectual level—not the only level when it comes to such personally engaging questions, but a key one nonetheless—it is in the university if anywhere that the encounter between Catholic faith and the various worlds of the other must meet. John Henry Newman insisted that the university

> is pledged to admit, without fear, without prejudice, without compromise, all comers, if they come in the name of Truth; to adjust views, and experiences, and habits of mind the most independent and dissimilar; and to give full play to thought and erudition in their most original forms, and in their most intense expressions, and in their most amble circuit.[12]

Here no honest stranger should be excluded. Every shibboleth is here open to challenge. For, as Newman also observed, "It is not the way to learn to swim in troubled waters, never to have gone into them."[13] Here above all the hard questions about how Christianity has entered into conversation with, or has merely mounted attacks on, or has tried to ignore its relations with the stranger must be asked. Looking back we perhaps can see what has been missed or what we today have forgotten, what was misapprehended or vaguely perceived. That is, we can learn from the past, both from Christianity's mistakes and from its successes.

It was with these thoughts in mind that a number of historical theology faculty members at Saint Louis University decided to reflect on the theme "Christianity and the Stranger" and to present the following historical soundings into the Christian, and especially the Catholic, experience of the stranger, each working on a historical topic connected with his or her special area of competence. Thus, the proper

---

[11]"Dogmengeschichte in meiner Theologie," in *Dogmengeschichte und katholische Theologie*, eds. Werner Löser, Karl Lehmann, and Matthias Lutz-Bachman (Wurzburg: Echter, 1985) 325. See also Walter H. Principe, "The History of Theology: Fortress or Launching Pad?" in *The Catholic Theological Society of America, Proceedings of the Forty-Third Annual Convention* (1988) 19-40.

[12]*The Idea of a University Defined and Illustrated,* ed. I.T. Ker (New York: Oxford UP, 1976) 369.

[13]Ibid. 197.

task of the historical theologian, within the larger Christian responsibility to enter into dialogue with the stranger, can commence. Though this collection is just a beginning, it illustrates the manifold dimensions of the question, as well as the fruitfulness of such self-examination and *ressourcement*.

The collection of essays begins with Bernhard Asen's foundational discussion of the Old Testament understanding of stranger (*gēr*). He reviews past studies of the concept where *gēr* calls for a response of protection, as well as more recent sociological examinations which stress the notion of inclusion. After rehearsing the various ways of becoming a *gēr*, the life of the *gēr*, and the problem of the stranger in prophetic tradition, Asen shows how the Old Testament tradition of protection and reception of the *gēr* evolved into the notion of proselyte, that is, into full spiritual participation of the *gēr* in the community. This essay lays the groundwork for the subsequent studies which take up various aspects of Christianity's fidelity to and failure to realize the ideal relationship with the stranger proposed by the Jewish scriptures. Not only are Christians called to accept the stranger, but they must also recognize that they too are strangers in this world; furthermore, they must acknowledge the stranger even within their own hearts.

The next three essays examine the question of the stranger in aspects of the Syriac, Greek and Latin traditions of early Christianity. Frederick McLeod retells the ancient legend of the holy man of Edessa and how that story functioned in the spiritual life of Syriac Christianity. That is, he tells the story of the mysterious stranger, who comes to Edessa as a poor beggar, begging not just for himself but also for the poor generally, who turns out to be an *alter Christus*, Jesus himself in a hidden form. The story eventually takes on the dimensions of myth, becoming a vehicle for the cultivation of social consciousness, an agent for social change in the Syriac world of late antiquity. In an appendix McLeod provides an English translation of the Syriac text of this legend.

The other two essays analyze aspects of the Christian situation of being "strangers and foreigners on the earth" (Heb 11:13). Like Abraham in search of a homeland, they realize that their true homeland is not in this world. Rather, "in Christ Jesus" they "are no longer strangers and aliens," as Christians seem to be in this world, but they have become "citizens with the saints and also members of the household of God" (Eph 2:13, 19). If Jesus came on earth in some sense as a stranger, and if Christians in becoming united to Christ take on a new citizenship, they, at the same time and in some respects, become aliens here below. This situation sets up both an interior and an exterior strangeness in the Christian experience. Richard Valantasis analyses the ways in which the Christian ascetic becomes a stranger both within and without. That is, the ascetic becomes an interior stranger through withdrawal from the typical life style of the world, and an exterior stranger through withdrawal from normal social relationships. Valantasis tells the story of his encounter with a modern hermit who had withdrawn from the high places of Western culture into a remote Greek hermitage. Valantasis then relates this contemporary story to a famous letter on asceticism by Basil the Great (330-79), addressed to his fellow bishop Gregory. Valantasis shows how Basil's ascetical teachings attempt to create a distinctively Christian culture out of elements of the philosophical and ascetical traditions of Late Antiquity. The essay also shows that asceticism illustrates how we are all in some sense strangers and therefore called to recognize each other as friends. God comes to all as a stranger. When we welcome this stranger, we become part of another world. Accepting this strangeness means also accepting all those other strangers who follow their own paths toward the Wholly Other, a path that Christian asceticism marks out in its own way.

This Christian situation of being somehow strangers also makes them citizens of two cities, as Saint Augustine (354-430) pointed out. Kenneth Steinhauser in his essay lays out the evolution of Christianity in three stages: from Jesus' announcement of the imminent arrival of the Kingdom of God, that announcement translated by Paul into the proclamation of Jesus himself as savior, and finally the adaptation of that message by Saint Augustine to the circumstances of his day so that Christians are described as citizens of two cities in his *De ciuitate dei*. That is, Steinhauser shows how Paul adapted the apocalyptic message of Jesus to the changed situation of Paul's day, drawing out the concrete implications of salvation for the individual. Then he indicates how Augustine adapted Pauline soteriology to the situation of an established Christian community now embedded in society and history. The mysterious strangeness of Jesus and his proclamation, becomes in Paul the mystery of personal salvation through Jesus, and then in Augustine the strangeness of the city of God in the midst of this world.

The kingdom becomes the city making all spiritual travelers sojourners and all genuine Christians strangers in a foreign land.

But if Christians, as strangers themselves, ought in imitation of Jesus be welcoming to other strangers too, there is one group of people, even within the Christian community, which down through history has been treated as strangers, namely women. Joan Range's essay describes women as "familiar strangers," and she spells out the tensions in this attitude by a close analysis of Gratian's twelfth century collection of law, the *Decretum*. Though Christians, following Paul's proclamation that "there is no longer male nor female; for you are all one in Christ Jesus" (Gal 3:28), knew that all were equal citizens of the city of God, they found it difficult to institutionalize that equality in the life of the community. Inheritor of Jewish ambivalence about the place of women in society, the revival of Roman law in the Middle Ages tended to perpetuate the assumptions of those Jewish and Roman legal traditions. Gratian conceived of the Church on the model of the family, but that symbolism led to inconsistencies when he tried to fit women into this model, all the while excluding them from ministry and from any public role in Church courts or in liturgical worship. Even the gradual enforcement of laws regarding clerical celibacy distanced women from the governance of the Church (and the clergy themselves from the direct influence of women and family). Range points out, however, that women sometimes exercised considerable authority within monastic life. Furthermore, women in various ways also enjoyed equality with their husbands within the family. But in all this there remained a fundamental inconsistency. The strangeness of women to a patriarchal ecclesiastical institution remains an anomaly to this very day, an alienation incorporated into Church law with Gratian.

Among the many strangers Christianity has had to cope with over the centuries, one of the most daunting in modern times has been the critical mentality of the Enlightenment. In the face of the discovery of new worlds and distant cultures, the rise of the physical sciences and experimental methodology, the growing sophistication of historical and anthropological studies, and the phenomenon of mixed religious allegiances within European culture, Christianity generally and the Catholic Church in particular found it very difficult to come to terms with how all this should affect its own self-understanding. For a long time, even up to nearly the present day, Christianity has tended to simply reject it all. And, in the midst of all these strange developments, the interpretation of the Bible, both for Protestants and Catholics, occupied a central place. The next essay on the life and work of Richard Simon (1638-1712), the founder of historical-critical treatment of the Bible among Christian scholars, shows how one scholar tried to respond to all these challenges. His attempt to incorporate the traditions and insights of non-Christian communities, Muslim and Jewish; scholars of all hues, Protestant and Catholic; as well as his willingness to call all customary assumptions about the nature and methods of interpreting the Bible to the bar of rational discourse, all this met with almost universal rejection. He is an illustration of how Christianity might embrace the stranger in the guise of modern critical mentalities without surrendering commitment to Christian faith, a lesson which, though partly accepted today, remains a continuing agenda for the Churches.

Ultimately, welcoming the stranger always comes down to an individual case. The Valantasis essay showed how the Christian ascetic embraces the stranger within and without. In the next essay by Kenneth Parker this drama is exemplified in the story of one of the most influential but also in certain ways one of the most ambiguous figures in modern Roman Catholic history, John Henry Newman (1801-90). Parker analyzes Newman's experience of estrangement as he passed from his early evangelicalism, through a period of moderate liberalism, to a certain variety of High Churchmanship, and finally conversion to Roman Catholicism—all against the background of the social and cultural changes taking place in nineteenth century English society. In the process Newman experienced a very painful sense of estrangement from family, friends, and an ecclesiastical home, all deeply treasured. His religious journey thus exemplifies the struggle involved in every authentic welcoming of the stranger.

Perhaps the most troubling relationship with a stranger for Christianity down through its whole history has been that with Judaism. Jews were tolerated within Christian society in ways that pagans and heretics were not, precisely as resident aliens witnessing to the superiority of Christianity. Ronald Modras in his essay traces how the Catholic perception of Jews went from alien to enemy and from underling to threat. As Modras points out, the myth of a Masonic-Jewish alliance to subvert Christian culture first flourished in France but found credulous audiences throughout Europe. Jews were seen as the foremost beneficiaries of the French Revolution and the Catholic

Church as its foremost institutional victim. Conservative Catholics came to attribute secularizing efforts anywhere to Masons and Jews, even, as in Spain, where there were no Jews. Every assimilated Jew, served both as a symbol and as a potential agent of political liberalism and all it stood for—separation of Church and state, state control of education, civil marriage and divorce. Perhaps because Catholics have come to accept these enlightenment principles themselves, they no longer regard Jews either as strangers or enemies.

If Catholicism has come to some sort of reconciliation with Jews and now rather comfortably relates with main-line Protestant groups, evangelical, or conservative, or fundamentalist Christians remain something else. In his detailed survey of the popular and scholarly Catholic comment on fundamentalism since 1976, William Shea discovers various aspects of typical tribal response. As he explains, we all belong to tribes and always tend to be suspicious of outsiders. Thus, he finds among this large collection of articles, books and official Church statements about Catholics and fundamentalism all sorts of responses, from outright hostility and misrepresentation, through a certain mixed and cautious invitation to Catholics to learn from the fundamentalists, to an honest interest and willingness to take fundamentalists as worthy conversationalists and fellow Christian believers. For the most part however, the Catholic response to fundamentalism has been more defensive and uninformed than welcoming. Here too Catholics, Shea maintains, have much to learn from this stranger.

All of these essays, then, revolve around the encounter of the Christian with the stranger. They begin with the biblical experience of God as stranger, the legal tradition of Israel with respect to strangers, and Jesus as a model and preacher of openness to the stranger. Then essays take up the Syriac tradition of the wandering holy man who teaches the Christian to be open to God who comes in the form of the stranger. Next, the ascetic ideal, particularly as explained by Basil the Great, shows how Christians should welcome the stranger within and without as friend. The way Augustine works out the implications of Christian faith for a community living somehow as strangers in this present age is analyzed. The special situation of women in Christian legal tradition and their status as familiar strangers is examined. How Richard Simon tried to integrate the strange insights of early Enlightenment criticism into Christian understanding of its foundational scriptures comes next. John Henry Newman's acceptance of messages from strangers in the process of his own religious conversion is presented as another model of personal response to God's approach in the stranger. The Jews, quintessential strangers for Christians, their emancipation and acceptance as part of the Enlightenment agenda, as well as the Church's initial inability to realize the justice of this change along with the other social contributions of the Enlightenment, are discussed. Finally, the phenomenon of Christian fundamentalism and the gradual awakening of a Catholic recognition of this way of God's coming in the form of the stranger is traced out. Thus, this collection of essays attempts to study various facets, both internal and external, at once personal and corporate, of the encounter between Christianity and the stranger.

God not only visited Abraham in the form of three mysterious strangers at the oaks of Mamre, but he also came to Jacob in the night at the ford of the Jabbok. There Jacob struggled with God in the form of another mysterious stranger. As dawn broke God gave Jacob a new name, Israel, a new identity, a fruit of this struggle. "Then Jacob asked him, 'Please tell me your name,' But he said, 'Why is it that you ask my name?' And then he blessed him" (Gen 32:29). God not only comes to us in the form of the stranger, we not only have to welcome God in the stranger, but this welcoming requires struggle. That is, the stranger summons us to change, to rethink our own identities, to reorder our cherished priorities. Darrell Fasching put the implications of this story with uncommon clarity.

> When we wrestle with God we become strangers to ourselves and thus are able to identify with the experience of the stranger and welcome the stranger into our lives as the one whose very strangeness or otherness mediates the presence of the Wholly Other. Through the story of Jacob's encounter with the stranger we come to learn that wrestling with the one who is alien or different does not have to lead to the victory of the one over the other. It can lead instead to mutual respect. Not all wrestling matches are zero-sum games in which there can be only one winner. Jacob wins; he prevails, but the stranger is not defeated and blesses him before departing.[14]

Though the experience of honestly welcoming the stranger can often

[14]Darrell J. Fasching, *Narrative Theology after Auschwitz: From Alienation to Ethics* (Minneapolis: Fortress, 1992) 2.

be a difficult and painful one, ultimately, if we cling to the stranger within and without as Jacob did, ultimately we will, like him, see God face to face, and he will bless us.

2

FROM ACCEPTANCE TO INCLUSION

The Stranger (גֵּר/gēr) in Old Testament Tradition

Bernhard A. Asen

U ntil recently, the major challenge facing religion was said to be secularization. Now, however, secularization has been replaced by the challenge of how to deal with the "other," the "outsider," "difference." Jacob Neusner claims that the "single most important problem facing religion for the next hundred years...is...how to think through difference, how to account, within one's own faith and framework, for the outsider, indeed for many outsiders."[1] How do we love one another without repelling, even hating, everyone who is not "like us?" Can religion not only tolerate, but welcome difference?

In his theory on the origins of violence, René Girard argues that it is the destruction of distinction that is at the root of violence. Whereas contemporary society emphasizes equality among people, eliminating economic and social distinction, primitive religion found such distinctions essential.[2] The reason, for example, that primitive societies hated twins was because they thought every individual had to be different. Today, however, we hate others not because they are different, but because they do not act and believe exactly the same as we do.

In a recent monograph, Jonathan Z. Smith notes that this challenge of the "other," "difference," is apparent from the increase of book titles on these topics. While social historians may discuss why the ideas are

---

[1]Jacob Neusner, "Thinking about 'The Other' in Religion: It Is Necessary, but Is It Possible?" in *Lectures in Judaism in the History of Religions* (Atlanta: Scholars Press, 1990) 17.

[2]René Girard, *Violence and the Sacred* (Baltimore: Johns Hopkins UP, 1977) 51. For a discussion and critique of Girard's work and its impact on Old Testament studies see Robert North, "Violence and the Bible: The Girard Connection," *Catholic Biblical Quarterly* 47 (1985) 1-27.

so popular at this time in history, "there is nothing inherently strange in the topic—it is a subject for thought at least as old as humankind."[3] The image Smith uses to distinguish those who are "like us" from those who are not is the threshold. It is the threshold "which separates those who belong, those who are welcome, from those who are not; those who are received by a host...from those who are repelled by a host."[4] This interest in the "other," "difference," those who are welcome and those who are not, is certainly part of Old Testament thought and is found in a variety of recent discussions on tribe, land, family and property in the Old Testament.[5]

The Bible uses a number of words that refer to the "other," "outsider," "foreigner," "alien" or "stranger." This essay will attempt only to describe the life and position of the *gēr* (stranger, resident alien, immigrant) in Israel. Particular attention will be paid to the general notion that there is a trajectory of thought in the Old Testament treatment of the *gēr* which moves from protection toward preparing the way for the proselyte, namely, the person who receives full admission into the Israelite community through the rite of circumcision. I argue that, while circumcision was required of the *gēr* to participate in the Passover meal, there were no special laws governing them. Israel was to welcome the stranger simply because the Israelites themselves had been strangers in Egypt (Lev 19:33). And if strangers were not welcomed, or worse, if they were treated unjustly or violently, they might in time become dominant.

While circumcision was the physical mark of inclusion into the community, ultimately it was spiritual, not physical circumcision that was the mark of inclusion. It is not accidental that many of the references to welcoming strangers are found in the Holiness Code (Lev 17-26) where care of the stranger is seen as a sign of holiness.

The importance of holiness in welcoming the stranger is carried through into the New Testament. The Septuagint translates the Hebrew *gēr* through the Greek *prosēlytos* (προσήλυτος). In the New Testament,

---

[3]Jonathan Z. Smith, "Differential Equations: On Constructing the 'Other,'" *The Thirteenth Annual Lecture on Religion* (Arizona State, 1992) 1.

[4]Ibid. 2.

[5]See for example Walter Brueggemann, *Interpretation and Obedience* (Minneapolis: Fortress, 1991); Norman K. Gottwald, *The Tribes of Yahweh* (Maryknoll, N.Y.: Orbis, 1979); Christopher J.H. Wright, *God's People in God's Land* (Grand Rapids: Eerdmans, 1990).

however, the word for stranger is not *prosélytos*, but *paroikos* (παροικος). Furthermore, the New Testament not only addresses the question of the stranger, the "other," but also the question of holiness. This is apparent in the parable of the Good Samaritan (Lk 10:23-37) where the Samaritan is not only the stranger, but the hated stranger, who is presented as a model of what it means to be "holy." And Jesus, after the resurrection, is the stranger welcomed into the home of the Emmaus disciples where he becomes host to the world.

The Stranger in Extra-biblical Sources

Translations of the Hebrew root *gwr*, from which the word stranger (*gēr*) derives, can have a variety of meanings—"to attack," "strive," "be hostile" or, in the subordinate form of *ygr*, "to be afraid."[6] In extra-biblical sources the translations of the word for stranger range in meaning from "take possession of," to "client," "patron," "protégé," and even "prostitute."[7]

A number of sources mention *gērîm* (strangers) who sought asylum at the sanctuary of the local god and thus became "temple-clients."[8] In 2 Kings 17:24-27, the King of Assyria sent priests back to the conquered cities of Samaria because the foreigners whom he had settled there were killed by lions sent by God. The priests were sent back to teach the settlers "the law of the god of the land" (2 Kings 17:27). The implication is that these foreigners were to become clients or patrons of Yahweh, and thus protected from harm. It is this idea of *protection* that permeates past definitions and studies of the *gēr* in the Old Testament sources.

---

[6]Diether Kellermann, *gûr* (גּוּר) in *Theological Dictionary of the Old Testament*, ed. G. Johannes Botterweck, Helmer Ringgren, Heinz-Josef Fabry; trans. John T. Willis (Grand Rapids: Eerdmans, 1975) 2:439-40.

[7]Ibid. In a Phoenician text from the third or fourth century BCE, *grm* (clients) are mentioned together with *klbm* (dogs). While the meaning of *gr* here is not clear, it has been suggested that the reference is to young prostitutes because elsewhere in the text a *klb'* (prostitute) is mentioned as the son of a *gr* (client). See also John R. Spencer, "Sojourner," in *The Anchor Bible Dictionary*, ed. David Noel Freedmann (New York: Doubleday, 1992) 6:104.

[8]Kellermann 441.

The gēr: Past Studies

Until recently, when discussing the stranger (*gēr*) in the Old Testament, the chief sources cited were the writings of Alfred Bertholet, Johannes Pedersen, and Roland de Vaux. According to Bertholet, a *gēr* is someone who leaves a particular society and enters a dependent relationship in a new society.[9] Pedersen describes the *gērîm* (plural) as "partly incorporated 'sojourners' of foreign, especially of Canaanite origin."[10] And de Vaux sees a connection between the Arabic *jar* who was a refugee seeking the protection of a tribe other than his own and the Hebrew *gēr* who was "essentially a foreigner [living] more or less permanently in the midst of another community, where he is accepted and enjoys certain rights."[11] William Robertson Smith defines the *gēr* as someone from "another tribe or district who, coming to sojourn in a place where he was not strengthened by the presence of his own kin, put himself under the protection of a clan or powerful chief."[12] Samuel Rolles Driver describes the *gēr* as a technical term denoting the "protected or dependent foreigner, settled for a time in Israel."[13] The common thread apparent in these definitions is that the stranger is entitled to *protection*. Nomadic life, says de Vaux, was such that it was impossible for an individual to live independently. Consequently, if someone was ostracized from his tribe or even left voluntarily, he had to seek protection in another tribe.[14] Group solidarity was essential and was evident above all in the tribe's "duty to protect its weak and oppressed members."[15]

When someone was separated from the tribe it was important to find shelter, food, and especially water. "Anyone may have need of...help,

---

[9]Alfred Bertholet, *Die Stellung der Israeliten und der Juden zu den Fremden* (Leipzig: 1896) 328-34.

[10]Johannes Pedersen, *Israel: Its Life and Culture* (London: Oxford UP, 1940) 4:583-84.

[11]Roland de Vaux, *Ancient Israel* (New York: McGraw, 1961) 74.

[12]William Robertson Smith, *The Religion of the Semites* (London: Black, 1927) 75.

[13]Samuel Rolles Driver, *Deuteronomy*, 3rd ed. (Edinburgh: Clark, 1902) 126.

[14]De Vaux 10.

[15]Ibid. 1.

and therefore everyone must give it."[16] The stranger was to be shown hospitality for three days, and even after leaving was entitled to protection. The time this protection was in force varied from tribe to tribe. Among some tribes it was "until the salt he has eaten has left his stomach"; for others it was for three more days and within a one hundred mile radius.[17] As soon as a stranger entered a tent or even touched the tent rope, he was safe.[18]

The laws of hospitality and asylum were meant to ensure that the stranger received protection. It was not only an affront to refuse to offer hospitality (Gen 19:6-10), but also to refuse to accept it (Gen 19:2).

When Yahweh appears to Abraham at Mamre in the form of three strangers, Abraham not only offers them water, rest and bread, but cakes, choice meat, curds and milk (Gen 18:1-8). And in 2 Kings 4:8-10, the widow of Shunem, in addition to offering Elisha a meal when he passes through town, goes so far as to ask her husband to build him a room in their house, complete with bed, table, chair and lamp.

Though not always honored (1 Kings 2:28ff), the right of asylum was given to anyone who committed unpremeditated murder (Ex 21:12-14; Deut 4:41-43; 19:1-13).[19]

The gēr: Recent Studies

In more recent sociological studies protection is still seen as an important element for understanding the position of the *gēr* in Israelite society. However, in addition to protection, *inclusion* of the *gēr* into the community to share its privileges also is seen as important.

In his discussion of the extended Israelite family (*bayit/bêt-'āb* [בַּיִת/אָב/בֵּית]), Norman Gottwald includes *gērîm* (גֵּרִים "resident aliens"). While no biblical statistics are available, Gottwald conjectures that a thriving *bêt-'āb* could include from fifty to one hundred persons.[20] The

---

[16]Ibid. 4.
[17]Ibid. 10.
[18]Smith 76.
[19]See also de Vaux, 160-63.
[20]Norman K. Gottwald 285.

story of Micah (Judg 17-18) is offered as an example of how a *bêt-'āb* may have looked. Micah's household, in addition to his widowed mother and at least two sons, included the Levite, Jonathan, grandson of Moses (18:30), who had been a *gēr* in Bethlehem. Jonathan became Micah's priest "in the house (*bêt*) of Micah" (17:12). According to Gottwald, since these members of Micah's household are mentioned only "in connection with their relevance to the plot, Micah's household doubtless had many additional members unnoted in the story."[21]

In the opinion of Christopher Wright, the place of "resident aliens" (*gērîm*) in the Old Testament is ambiguous. Though they were not land owners, the *gērîm* did experience some inclusion within the community.[22] They could, for example, participate in major festivals (Deut 16:11,14), and were present at covenant renewal ceremonies or readings of the law (Josh 8:33; Deut 29:11; 31:12). Though Ex 12:43-48 appears to distinguish between the "sojourner" (*tôšāb* [תּוֹשָׁב]), "hired servant" (*śākîr* [שָׂכִיר]) and "stranger" (*gēr*), it "seems incorrect," says Wright,

> to differentiate the "stranger" (*gēr*) from the "alien" (*tôšāb*) and the "hired laborer" (*śākîr*) in terms either of social status or of essential function. Rather, the most acceptable view is that "stranger" was the general term, within which "alien" and "hired laborer" were subdivisions according to respective occupations and means of livelihood.[23]

Anthony Spina connects the meaning of *gēr* with the origins of the *'apiru*. From the state's perspective the *'apiru* was an "outlaw." But a *'apiru* could also be a "fugitive," if "for any reason he had been driven out of his original social setting."[24] Both *gēr* and *'apiru*, claims Spina, "refer to people away from their original homes. Both have to do with situations of social unrest, conflict or instability. And both have to do with the status of 'outlaws, fugitives and immigrants.'"[25]

Spina also sees an analogy between the Hebrew *gērîm* and American history which enacted laws to protect aliens and minorities who were

[21]Ibid. 291.
[22]Wright 101.
[23]Ibid. 101-02.
[24]Frank A. Spina, "Israelites as *gērîm*, 'Sojourners' in Social and Historical Context," in *The Word of the Lord Shall Go Forth*, ed. Carol L. Meyers and M. O'Conner (Winona Lake, IN: Eisenbrauns, 1983) 331.
[25]Ibid. 323.

often subjected to discrimination.[26] Spina prefers to translate *gēr* as "immigrant" because it contains the "nuances inherent in 'resident alien' and 'sojourner,'" and also because it "calls attention to the original circumstances of social conflict which are inevitably responsible for large-scale withdrawal of people."[27]

Using the work of Spina as a departure point, Walter Brueggemann concludes that those who became the Old Testament "people of God" were among those whom the empire had declared "stranger," "outsiders," a "threat."[28]

For Brueggemann, the Israelites who were considered "outlaws" and "strangers" are given a new status because God hears their cry and gives them a "special identity, status, vocation."[29] This new status of strangers means that they become covenant partners with God and each other. "Outsiders" become "insiders," "chosen" people. Until then, they were only Hebrews (*'apiru*), "socially marginalized masses without status or identity. Now they are given a new social possibility."[30]

This community of "outsiders" become "insiders" now endorses "a different ethic." In the covenant relationship, Israel adopts a social practice that the empire considers "subversive, treasonable, and foolish"[31] because it "unsettles" the systems of power to which people become accustomed.[32]

Spina's preference for translating *gēr* as "immigrant" is instructive when one considers the social factors which contributed to someone needing protection and seeking inclusion into a new community.

Reasons for Becoming a gēr

The biblical sources provide the following reasons for becoming a *gēr*:

1. *Famine*. The first and major reason appears to have been famine. Abram went down to Egypt "to reside there as an alien [*lāgûr* (לָגוּר)]

---

[26]Ibid.
[27]Ibid.
[28]Ibid.
[29]Brueggemann 293.
[30]Ibid. 297.
[31]Ibid. 298.
[32]Ibid. 299, 304.

for the famine was severe in the land" (Gen 12:10). Joseph's brothers come before the Pharaoh of Egypt and say they have "come to reside as aliens [*lāgûr*] in the land...because the famine is severe in the land of Canaan" (Gen 47:4). In Gen 26:1 we are told that "besides the former famine...in the days of Abraham," there was another famine. This famine prompted Isaac to go to Abimelech, king of the Philistines. Yahweh then appears to Isaac and says, "Do not go down to Egypt.... Reside in this land as an alien [*gûr*], and I will be with you and will bless you." (Gen 26:2-3) Elijah resides [*mitgôrēr* (מִתְגּוֹרֵר)] with the widow of Zerephath because of a famine (1 Kings 17:20), and Elisha instructs the Shunemite woman whose son he had restored to life to "reside [*gûrî* (גוּרִי)] wherever you can; for the Lord has called for a famine" (2 Kings 8:1). And in Ruth 1:1, Elimelech moves his entire family and resides [*lāgûr*] in Moab because of a famine.

2. *Military conquest.* A second reason for becoming a *gēr* was military conquest. The people of Beeroth fled to Gittaim and "are there as resident aliens [*gārîm* (גָּרִים)] to this day" (2 Sam 4:3). Their flight was probably due to a battle between the Canaanite inhabitants of Beeroth and the invading Benjaminites.[33] And Isa 16:4 exhorts the people to allow the outcasts of Moab to settle [*yāgûrû* (יָגוּרוּ)] and find refuge in Judah. Jeremiah combines the factors of famine and military conquest when he warns the people that if they try to escape the Babylonian invasion and become residents in Egypt they will encounter the very famine and death they want to escape (Jer 42:15,17,22; 43:2,5; 44:8-9,12,14,28).

3. *Other factors.* In addition to famine and war, other factors that could result in one's becoming a *gēr* included the desire to preserve the "nomadic ideal," as the Rechabites did (Jer 37:7), or to avoid punishment for a crime, as Moses did when he killed an Egyptian (Ex 2:12) and became a *gēr*. While in Midian, Moses married Zipporah and she bore a son who was named Gershom; for Moses said, "I have been an alien [*gēr*] residing in a foreign land" (Ex 2:22).

[33]Kellermann 443.

The Life of the gēr

The way of life of the *gēr* is known primarily from three major Old Testament traditions: (1) the Book of the Covenant (Ex 20, 22-23, 33); (2) the Deuteronomic law (Deut 12-26) and (3) the Holiness Code (Lev 17-26).

In the past, the tendency has been to distinguish what is said about the stranger in Israel's "legal" texts from what is said in the ritual or "holiness" texts. According to de Vaux, the majority of the "holiness" texts were written rather late in Israel's history (shortly before the Judean exile in 586) when there was a large influx of the *gērîm* into Judah, many of them from the former Northern Kingdom.[34]

However, as H. Eberhard von Waldow has pointed out, "the existence of a particular ordinance within one of these codes does not establish anything with regard to the actual age of the ordinance."[35] The use of the apodictic formula "you shall not" (second person singular), while not exclusively confined to Israel, is one of the oldest law forms in the Old Testament.[36] This formula is found, for example, in the Book of the Covenant: "You shall not wrong or oppress a resident alien [*gēr*], for you were aliens [*gērîm*] in the land of Egypt" (Ex 22:21), and in the Deteronomic law: "You shall not deprive a resident alien [*gēr*] or an orphan of justice.... Remember that you were a slave in Egypt." (Deut 24:17) The eating of the Passover meal did require that the *gēr* be circumcised, but if circumcised he could participate in the feast like a native Israelite (Ex 12:44-49; Num 9:14).

The Holiness Code (Lev 17-26) confirms this status of the *gēr* in Israelite society:

> When an alien [*gēr*] resides with you in your land, you shall not oppress the alien [*gēr*]. The alien [*gēr*] who resides with you shall be to you as the citizen among you; you shall love the alien [*gēr*] as yourself, for you were aliens [*gērîm*] in the land of Egypt. I am the Lord your God. (Lev 19:33-34)

The code requires the same purification for an Israelite and a *gēr*

---

[34]De Vaux 75.

[35]H. Eberhard von Waldow, "Social Responsibility and Social Structure in Early Israel," *Catholic Biblical Quarterly* 32 (1970) 182.

[36]Ibid. 183.

guilty of eating "what dies of itself" (Lev 17:15), and the same injunction against idolatry is directed against both (Lev 20:20). Furthermore, important cultic acts could be performed by Israelites and strangers (Lev 16:29, fasting; 17:8-16, sacrifice; 22:18, offerings).

However, the Holiness Code is not thoroughly consistent in its instructions concerning the *gērîm*. The code forbids buying *Israelite* slaves, and suggests that they be bought instead from among the *gērîm* (Lev 25:45). And while Lev 17:15 requires the same purification for eating unslaughtered animals, Deut 14:21 states that Israelites should leave such animals to the *gērîm*.

While the Holiness Code comes from a later period of Israel's history, it no doubt contains material from much earlier times. The inclination to separate what is stipulated in the Holiness Code from what is said in the Book of the Covenant is unnecessary. According to Brevard Childs,

> Not only are the ritual and purity laws treated in the Pentateuchal sections of the Old Testament, but extended interpretations are offered within the other parts of the canon which are not merely to be harmonized or arranged in a developmental sequence, but rather used for theological reflection from the perspective of the whole corpus of scripture.
>
> One of the striking features of the ritual and purity laws, which they share with the Decalogue, is that the underlying motivation for a particular law is seldom offered. Rather, the emphasis falls heavily upon the purpose toward which the law points. Israel, as a covenant people, is separated unto God and her life is to reflect the nature of God which is above all holiness (Lev 19:1ff).[37]

The connection between cultic and social laws present in the Book of the Covenant is further elaborated in Deuteronomic law which shows great concern for the Levite, stranger (*gēr*), orphans and widows (Deut 14:28-29). Because these ritual laws were seen as part of covenant law "the Deuteronomic writer could move freely between laws directly affecting God and those chiefly social in nature as portions of the whole (27:9-29)."[38]

Taken all together, the major sources give us the following portrait of the life of the *gēr*:

[37]Brevard Childs, *Old Testament Theology in a Canonical Context* (Philadelphia: Fortress, 1985) 86-87.
[38]Ibid. 88.

1) They were counted among the poor of the land (*personae miserabiles*)[39] who were to receive the "gleanings" of the harvest (Lev 19:9). Vineyards were not to be stripped bare, and fallen grapes were to be left where they fell for the poor and the alien to gather (Lev 19:10).

2) Apparently strangers supported themselves as hired hands because they, along with the rest of the family, were required to remember the Sabbath day (Ex 20:10). And, according to Deut 24:14, wages were not to be withheld from poor and needy laborers whether Israelites or aliens (*gērîm*).

3) The resident aliens, together with the Levites, orphans and widows, were to receive the produce tithe every third year (Deut 14:28-29).

4) The *gērîm* were subject to the same law of purification as the Israelites, if they ate unslaughtered animals (Lev 17:15).

5) While slaves could not be bought from among Israelites, they could be purchased from among the *gērîm* (Lev 25:44-46).

6) Because its members were dispersed among the tribes, the Levites were counted among the widows, orphans and *gērîm* (Deut 12:12,19; 14:27,29; 16:11,14; 26:11). Because they had no inheritance they, together with orphans and widows, were to receive the produce tithe every three years. Though the Levites are never called strangers, they are ranked with widows and orphans because they are landless and therefore qualify "for specific assistance from the larger population."[40]

7) The eating of the Passover meal required that the *gēr* be circumcised, but if circumcised he could participate in the feast like a native Israelite (Ex 12:44-49; Num 9:14).

While the life of the *gēr* was lived primarily on the margins of Israelite society, it appears that strangers could also prosper. Lev 25:47, for example, provides for the redemption of an Israelite who has fallen into "difficulty" with a prosperous *gēr*.

Perhaps the most powerful and instructive text in this regard is Deut 28:43. In the warnings against disobedience of the covenant the author states that one of the consequences of disobedience will be: "Aliens residing among you shall ascend above you higher and higher, while

---

[39]Waldow 182.

[40]John R. Spencer, "Sojourner," in *The Anchor Bible Dictionary*, ed. David Noel Freedmann (New York: Doubleday, 1992) 6:104.

you shall descend lower and lower. They shall lend to you but you shall not lend to them; they shall be the head and you shall be the tail." (See also 28:13; Isa 9:14.) The implication is clear: If strangers are not cared for, if the laws concerning them are disobeyed, they will, in time, become dominant. And it is noteworthy that just prior to this verse the author of Deuteronomy refers to the Assyrian invasion of the Northern Kingdom (721 BCE) when many Israelites were taken into captivity (Deut 28:36). And one of the reasons for that captivity, according to the prophets, was trampling on the marginalized—the widow, the orphan, and the resident alien.

Though it appears possible for the *gērîm* to prosper, generally speaking they were counted among and poor and needy. With the exception of circumcision in order to eat the Passover meal, it does not appear that they were subject to any special laws. The *gēr* and the freeborn person were to be judged according to the same laws: "Judge rightly between one person and another, whether citizen or resident alien (*gēr*). You must not be partial in judging: hear out the small and the great alike; you shall not be intimidated by anyone, for the judgment is God's." (Deut 1:16-17)

The *gērîm* were not those who had been integrated into God's people through acceptance of Israelite law and faith. Rather, strangers in Israel had precisely the same position as the Israelites in Egypt. Dealing with the stranger on the basis of justice and love had no pre-conditions.

The gēr *in the Prophets*

Given their strong interest in the marginalized, weak and oppressed, it is striking that the prophets do not show more interest in the stranger. The word *gēr* does not appear in Amos, Hosea or Micah, and is used only once in First Isaiah (14:1).

There is the interesting twist on the verb *gûr* which is used in connection with the warning against migration to Egypt.[41] However, specific references to the stranger in the prophets occur in conjunction with the widow, orphan, poor and oppressed (Jer 7:6; 22:3; Ezek 22:7,29; Zech 7:10; Mal 3:5). These references show deuteronomic

---

[41]See above p. 8.

influence, even though the exact deuteronomic formula (stranger, widow, orphan) is not always used.[42] The same formula also appears in two post-exilic texts from the Psalter (Ps 94:6; 146:9) that are independent of the deuteronomic formula.[43]

When we attempt to address the reason for the prophets' apparent lack of interest in the stranger we need to keep in mind that the majority of the specific laws regarding the *gērîm* came from a time after Amos, Hosea and Micah, and after the fall of the Northern Kingdom and the destruction of Samaria when there was an influx of strangers into Judah. It has been conjectured that the laws in Deut 23:2-8 forbidding Ammonites and Moabites from admittance into the "assembly of Yahweh," and making it easer for Edomites to enter, was meant to make full citizenship of the *gērîm* from the Northern Kingdom easier.[44]

On the one hand, the reason the eighth century prophets do not show more explicit interest in strangers may be because their presence was not yet an issue. The prophets Amos and Micah, for example, prophesied during the halcyon days of the Northern Kingdom, before the fall of the North and the southern migration of the *gērîm*. But on the other hand, it may be because both Amos and Micah were concerned with everyone, anyone who was exploited and treated unjustly, and not because there were no specific laws, or because they were unaware of any.[45]

For Amos, election was not protection against God's judgment. In fact, it was precisely because of Israel's chosenness that more was required of Israel than of the foreign nations. The oracles in Amos 1-2 castigate the foreign nations for crimes against humanity. However, in the oracles against Judah (2:4-5) and Israel (2:6-8), Amos centers not on war crimes, but on crimes against sisters and brothers in community—rejecting the Torah (2:4), selling the righteous for silver, the needy for a pair of shoes, trampling the poor into the dust of the

---

[42]Thomas Krapf, "Traditionsgeschichtliches zum Deuteronomischen Fremdling-Waise-Witwe-Gebot," *Vetus Testamentum* 34 (1984) 89.

[43]Ibid.

[44]A. van den Born, "Stranger," in *Encyclopedic Dictionary of the Bible,* 2nd ed., ed. Louis Hartman (New York: McGraw, 1963) 2334.

[45]See Amos 5:11-12 and the discussion of these verses in Shalom Paul, *Amos* (Minneapolis: Fortress, 1991) 171-75; also the discussion of *dal* [דָּל] in *Theological Dictionary of the Old Testament* 3:208-30, esp. 222-23.

earth, and so on (2:6-8).

Recalling the Exodus when God brought Israel "up out of the land of Egypt" (3:1), Amos bellows, "You only have I known of all the families of the earth; therefore I will punish you for all your iniquities" (3:2). The key word here is *therefore* (*kî* [יכ]). Amos is not calling Israel's election into question. But Yahweh's saving action is only one side of election, the other side is Israel's responsibility in that election.[46]

But there is still more. In Amos 9:7, the prophet disputes the notion that Israel has a special place in God's heart because of the Exodus. "Are you not like the Ethiopians to me, O people of Israel?... Did I not bring Israel up from Egypt, and the Philistines from Capthor and the Arameans from Kir?" (9:7) These nations also experienced exodus.

> The deliverance from Egypt, historically speaking, affords no special assurance or preference for Israel, for it is not unique. It is merely another example of the Lord's universalistic impartiality. The fact is not debated.... What is objected to are the theological conclusions that Israel has repeatedly, and incorrectly, drawn from this event. Election is not predicated upon exodus.[47]

Because Israel did not remember its stranger status in Egypt, it would fall.

The fall of the Northern Kingdom came in 722 and not only had serious consequences in the North, but in the South as well. Archaeological data show that in the late eighth century, "Jerusalem grew to three or four times its previous size."[48]

In his discussion of the social and economic conditions during Micah's time, Delbert Hillers refers to various features that comprised "movements of revitalization"[49] and cites Micah 4:6,7a:

> In that day, says the Lord, I will assemble the lame; and gather those who have been driven away, and those whom I have afflicted. The lame I will make the remnant, and those who were cast off, a strong nation.

[46]See Hans Walter Wolff, *Joel and Amos* (Philadelphia: Fortress, 1977) 104-06.

[47]Paul 283.

[48]Delbert R. Hillers, *Micah* (Philadelphia: Fortress, 1984) 5.

[49]Ibid. 6.

Because the language of these verses is poetic it is difficult to be precise about the time they were written. While many commentators assign these verses to exilic or post-exilic times because of the reference to the "remnant," surely the fall of the Northern Kingdom would have given "sufficient cause to speak of the people as 'limping' and 'driven away.'"[50] In any event, the message of these verses involves the expectation that "underdogs will come out on top"[51] and is reminiscent of Deut 28:43 where it is stated specifically that one result of covenant disobedience will be the ascent of the *gērîm*.

When Jeremiah speaks of the oppression of the *gēr* in his Temple Sermon, he does so in conjunction with the widow and the orphan (7:6) at a time when people were trusting in the holiness of the temple rather than living holy lives of advocacy for the oppressed.

Because Yahweh dwelt in the temple the people believed all would be well. But for Jeremiah even Yahweh becomes a *gēr* because of the people's corruption.

O hope of Israel, its savior in time of trouble, why should you be like a stranger [*gēr*] in the land, like a traveler turning aside for the night (14:8).

A similar note is sounded in 9:2 where Yahweh laments the slain, and wants to find a traveler's lodging place in the desert rather than reside with the people. The desert (wilderness) is generally at the "edge of Yahweh's touch," and thus Yahweh prefers to be out of touch rather than dwell in Jerusalem where the people move from "evil to evil" and do not know Yahweh (9:3).[52] Has the land become so identified with Sheol that even Yahweh has become a stranger? (14:2, 18:15:7)[53]

Jeremiah not only challenges the misconception that Jerusalem and the temple are Yahweh's dwelling place, regardless of the nation's conduct, but also that circumcision, the mark of covenant membership, was a guarantee of Yahweh's favor. Only if the people return to Yahweh, remove their abominations and live justly will blessings come (4:1-2). "Circumcise yourselves to Yahweh, remove the foreskin of your hearts...or else my wrath will go forth like fire...because of your

---

[50]Ibid. 55.
[51]Ibid.
[52]William L. Holladay, *Jeremiah 1* (Philadelphia: Fortress, 1986) 299.
[53]Ibid. 433.

evil doings" (4:4).

More important than physical circumcision is circumcision of the heart. Whether Jer 4:4 is translated be circumcised "by Yahweh" or "for Yahweh" it must "make a genuine difference in the life of the people."[54] This same idea is found in Deut 10:16 ("Circumcise the foreskin of your heart.") in the context of God's lordship over everyone. This exhortation is followed in Deut 10:17 by the statement that God "executes justice for the orphan and the widow, and who loves the strangers (*gērîm*), providing them food and clothing."

Furthermore, in 9:25 Jeremiah reminds the people that they are not the only ones who practice physical circumcision. Evidence shows that the Egyptians and Edomites also circumcised.[55] But even non-Israelites, though they circumcise, are not members of the covenant community.

Ezekiel also shows concern for strangers (14:7), and chastises the people for extorting and robbing them (22:7,29). Looking forward to the return of God's glory to the temple (ch. 43), Ezekiel provides ordinances, and among them is one that excludes foreigners (*nēkār* [נֵכָר], not *gērîm*) who were not only uncircumcised in the flesh, but also in the heart (44:7,9). And in the new allotment of the land strangers (*gērîm*) are to receive their portion (47:22,23). Walther Eichrodt calls the admission of strangers to the right to hold property "a great and daring step towards putting the alien on the same footing as the native born."[56] The status of the *gērîm* "gradually kept approaching that of proselytes."[57]

Proselytes

Past treatments of the stranger's place in Israel's life and faith generally end with some variation of Eichrodt's comment above.[58] The Septuagint does translate the Hebrew *gēr* by the Greek

[54]Ibid. 130.

[55]Ibid. 319-20.

[56]Walther Eichrodt, *Ezekiel* (Philadelphia: Westminster, 1970) 592.

[57]Ibid.

[58]E.g., de Vaux says that the gradual assimilation of the *gērîm* into Israel "paved the way for the status of proselytes," p. 75. See also Pederson 603.

prosēlytos, which denotes a Gentile who becomes a full Jew through the rite of circumcision.[59] However, this translation has led to misunderstanding because strangers were not those who had been assimilated into God's people through acceptance of Israelite law and faith, as the later Greek meaning of "proselyte" could suggest. Rather, as we have seen, strangers in Israel had precisely the same position as the Israelites in Egypt (Lev 19:34), and even physical circumcision was no guarantee that one was a member of the covenant community. Furthermore, the Septuagint word for stranger is not *gēr,* but *xenos* (ξένος), and "*xenos* is not the chief equivalent of any of the Hebrew terms" for stranger, foreigner, outsider, and the like.[60]

In a brief reflection on the meaning of the stranger, Olaf Schumann reminds us that the responsibility of God's people to conduct themselves with justice and love was not limited to one's own people. "Everyone, including and especially the stranger, was to be treated in the same way."[61] While a distinction was made between the fellow citizen (*rē'a* [רֵעַ]) and the stranger (*gēr*), there was no distinction concerning how both were to be treated.

> Dealing with the stranger on the basis of justice and love had no pre-conditions. There was no requirement for "integration," "assimilation" or any other form of accommodation. The stranger was to be dealt with justly and in love simply by virtue of being a stranger.[62]

The history of the change in meaning between *gēr* and *prosēlytos* in the Septuagint is unclear. However, the change does reflect the population changes that occurred after the fall of the Northern Kingdom, and the later Babylonian dispersion when the Jewish community became more concerned with gaining converts.[63]

One of the most instructive texts in this regard is Isa 56:1-8 where not only foreigners but eunuchs will be joined to Yahweh (56:3-4). Deut 23:1 had excluded eunuchs from the community. Here, however,

[59]See *prosēlytos* in *Theological Dictionary of the New Testament,* ed. Gerhard Kittel, Gerhard Friedrich (Grand Rapids: Eerdmans, 1968) 6:730.

[60]See *xenos* in *Theological Dictionary of the New Testament* 5:8.

[61]Olaf Schumann, "Reflexionen über die Bedeutung des 'Fremden,'" *Zeitschrift für Mission* 13 (1987) 164.

[62]Ibid. 165.

[63]Marvin H. Pope, "Proselyte," in *The Interpreter's Dictionary of the Bible* (New York: Abingdon, 1962) 3:924ff.

they are provided "a monument and a name better than sons and daughters" and "an everlasting name that shall not be cut off" (Isa 56:5). Not circumcision, but holding fast to the covenant and keeping the sabbath are the criteria for belonging to Yahweh's community. In short, holiness of life is the sign of covenant inclusion.

The Stranger in the New Testament

Though the Septuagint does translate *gēr* with *prosēlytos*, the New Testament uses the word *prosēlytos* only four times (Mt 23:15; Acts 2:11; 6:5; 13:43), and its usage is not helpful for understanding how the concept of the stranger is treated in the Christian scriptures.

A New Testament word closer in meaning to the Hebrew *gēr* is *paroikos*. While it is not our purpose to explore the concept of the stranger in the New Testament in any depth, it is noteworthy that in many of the New Testament references where *paroikos* is used there is either a quotation from, or an allusion to, some event from Israel's past. In Acts 7:6, Stephen says, "And God spoke in these terms, that his descendants would be resident aliens [*paroikon*] in a country belonging to others, who would enslave them and mistreat them during four hundred years" (see Gen 15:13). And in Acts 7:29, Stephen refers to Moses' flight to Midian where he became a resident alien (*paroikos*; see Ex 2:15). Paul mentions the sojourn (*paroikia*) of Israel in Egypt (Acts 13:16; see Ex 6:1,6).

Heb 11:9 states that by faith, Abraham "stayed for a time (*parōkēsen* [παρῴκησεν]) in the land he had been promised, as in a foreign land, living in tents, as did Isaac and Jacob." The reason Abraham sojourned was because he looked toward the "city that has foundations, whose architect and builder is God" (Heb 11:10). Abraham, Isaac and Jacob all "died in faith without having received the promises, but from a distance they saw and greeted them. They confessed that they were strangers [*xenoi*] and foreigners [*parepidēmoi* (παρεπίδημοι)] on earth" (Heb 11:13).

And, according to Paul, what is true of ancient Israel is true also of the Church, the new Israel: "So then you are no longer strangers [*xenoi*] and aliens [*paroikoi*], but you are citizens with the saints and members of the household of God" (Eph 2:19; see also Heb 13:14). But on the other hand, 1 Peter 2:11 urges the community to live as "aliens [*paroikous*] and exiles" and "to abstain from the desires of the flesh that wage war against the soul."

Thus, on the one hand, we are all citizens and, on the other, we are all strangers. The New Testament lives in this tension between being a part of and apart from the world.[64] But we are also strangers within the world who in our strangeness are called to transform the world through love. To be a stranger means to live a life of love and to seek to reconcile the world through that love which has its origins in the God who loves and welcomes strangers.

The New Testament word for this love is *agapē* (ἀγάπη), and *agapē* always implies *philoxenia* (φιλοξενία, love of the foreigner). In contrast to other ideas during Jesus' time, the neighbor was understood in the broadest terms possible. There were no limitations on who the "neighbor" was. This is made clear especially in the parable of the Good Samaritan (Lk 10:23-37) where not only the question of the stranger, the "other," but also the question of holiness is addressed in an exemplary way.

In this parable, which Olaf Schumann calls "the pinnacle of the holiness code," the love command is not fulfilled by those who had a special responsibility to do so—the priests and Levites—who were themselves ranked among the *gērîm* in the Jewish scriptures.[65] Rather, the divine command is fulfilled by one who not only belonged to the "nations" (*gôyim* [גּוֹיִם]), but who was accused of knowingly rejecting the laws of holiness. It was the Samaritan, the "other," who helped the beaten man.[66]

The Samaritan's actions make clear that not only the related neighbor and stranger, but also those who are cultically or societally excluded stand within the horizon of the love commandment. This command, not circumcision, is the test of holiness.[67] Samaritans also practiced the ancient rite of circumcision. But here the one who is considered "unclean" is the one who shows himself to belong to God

---

[64]For a discussion of Jesus and the tension of being a stranger in early Christianity see Peter Lampe, "'Fremdsein' als urchristlicher Lebensaspekt," *Reformatio* 34 (1985) 58-62.

[65]Schumann 165.

[66]The word *allogenēs* (ἀλλογενής) and related forms means "alien" or "foreign." It is used in the NT only for the Samaritan who returns to thank Jesus in Lk 17:18.

[67]Schumann 166.

through his deeds. It is now the Samaritan, as it were, who teaches the "law of the god of the land." The departure point of this parable is not some theoretical question: "Who is my neighbor?"

> Faith is not a philosophy or a worldview, but an action in which the believer shows an orientation toward God's will and is thus "holy," i.e., belongs to God.[68]

The image of the threshold once again comes to mind. Not only does the threshold separate those who are welcome from those who are not, it also leads into the place of the holy (see 2 Kings 12:9; Ps 84:10). Where true holiness is lived out, the barriers between self, neighbor and the stranger are broken down. In Luke's Emmaus road narrative, the resurrected Jesus is asked: "Are you the only stranger [*paroikos*] in Jerusalem who does not know the things that have taken place in these days?" (24:18). It is this stranger who is persuaded by the Emmaus disciples to cross their threshold and stay with them. And at table Jesus, the stranger, becomes host, and "then their eyes were opened" (Lk 24:31).

---

[68]Ibid.

3

THE STRANGER AS A SOURCE OF SOCIAL CHANGE

IN EARLY SYRIAC CHRISTIANITY

Frederick G. McLeod, S.J.

"Stranger" is a multifaceted term whose meaning alters like the colored patterns in a kaleidoscope rotated to new settings. In one context, stranger signifies someone who is quaint, peculiar, queer; in another, an unfamiliar person—an outsider, alien or foreigner; and in still another, one feared as a source of danger. As these different shades of meaning reveal, stranger is a word that must be examined in its own proper context. The following study explores an interesting facet of the term "stranger," emerging from a pious Syriac legend about the holy man of Edessa. Though a stranger, he became, through the story of his life, a source of social change in the Syriac Christian world.

I will first recount the legend, then seek the primary purpose for its composition through an examination of its literary structure. This process will entail a twofold consideration: (1) how the story of the holy man of Edessa reflects the economic, social and religious milieux of the times, and (2) how his legend became a religious myth which changes the way a person looks at and cares for destitute strangers. This latter insight is one that modern hagiographers, influenced by political and liberation theologies, now seek in the lives of the saints. That is, they ask how saints' stories disclose social needs and religious challenges.

In other words, the life of the holy man of Edessa will be examined not merely to see the specific ways he achieved sanctity but also for the wider insight into the background of his time which his life provides, as well as the role this story played in shaping religious attitudes and social values among Syriac-speaking Christians of the late fifth century. I focus on two questions: What were the cultural attitudes towards the holy person and "stranger" in late Syriac antiquity? and

What changes did the legend of the holy man of Edessa attempt to accomplish in these views? I will then discuss how the outlook promoted by the legend concerning the "stranger" has been inspired by Christian scriptures, and I will conclude this study with a consideration of how the concept of "stranger" is linked to that of the holy and how, again, this kind of story can evoke social change.

The Legend of the Holy Man of Edessa

The Syriac-speaking Christians of late antiquity propose a very peculiar type saint whose ascetical life style may strike many today as unusual, to say the least. This type appears in concrete form in the Syriac version of the legend of the holy man of Edessa.[1] The story narrates the life of a man born in Rome to exceedingly rich and powerful parents. He was their only child, a divine favor bestowed in response to prayer. As he grew older, he devoted himself to a search for truth, holding all else in disdain. One day his parents arranged for his wedding and hosted a festive celebration to which the whole city was invited. But on his wedding day, the holy man left his bride and secretly set sail for Seleucia in Syria. From there, he journeyed overland to Edessa,[2] where he remained until his death, fasting and begging for alms at the church door. He generously bestowed on others whatever was not required for his own most basic needs.

At night, when all others in the church courtyard were asleep, he used to pray with his arms extended in the form of a cross. One night a church sacristan noticed him and inquired where he was from. After persistent questioning, the holy man revealed that he was the only son of a noble Roman family. When he later fell seriously ill, the sacristan

---

[1] Since the legend in its entirety is only found in Arthur Amiaud's *La Légende syriaque de saint Alexis, l'homme de Dieu*, Bibliothèque de l'École des Hautes Etudes 79 (Paris: Vieweg, 1889), I have included my own English translation, based on the critical Syriac text that Amiaud has established, in an Appendix at the end of this paper. See also the article on "Alexius," in *The Catholic Encyclopedia* (1907) 1:307-08. This entry has not been included in the *New Catholic Encyclopedia* (1967). I am also indebted to Han J.W. Drijvers, "Hellenistic and Oriental Origins," in *The Byzantine Saint*, ed. Sergei Hackel, Studies Supplementary to *Sobornost* 5 (London: Fellowship of St Alban and St Sergius, 1981) 26-27.

[2] Now the modern city of Urfa in Turkey.

was so concerned that he brought the holy man to a hospital for care. One day when the sacristan was unable to visit, the holy man died and was buried in a cemetery for strangers. When the sacristan later learned what had happened, he hastened to Bishop Rabbula (d.435) and told him the story of the holy man. Then they both hurried to the cemetery, where the bishop immediately ordered his grave opened. They thus discovered that the body of the holy man had disappeared. Only his rags remained. Deeply moved by this experience, Bishop Rabbula put aside his building activities and devoted himself wholeheartedly to the care of poor strangers, who were neglected in Edessa and in other cities of Syria.

Recent research traces this legend back to a Syriac manuscript of the late fifth century.[3] In time, this story became part of the hagiographical traditions of Byzantium, Rome, and medieval Christianity. As the text was passed on, substantial changes were introduced, however. The holy man was later called Alexius and was said to have died in 417 as a stranger, not in Edessa, but as a beggar under the stairway of his parents' palace in Rome. According to these much later versions, a document was found on his body, revealing his true identity. When this fact became widely known, the story ran, he was recognized and venerated as a saint. His father's house was later converted into a Church dedicated to the memory and patronage of St. Alexius.

How much factual history is actually contained in this Syriac/Byzantine/Roman legend is impossible to determine. Perhaps all we can reasonably affirm is that a pious ascetic lived the life of a beggar at Edessa and was later widely venerated as a saint. But this historical ambiguity raises a fundamental question. What was the primary purpose of the Syriac legend? Was it simply written to glorify the ascetical prowess of a holy beggar, or did it have a deeper intent? The next section will discuss this question in general. Afterwards, I will outline the insightful answer Han J.W. Drijvers proposes in light of his literary analysis of the Syriac legend.

---

[3]See Amiaud i. Also the article "Alessio" in the *Bibliotheca sanctorum* (Rome: Istituto Giovanni XXIII, Pontificia Università Lateranense, 1961) 1:814-22.

The Purpose and Value of Early Hagiography

The legend of the holy man of Edessa may strike many today as typical of the rigorous asceticism ascribed to the lives of saints in late Syriac antiquity. Probably the best known story from this tradition is that of Symeon the Stylite who perched for thirty-seven years on the top of a tall column. While such fantastic and even bizarre feats may arouse the interest of those looking for a trendy psychological explanation for such behavior, most others may simply dismiss these accounts as a manifestation of an unhealthy, or even a crazed, outlook on life, with little or no historical value. Others may even confess that they feel as baffled and appalled before such uncompromising life styles, as were Edward Gibbon[4] and E.R. Dodds[5] who severely condemned the penitential practices of the early Church.

The attitude of contemporary scholars towards the lives of saints of late antiquity has changed remarkably from these unsympathetic and highly negative opinions. Peter R.L. Brown,[6] Stephen Wilson,[7] Henry Chadwick,[8] Han J.W. Drijvers,[9] and Elizabeth A. Johnson[10] have—each in his or her own way—argued persuasively that, although these lives of the saints may be wholly or partially unreliable as biography, they do provide us with an invaluable source of other kinds of information. Relying on a more nuanced view of what it means to be "historical," these authors show how these devotions to the saints

---

[4]Edward Gibbon, *The Decline and Fall of the Roman Empire* (New York: Dutton, 1956), chapter 37.

[5]E.R. Dodds, *Pagan and Christian in an Age of Anxiety: Some Aspects of Religious Experience from Marcus Aurelius to Constantine* (New York: Norton, 1970) 34.

[6]See Peter R.L. Brown, "The Rise and Function of the Holy Man in Late Antiquity," *Journal of Roman Studies* 61 (1971) 80-101; *The Making of Late Antiquity* (Cambridge: Harvard UP, 1978); and *The Cult of the Saints: Its Rise and Function in Latin Christianity* (Chicago: U of Chicago P, 1981).

[7]Stephen Wilson, ed., *Saints and Their Cults*, (Cambridge: Cambridge UP, 1983), especially his Introduction, page 153.

[8]Henry Chadwick, "Pachomios and the Idea of Sanctity," in *The Byzantine Saint* 11-24.

[9]Drijvers 25-33.

[10]Elizabeth A. Johnson, "Saints and Mary" in *Systematic Theology: Roman Catholic Perspectives*, eds. Francis Schüssler Fiorenza and John P. Galvin (Minneapolis: Fortress, 1991) 2:145-77.

reflect a whole spectrum of political, social, economic, and religious conditions in the societies. Conversely, these cultural forces have significantly shaped the role that a holy person was expected to assume in society.

Peter Brown has played the most prominent role in the current reassessment of the meaning of these devotions in late antiquity. He believes that the Roman system of patronage was the primary force molding societal views about who were saints and what their function in the local community would be. This idea helped convince ordinary people that saints were exceptionally powerful advocates before God. Being in close contact with the divine, saints were able to mediate God's power, performing miraculous deeds either by their own personal touch, through their holy relics, or even at times through pilgrimages to their tombs.[11]

Stephen Wilson agrees with Brown that the lives of the saints of late antiquity reflect the fabric of the societies which both created and nourished them. For Wilson, lives of saints indicate "not only modes of religious perception and feeling but also social relationships and political structure."[12] From his own analysis of the material, he concludes that devotion to saints has a variety of purposes in society. He groups these goals under three, often overlapping, headings: universal assistance, patronage, and political functions.[13] As he probes the lives of the saints in these ways, he is mainly concerned about two interrelated, critical questions: Are early devotions to saints used as a means to legitimize and sacralize a certain social order? and, Are these stories subtle instruments of social control?[14]

Syriac Tradition

H.J.W. Drijvers adds another element to these new insights into the lives of saints, beyond the social and political elements abstracted from

---

[11]See Brown, "The Rise and Function of the Holy Man in Late Antiquity."
[12]Wilson 1.
[13]Wilson 16. For a study of the political role of the holy man, see Cyril of Scythopolis, *Lives of the Monks of Palestine*, trans. R.M. Price, Introduction and notes by John Binns (Kalamazoo, MI: Cistercian, 1991), especially page xxxvii.
[14]Wilson 38.

their stories. In his response to Peter R.L. Brown's opinion[15] that sociological conditions provide sufficient explanation for the origin and function of the holy man in the third and fourth centuries, Drijvers calls attention to the more basic role that culture plays in this whole process. He believes that Brown's emphasis on the need for a mediating patron during late antiquity's crises, a patron who could intervene on behalf of others, prevented Brown from asking what should be a more central question: What is specifically Syriac in all this?

In other words, Drijvers believes that Brown—the same could be said of Wilson—has focused so exclusively on the *general* sociological and political attitudes of the Greco-Roman world that he has overlooked the *specific* cultural and religious forces that molded the lives of the holy men and women of Syria and Mesopotamia.[16] To corroborate and illustrate his claim that these forces, in fact, played a primary role in the development of early Syriac hagiography, Drijvers subjects the structure of the legend of the holy man of Edessa to literary analysis. He believes that this analysis highlights what he considers the chief characteristic of a holy person in Syriac literature: the saint is first and foremost an *alter Christus*.

Drijvers points out that major details of the life of the holy man of Edessa are structured along the lines of Jesus' life. Even a superficial comparison of the two lives shows how closely they resemble each other. The young holy man of Edessa advanced, as Jesus did, "in wisdom and in years, and in divine and human favor" (Lk 2:52). So too, just as the Word renounced heavenly glory to become man, the holy man of Edessa abandoned the wealth of his noble state. And, like Jesus, the saint left his family and had no place to call his own, in order to dedicate himself wholly to God. But this dedication in no way prevented him from also devoting himself totally to God through daily care for the poor and others in need.

Likewise, the holy man's nightly prayers, with arms extended in the form of the cross, evoke images of Jesus praying in the Garden of Gethsemani and his dying on the cross. Bishop Rabbula and the sacristan hastening to the cemetery recall the incident in John's gospel (20:1-10) where Peter and John rush to Jesus' tomb only to discover

---

[15]Brown, "The Rise and Function of the Holy Man in Late Antiquity" 82.
[16]Drijvers 25.

his burial clothing lying there and his body missing. The passage in John 21:1-19, where the risen Jesus unexpectedly appears to his disciples as a stranger on the shore of the Sea of Tiberias and urges Peter to care for his sheep, parallels the conclusion of the legend where Bishop Rabbula is so affected by the mysterious disappearance of the holy man's body that he commits himself to pastoral care of the poor and strangers.

Drijvers argues from all of these similarities that the legend of the holy man of Edessa does not substantiate Brown's theory that devotions to a saint in late antiquity were based merely on the desire for a good and powerful *patronus*, who could intervene on behalf of a supplicant. According to Drijvers, the story portrays the holy man of Edessa as another Christ. This Christ-like identification is especially clear in what Drijvers believes is an essential part of the story—the miraculous way the holy man's body vanished, just as Jesus' body disappeared from the tomb. This parallel indicates that the major details of the story were chosen to symbolize, in a highly stylized and ritualized way, how the life of the holy man of Edessa represents "an ideal life that *asks for imitation* in exactly the same way as Christ's life."[17] But what does it mean "to imitate Christ" in the Syriac world of the fourth and fifth century?

The Syriac Understanding of an Alter Christus

In early Syriac spiritual literature, a person who sought to live a life in close imitation of Christ was called an *iḥîḏāyâ* (ܝܚܝܕܝܐ). This term can be understood, as recent studies[18] have brought out, in various ways. It can signify a person who is "single-minded," or a "single" person who has left his or her family and continues to remain unmarried, or one who enjoys "a very special relationship to Christ as the only-begotten Son of God." By the fourth century, the word acquired a technical sense, embracing all these nuances. That is, it

---

[17]Ibid. 28. Emphasis mine.

[18]See Robert Murray, *Symbols of Church and Kingdom: A Study in Early Syriac Tradition* (New York: Cambridge UP, 1975) 12-14; and Arthur Vööbus, *History of Asceticism in the Syrian Orient II*, in *Corpus Scriptorum Christianorum Orientalium* 197, Subsidia 17 (Louvain: CorpusSCO, 1960) 332-42.

designated a person who had "put on" Christ, the "only-begotten" Son of God, by living a "single-minded" kind of life, consecrated to virginity and asceticism. A person living this kind of life then belonged to a group known as "the sons and daughters of the Covenant." These formed, as it were, "a Church within the Church," in the sense that they were recognized in their day as being not only a distinguishable body[19] within the Church, but a special group in the heart of the community, ones who tried to live the Christian life as fully as possible.[20]

An *îḥîdāyâ*, therefore, is one who freely strives, in a single-minded way, to follow Christ within the heart of the community. Such a person manifested a special calling by living, as Jesus did, a life of consecrated virginity and seeking to attain through ascetical practices a state highly admired in the early Church, that of *apatheia*, in which a person exercises firm control over passions. Those who have aspired to this state believed that, by overcoming temptations through a uncompromising ascetical life, they would thereby manifest God's saving plan for all humanity and actually participate in the work of salvation through their imitation of Christ's life.

When we set the legend of the holy man of Edessa against this cultural background of Syriac esteem for the life of an *îḥîdāyâ*, we can readily understand how his life story reflects these specific ascetical ideals. This background also provides insight into why Drijvers categorically rejects Dodd's opinion that hatred of the body as such was prevalent among Syriac Christians of late antiquity,[21] and especially Drijvers' objection to Arthur Vööbus' claim that Syriac asceticism was due to Manichaean influence.[22] Since Drijvers' argument here touches on the central concern of this paper, it requires further elaboration. He points out that the Manichaeans regarded themselves as a religious elite who avoided involvement in the cares and troubles of others. This attitude is certainly at odds with the lesson inculcated by the legend of the holy man of Edessa who reaches out

---

[19]See Vööbus 332. While some of these "sons and daughters of the Covenant" lived together in small communities, they do not appear, generally speaking, to have lived apart from the laity in the third and fourth centuries.

[20]Murray (page 14) notes, however, that they were not monks or nuns in the strict canonical sense.

[21]Drijvers 30.

[22]Ibid. 30-32.

to those who are poor like himself and inspires others to become similarly involved. His life style shows him to be an *iḥîḏāyâ*, who is not merely close to God, but an *alter Christus* who has had a decisive social impact on his community.

The Economic and Religious Milieux of Late Syriac Antiquity

To understand how the holy person served as an integrating force within late Syriac antiquity, one has to be aware of the major cultural influences at work. I will consider first, briefly, evidence indicating general economic and political conditions during the fourth and fifth centuries, then monastic ideals relevant to the treatment of strangers. This background will clarify the role the holy man of Edessa was expected to play in his society. This analysis will then lead to an examination of how the Christian scriptures have influenced the presentation of the holy man as an integrating and challenging force in late Syriac antiquity.

The documents that have come down to us afford some knowledge of the economic and political situation during the fourth and fifth centuries.[23] They paint an exceptionally grim picture of the social conditions of larger cities of Syriac-speaking Syria and Mesopotamia, crowded with many poor, starving and homeless strangers. This situation was especially harsh during the winter time, particularly when Roman and Persian armies were devastating the countryside and when Persian persecutions were forcing Christians to flee for safety. Confronted with this calamity, committed Christians had to face the personally challenging question: How are these oppressed people to be treated?

Other documents suggests that the legend of the holy man of Edessa was historically accurate when it related that Bishop Rabbula, touched by the miraculous disappearance of the holy man's body, undertook works of charity for social outcasts.[24] A series of canons ascribed to

---

[23]Drijvers, page 28, cites J.B. Segal, "Mesopotamian Communities from Julian to the Rise of Islam," *Proceedings of the British Museum* 41 (1955) 116ff, for economic and political background. See also Segal's *Edessa: The Blessed City* (New York: Oxford UP, 1970).

[24]Georg Günther Blum, *Rabbula von Edessa: Der Christ, der Bischof, der Theologe,* in *Corpus Scriptorum Christianorum Orientalium* 300, Subsidia 34

Rabbula seems to verify this fact. These canons direct the monks of Rabbula's day to be compassionate whenever strangers appeared at their gate or cell.[25] This concern is evident in the following admonition: "They [the monks] shall receive strangers kindly, and shall not close the door before any of the brothers."[26] This bedrock principle became so ingrained in monastic tradition that it calmed any fears the monks may have harbored about strangers taking advantage of their generosity. According to Vööbus, the admonition even affected those monks who were committed to absolute isolation from the world. These monks too welcomed whoever chanced upon them in the wild and offered such strangers whatever assistance they could.[27]

In his study of Syriac asceticism, Vööbus calls attention to how the monks were inspired to be more than simply open to strangers. They were urged to provide for strangers as if they were serving Christ himself. We can detect this generous spirit in James of Serug's summation of the Syriac monks' vocation in life: "Build great monasteries...and open their gates to strangers, that they may please God through the vexed ones that come to them; and (in this way) they become beautiful vessels to men because of the love of God."[28] Vööbus proposes two reasons for the monks' attraction to poverty-stricken strangers. First, the monks felt a keen sense of being personally identified with them, since they used the same Syriac word, *meskine* (ܡܣܟܢܐ), to designate both these poor people and themselves.[29] Secondly—and much more closely allied to the point of this paper—the monks were convinced that God came to them at times in the guise of a complete stranger to test their fidelity. Vööbus sums up the impact of this outlook:

> The great thought concerning Jesus—that He, in the disguise of a pitiful human being of pitiful appearance and in need, appears incognito in order to test the love and loyalty of His believers—was the secret power among the Syrian monks which stimulated them to service. Thus the same profound concept which was brought to mind in relation to travellers had

(Louvain: CorpusSCO, 1969) 70ff.

[25] See Vööbus, especially chapter eleven on "Asceticism and Social Concern" 361-71.

[26] Ibid. 361.

[27] See Vööbus 365.

[28] Vööbus cites James of Serug on page 364.

[29] Vööbus 366.

the same implications here. In the sources, these duties often appear side by side, as shown also by the Jacobite calendar, which has a special day, January 4, devoted to both categories, travellers and the poor.[30]

The Legend of the Holy Man of Edessa as Myth

From this brief overview of *îḥîdāyâ*, the economic and political conditions in Syria and Mesopotamia, and the monastic ideals regarding hospitality to strangers, we can now see how the legend of the holy man of Edessa contains all the elements just outlined. He is described as living the life of an *îḥîdāyâ*, in an environment of widespread poverty, where individuals, especially monks, undertake works of mercy on behalf of homeless people. His life is a classic example of how Christian hagiography illumines the concrete situation of a certain period and provides an understanding of the social and religious challenges confronting religious peoples. After noting how the legend of the holy man of Edessa reflects conditions of its time, Drijvers urges scholars

> to analyze some Lives of Eastern saints more closely, not only to analyze these images as products of the society around the holy man, but also to have a closer look at the inherent ideology in a characteristic lifestyle. His life is symbolic, his actions, cures and deeds of power refer to a religious myth.[31]

In other words, the life of the holy man of Edessa should not be read merely as a quaint, edifying story about an ancient Syrian ascetic. Rather, it is a myth designed to awaken a sense of social consciousness in readers. Like all myths, it aims at revealing the core convictions of a society and stirring it to live accordingly to those ideals. Specifically, it has two functions as religious myth. It seeks to highlight what an authentic Christian's attitude towards poor strangers ought to be. More than that, it attempts to change attitudes and behavior among the Syriac people of late antiquity.

The author of the legend wants to emphasize that caring for a poor, hungry, thirsty, and scantily clothed stranger is—as the Final Judgment scene in Matthew's gospel (25:31-46) brings out—equivalent to serving

[30]Ibid.
[31]Drijvers 26.

Jesus himself. This is what Bishop Rabbula realized when he discovered that the holy man's body had vanished from his grave. This holy stranger was really Christ himself. This conviction impelled the bishop to undertake works of charity on behalf of all strangers. His reaction was meant to be both an example and a challenge for all those who heard about it. The story's purpose was, so it seems, to break down negative social attitudes towards strangers in Edessa and to challenge well-to-do Christians to be charitable and just toward those who might otherwise be regarded as burdens on or threats to society.

Scholarly interest in hagiography is much in vogue today. Elizabeth Johnson, for example, emphasizes the mythic character of such stories. She points out the symbolic role saints exercise for us in general:

> Saints are also significant for the community because in response to the impulse of the Spirit they took risks and were successful in shaping new styles of holiness suitable for particular ages. As both redeemed sinners themselves and creative models of holiness for others, they are a vital part of the history of grace in the world.[32]

To flesh out how the lives of the saints can reflect and promote a certain emphasis in the spiritual life, Johnson turns to J.B. Metz' political theology, above all to his use of memory, narrative, and solidarity.[33] She applies these themes to the lives of the saints and to Mary, showing how their stories contain a mythic power, urging hearers to actions in behalf of justice.[34] Saints witness how grace not only empowers one to enter into a deeper relationship with God but, once freely assented to, grace also impels one to socially responsible living, to "a faith that does justice."

If the legend of the holy man of Edessa is understood as myth, it is quite easy to grasp its import. It was written to counteract what must have been a prevailing indifference to penniless strangers, perhaps seen as annoying nuisances or even as contemptible parasites on the Edessa community. If so, then hospitality was most likely a form of what we today call "interested hospitality." For example, if those strangers who

---

[32]Johnson 161.

[33]See Elizabeth A. Johnson's "Saints and Mary," in *Systematic Theology: Roman Catholic Perspectives* 2:150.

[34]See Johnson 162. Also Johannes Baptist Metz, *Faith in History and Society*, trans. Davis Smith (New York: Seabury, 1980).

arrived in Edessa were well-to-do travellers with money to spend or skilled tradesmen with talents needed in the city, they would undoubtedly have been welcomed with open arms. Those, however, who came begging for alms and had nothing to offer would be brushed aside or reluctantly tolerated. And, once they posed a serious burden or became a personal threat to the community, they would undoubtedly be quickly arrested or forced out of the city.

The originator or redactor of the legend of the holy man of Edessa structured the ending of the story to impress upon his readers the need for a positive reaction towards strangers. As Drijvers argued, the story teller's purpose was not to present the holy man as a powerful *patronus* who could intercede for others because of the holy man's intimate relationship with God, but to urge his readers to imitate Bishop Rabbula's conduct towards strangers.[35]

The Scriptural Basis of the Legend

The author of this legend derived key elements of its message concerning treatment of strangers from what the Christian scriptures reveal about Jesus' special love for the poor. I do not wish to repeat here what Bernhard Asen has already said in an earlier essay in this collection on the biblical use of the term "stranger." My purpose is more modest. I summarize the cultural and ethical ideals evident in both Jewish scriptures and the Christian gospels about how a stranger should be treated. Then I will show how these ideals correspond to those present in the legend of the holy man of Edessa.

The ancient Middle East was home to many nomadic peoples. These groups practiced a form of clan hospitality which respected passing strangers and guaranteed them food and lodging as long as they were guests of the family or tribe.[36] This hospitality tradition seems to have been based on a folk belief that the entry of an outsider could be a divine visitation in disguise. Traces of this concept appear in the tales about Abraham welcoming three mysterious strangers in Genesis 18:1-

[35]Drijvers (pages 31-33) sketches how early Syriac Christology may also have influenced the expected life style of saints in late Syriac antiquity.

[36]For a summary treatment of hospitality in the ancient world, see John Koenig, "Hospitality" in *The Encyclopedia of Religion* (1987) 6:470-73.

15 and about Jacob's wrestling with an angel or with God himself in Genesis 32:23-33. Most likely, these stories were originally part of popular folklore, here adopted by biblical redactors. At any rate, these stories reflect a widespread belief that God or his angels could indeed appear to a privileged individual in the guise of a mysterious stranger, and, if properly acknowledged, the visitor could shower divine blessings upon the host.

As Israel's faith awareness grew, it enlarged upon this indigenous hospitality tradition. Israel considered a stranger's unexpected arrival a test of its fidelity to her covenant with Yahweh. Israel came to this realization through becoming herself a stranger in foreign lands, particularly when, as the biblical tradition believed, Yahweh allowed the Jewish nation to be enslaved in Egypt and later exiled to Babylon. But during such times of trial, biblical faith believed that Yahweh still reached out and cared for Israel. These experiences convinced Israel that strangers should be welcomed as an opportunity, not merely for coming into contact with the divine world above, but more especially for imitating the gracious way in which, it believed, God had extended a helping hand to Israel. This conviction was eventually codified in Deuteronomy 10:12,17-19. Here Israel is told to show her love for Yahweh by befriending the stranger.

> So now, O Israel, what does the Lord your God require of you?...to walk in all his ways, to love him, to serve the Lord your God with all your heart and with all your soul.... For the Lord your God is God of gods and Lord of lords, the great God, mighty and awesome, who is not partial and takes no bribe, who executes justice for the orphan and the widow, and who loves the strangers, providing them food and clothing. You shall also love the stranger, for you were strangers in the land of Egypt.

The New Testament expanded this Jewish tradition. Throughout the gospels, Jesus himself is depicted as a stranger. The prologue of John's gospel proclaims that the Word came into the world as a stranger among his own, but they did not receive him (Jn 1:11). Surprisingly, Jesus is never portrayed during his earthly life as host to others. He is always the guest who must rely on the hospitality of those he meets. Rather than an oversight, this apparent omission seems deliberately arranged to offer an insight into Jesus' message and person. If so, Jesus as guest emphasizes that he does not force himself on others. Jesus allows followers to welcome him as Martha and Mary did (Lk

10:38-42), or, on the contrary, in the cold, calculating, insensitive way that Simon the Pharisee acted as his host (Lk 7:36-50).

The gospels especially portray Jesus as stranger during his passion. Here he is not only rejected by his own people, but he is also abandoned by his friends. Jesus' death on the cross dramatizes how completely he assumed the role of stranger. Jesus' role as stranger does not change, even after his resurrection. For instance, his disciples do not recognize Jesus on the road to Emmaus—until they welcomed him as guest (Lk 24:28-32). Nor do his seven disciples fishing on the Sea of Tiberias realize who he is, when he first calls out to them and directs them to fish in a new area (Jn 21:4-6). He seems to wait until the disciples accept him as a stranger and reach out to him as such.

This New Testament theme emphasizes, as the Jewish scriptures did, that being hospitable to strangers is an exercise of religious faith. Welcoming another person, different from oneself, involves an acceptance of an unknown. Jesus insists that his followers should not merely welcome their own. Even the Gentiles do that, Jesus says (Mt 5:43-47). Rather, Christian should offer assistance even to those who have nothing to give in return—the hungry, thirsty, naked, sick, and those in prison (Mt 25:31-46). The parable of the Good Samaritan (Lk 10:29-37) especially brings this out. Jesus even wants his disciples to be open to their traditional enemies.

Little has to be said, I believe, to show that the legend of the holy man of Edessa promotes the same attitude towards strangers as the one just described in the New Testament. This holy man is pictured as a living embodiment of Christ who comes to challenge readers of the legend to treat strangers in a caring way, as if they were other Christs. What needs to be addressed at this point are two closely related questions: Why should the legend of the holy man of Edessa evoke a positive response to strangers? and How was the story structured to accomplish this? Answers to these questions can be found in the skillful way the legend understands this man of Edessa as both stranger and holy.

Rudolph Otto's famous analysis[37] of the psychological dimensions of the experience of the holy show how stranger and holy are connected. Otto's insights, applied to the legend of the holy man of Edessa, explain why the legend was so effective in fostering a faith

---

[37]Rudolph Otto, *The Idea of the Holy* (London: Oxford UP, 1973).

response leading to social responsibility.

Otto begins his study of the holy by stressing that the feeling "elements" he is about to explore should not be regarded as constituting the whole experience itself. Rather, they intermingle with each other to form a unique experience. They are like a shadow pointing to its source, thereby providing some insight into an experience of the holy. He then designates the object of this experience the "numinous" or the "Totally-Other," whose mysterious power is experienced as both fascinating and fearful. In the presence of this majestic power, one becomes conscious of one's own creaturehood and one's moral failings, while at the same time being openmouthed with wonder and filled with heartfelt praise, thanks, and worship for being found acceptable, despite one's creaturehood—and forgiven, despite one's sinfulness. This experience then flows into a sense of personal atonement or, as the English root indicates, an at-one-ment with the divine, with oneself, with others, with nature, and with the cosmos itself.

Another aspect of the holy, which Otto mentions but does not spell out, is how the power of the holy urges a person to a personal response.[38] Isaiah's Temple Vision story, for example, is a classic description of an experience of the holy. After encountering God as the Lord Almighty, Isaiah responds to Yahweh's inquiry "Whom shall I send?" with an unconditional reply: "Here am I; send me!" To which Yahweh answers: "Go and say to this people..." (Isaiah 6:8-9).

Isaiah's response to the vision highlights how an experience of the holy includes a spiritual impulse that urges a person to both witness to and faithfully serve the mysterious power which has transformed one's life. This practical aspect of an experience of the holy is significant for our study, since it explains why an encounter with a holy stranger can be a stimulus to social change.

Otto also points out that an experience of the holy can be promoted by creating a setting and mood which arouse feelings similar to the ones mentioned above.[39] While insisting that neither this setting nor this mood can guarantee an experience of the holy, Otto maintains, nonetheless, that these conditions can still spark this experience, intensify and channel its spiritual impulses in a certain direction.

[38]Otto 23-24.
[39]Ibid. 42-43.

However, a person is not always explicitly aware of this kind of experience, or able to describe the full spectrum of "elements" enumerated above.

The Stranger as Symbol of the "Totally-Other"

It should now be clear why the legend portrays the holy man of Edessa as a stranger. A stranger is by definition a person separate and different from others, and therefore a mysterious "other." When such a person is encountered face to face, the mysterious inner nature of the stranger's personality stirs ambivalent feelings. One may be fascinated by the possibility that this meeting is a unique opportunity to encounter God in one's life. Or one may react negatively, as many spontaneously do, since one sees the stranger as a threat to one's own well being.

When a Christian responds generously to a complete stranger, however, believing this event is an opportune moment for meeting Christ in one's life, this response reveals how deeply scriptural ideals concerning care of strangers has taken hold in one's life.

Respecting and caring for strangers as mediators of Christ's presence concretizes what spiritual writers refer to when they speak about self-emptying love that leaves one poor in an ontological sense. Experiences of the holy teach one the limits of human existence and one's reality as creature. One can also sense one's poverty when, in giving oneself to others in a disinterested way, one feels that one has given oneself away totally. This is what the holy man of Edessa did and what Christian scriptures describe as dying to oneself.

Self-sacrificing love can be a terrifying experience for anyone. Christians, however, can draw strength from their personal faith. Those who share in Christ's death are also destined to share his resurrection—if not in this life, then certainly in the life to come. The legend of the holy man of Edessa expresses this truth of Christian faith when it relates how the holy man's body vanished from the grave just as Jesus' did on Easter morning.

Conclusion

As this study shows in broad strokes, the legend of the holy man of Edessa stands as a multi-layered story, appealing to a variety of audiences. First, as its widespread popularity in Syriac, Byzantine, and Latin traditions of late antiquity and of medieval times demonstrates, this legend has become an established Christian classic. It also shows how ancient hagiographers gathered facts and memories, then embellished them with incidents based on biblical models and legendary patterns.[40] We see this practice at work in the literary freedom exercised by Byzantine and Roman redactors who amplified the original legend of the holy man of Edessa. His story is also quite interesting for the ancillary information it provides about social and religious milieux of Syriac Christian antiquity.

While all these aspects are interesting in their own right and relevant to the present topic, I especially want to present the life story of the holy man of Edessa as a religious myth with a twofold purpose. It teaches Christians how to look at strangers, then moves them to treat strangers in a compassionate way. The story attempts to instill a central message of the Gospel: God loves and cares for the well-being of destitute strangers. Further, as Bishop Rabbula is reputed to have done at the conclusion of this legend, Christians are encouraged to undertake charitable acts on behalf of the poor.

The legend succeeds in achieving these purposes because the original hagiographer skillfully interwove key "elements" of the holy into the life story of the poor man of Edessa. His fantastic exploits and achievements, particularly his severe, ascetical life style, climaxed by the sudden disappearance of his body from the grave, suggest the presence of a mysterious power, hovering like an aura over his life. Even though one might be appalled by his ascetical practices, they are, in their own strange, paradoxical way, fascinating, evoking feelings of awe bordering on fright, especially if a person realizes that God may make similar demands upon oneself.

While it is possible that the original Syriac version of the legend, and especially its later redactions, were simply composed to spread an edifying story about a Syriac *îḥîdāyâ*, or holy man, the author or authors have—wittingly or unwittingly—cast the story in such a way that it takes on aspects of myth, capable of evoking and promoting an experience of the holy. Its widespread popularity proves that the story

---

[40]See Flor Van Ommeslaeghe's "The *Acta Sanctorum* and Bollandist Methodology," in *The Byzantine Saint* 153-62; also Lennart Ryden's "The Holy Fool" in the same work 106-13, especially page 110.

has served as an effective means of challenging its readers to regard strangers with the respect and loving care that both Jesus and Bishop Rabbula showed. Its later wide acceptance in late Syriac antiquity also suggests that the legend hit a proverbial raw nerve. Many came to recognize that something had to be done to counteract the shabby treatment accorded destitute strangers at Edessa and in other Syriac cities and towns.

The legend, of course, could rely on—and would actually be appealing to—attitudes and values already instilled in Syriac Christians, especially through those scriptural stories which relate Jesus' special love for the poor and which urge a similar love for strangers. The legend could affect readers in two other ways. First, the story could elicit a faith experience that would prompt readers to serve God in some way. Then, second, it could channel this energy in creative directions. By emphasizing Bishop Rabbula's care for destitute strangers, the legend's Syriac author is pointing out, even if unintentionally, that one ought to respond as Bishop Rabbula is said to have done. Christians should care for the material well-being of strangers they meet. In fact, the myth and its social consequences suggest parallels with contemporary forms of political and liberation theology.

The legend of the holy man of Edessa was written to invest the word "stranger" with a new connotation. The story itself suggests this by employing the Syriac word *'aksneyâ* (ܐܟܣܢܝܐ), a derivative of the Greek word *xenos* (ξένος) rather than *gîyûrâ* (ܓܝܘܪܐ), which comes from the Hebrew *(gēr)*. *'Aksneyâ* conveys several ideas. Besides indicating a person who is a stranger and a foreigner, it also signifies one who is a guest or a pilgrim, or even one living the life of an anchorite. Underlying these latter meanings is doubtless the primitive folk tradition that, whenever strangers arrived, they should be treated hospitably, as though they mediated a visit from the gods.

The legend expands and clarifies this tradition. It specifies, at least for Christians, that a visit from a stranger can be an encounter with Christ himself. So understood, this conviction could encourage those who meet a destitute stranger to act in a caring way towards such a person, to be like Bishop Rabbula, more socially concerned about the plight of poor strangers in their own community. We see, therefore, both implied in the Syriac word and explicitly expressed in the legend of the holy man, a religious message that we have lost in contemporary

English. The word "stranger" can connote an opportunity to serve God through one's hospitality to the poor. The words, attributed to Bishop Rabbula at the end of the legend, sum this idea up well: "Henceforth far be it from me, my Lord, that there be any other work for me, but only a diligent care of strangers! For who knows how many others there are, similar to this holy man, who delight in humility and other works pleasing in themselves to God, but not known to us humans because of their humble nature."

APPENDIX

Since the full text of "The Legend of the Holy Man of Edessa" is accessible only in Arthur Amiaud's French translation from the last century, I here provide an English translation for those who wish to see it in its entirety. The following translation is based on the critical Syriac text[41] published by Arthur Amiaud in his La Légende syriaque de saint Alexis, l'homme de Dieu. *I have tried to remain as close as possible to the Syriac text, adapting it only where necessary to provide a more readable rendition in English. It differs in many minor ways from Amiaud's own French translation.*

The Text

The life of the Man of God from the city of Rome, who attained victory because of his exploits in poverty and was crowned with glory in the city of Edessa, during the days of the illustrious and holy Bishop Rabbula of the same city of Edessa.

We will speak of the life of an extraordinary man—if indeed it be the story of a man. [We prefer] not to term him as such, but rather call him an angel who despised all the pleasures of the world. This then is his story.

This man was reared in great wealth. But he himself chose to be at enmity with wealth and substituted in its place a love for poverty. But this was not ordinary poverty, but one of extreme shame and reproach. For it was through his abasement that he achieved the destruction of pride and, through his voluntary poverty, that of haughtiness. He was a promoter of the eremitical life[42] and of humility. He was also a man

---

[41]For information about the Greek text, see F.M. Esteves Periera, "Légende grecque de l'homme du Dieu: Saint Alexis," *Analecta Bollandiana* 19 (1900) 241-56 (which includes one of the Greek texts); for the Latin text, see Luis Vasquez de Parga, "La mas antigua redacción latina de la legenda de San Alejo?" *Revista de bibliografia nacional* 2 (1941) 245-58, and B. de Gaiffer's review in *Analecta Bollandiana* 62 (1944) 281-83.

[42]Literally the text says "builder of the apostolate." Because this makes little sense in the context, Amiaud translates it as "the apostle of despoilment." I prefer to see a mistake in the text. I suspect that the reading should be *šalyûtâ* (ܫܠܝܘܬܐ) instead of *šlîḥûtâ* (ܫܠܝܚܘܬܐ).

of total fasting, weaning himself away from food. For he did not assent to becoming enslaved to his belly, as Esau did. He acted as a vigilant and circumspect[43] guardian of his body, especially in the ways he shunned marriage and fornication. For virginity and sanctity dwelt purely in his body, as though it were exempted from lust.[44]

Then as Abraham did, he joyfully left his family and his country. For his [whole] desire was to be inscribed and known in the heavenly Jerusalem and insisted [upon this] in his prayer of petition. And what [more can] I add to extol his grandeur than this that his final crowning surpasses every verbal attempt to tell of it! Behold then this man whose life is more impressive than ours and so imperfectly portrayed by us. Our story about him begins thus.

His parents were from the city of Rome—for from here it is fitting to begin our inquiry. They were known for their wealth and their fame as a noble family. They were, however, deprived of any offspring. And as their wealth grew and expanded, so too did their sadness increase with their wealth. For they did not see an heir for their treasures and did not know for whom they were amassing [all this]. For if Abraham, the father of all believers, could say with sadness to his Lord: "My Lord, what will you give me, I who am journeying [throughout life] without children," how much more do they mourn, whose minds cling to their wealth.

Then because of their tears and numerous prayers and vows, there was born to them a son—the subject of our present story. He was loved by God and his parents and those who saw him. His parents were then comforted in their grief. While still a nursing child, he had noble powers heaped upon him. But these honors came to him from his parents.

Then when he reached the time to study, he went to school in grand style with a great retinue of servants. Not only did he not attend to these wearying, transitory things that vanish, but he preferred their opposites. For he exercised himself in humility, being peacefully intent upon his studies, even though many of his peers were attempting to draw him away from his pursuit of great knowledge. But he did not weaken in his perseverance. The parents, however, of this child, because they did not recognize that he was an instrument chosen by

---

[43]I have followed Amiaud's translation of this word.

[44]Literally, "by a desirable (or lustful) law."

God, began to be sad and lament, convinced that he was foolish and incapable of coping with this world.

His parents then secretly conceived a plan, so that their child would become sophisticated and skilled in the ways of this world. His father commanded his servants to be lewd with him and wean him in the ways of wantonness. But with his habitually humble manner, he rebuked them and set them right. He then turned away from them in a dignified way with his eyes lowered. His mother for her part also prepared beautiful-looking maidens, adorned with all sorts of comely, worldly attires, and commanded them to serve him. This youth did not openly chase them away from him, but in his own customary manner commanded them to leave his presence, so that he could be alone by himself. Then the beloved's mother asked her well-groomed maidens whether he spoke with them and made merry with them. These responded: "Not only did he not make merry with us, but we did not even dare to look at him, because the gravity [of his demeanor so] overwhelmed us."

He continued to act in the same way for a long time. Then later when he reached his full youthful maturity, his parents were resolved to betroth him, as was customary, to a woman. This is, in fact, what they did. When the time came for the wedding feast, they prepared everything in a glorious and magnificent manner and set up a sumptuous marriage bed for him. And the whole city was invited to the feast.

Then early on the day of the marriage, when the bride was being prepared for her entrance in a solemn procession, this holy thought suddenly occurred to the saint. So he asked one of his groomsmen to go with him to the port. The groom, however, believed that he was saying this as a joke. Then when he indicated that he truly wanted to do this, he sought to prevent him, saying: "Behold, the whole city is invited today to your house to rejoice and be glad, and are we to rush out into deserted areas? Who will welcome us? Who will not scoff at us, when we act in a way that will change joy into sadness and turn for everyone awaiting your festival their great cheerfulness into sorrow."

But as often as his friend contrived to restrain him, this beloved one persuaded him that they should go. Since his groom revered him, he felt compelled to obey the humble man's wishes. They at once took two horses and departed for the port, with no one else in attendance. The holy man said to his friend: "Stay and keep this mare for me, while I take a relaxing walk. Then we will return together to the wedding feast." This man, however, being unaware of what he was planning to do, did as he commanded him. Having been persuaded by him, he said: "Let us return quickly and not delay and be mocked."

Then the blessed one, as he was moving away from his friend, prayed thus, saying: "O You whose gifts are [far] superior to our petitions, open for me your door on which I have knocked and grant me at this moment my heart's desire." And as he prayed thus, behold a galley appeared before him that was departing for Syria. He then embarked upon it, and a great wind came up and brought him by the providence of God without delay to the port of Seleucia in Syria. Afterwards, the blessed departed from Seleucia and moved inland begging [on the way]. He was led to the city of the Parthians, called Edessa, where he remained as a vagrant until his death.

This then is the blessed's manner of life in Edessa. Every day he came regularly to the church and to the *martyrium*,[45] accepting nothing from anyone. He also did not want to be in need for food during the day, so that he might keep his fast until evening. Then when evening came, he stood at the door of the church with his hand extended and received alms from those entering the church. But as soon as he received from them whatever was sufficient for his needs, he stopped. For his food allowance was ten *menîn*[46] of bread and two vegetables. Then if by chance he received more, he immediately gave it to another and from the alms [he received] bestowed alms. Because of this [practice], many tested and tried the Man of God. Yet he did not live apart from the poor. In the evening when all the poor—of which he was one—slept, he arose, extending his arms in the form of a cross towards a wall or a column, and prayed. Then with those coming to visit the Church for prayer, he entered and [remained there] until matins. All his days were spent in this way. He told no one about his previous patrician way of life. He did not even want to reveal his name to anyone, lest someone would find out and discover through his name his [true] background.

His groom friend, after having waited for a long time and [concerned that] he had not returned, wandered through the entire port

[45]This would be the sanctuary of the church where the relics of the martyrs were kept and venerated.

[46]Amiaud notes that a *menîn* (ܡܢܝܢ) is equivalent to an ounce and a half.

and inquired in search of him. Then when he learned by what boat he had sailed, he returned to the blessed's house, announcing what had happened. Words cannot describe the chagrin and sorrow that took hold of the humble man's parents. Then as befits their wealth and influence, they sent him to search out for him in all the ports and nations.

Afterwards there was one of his Christian stewards among those sent out in search of the holy man. While moving among the cities, they came finally to Edessa, while the holy man was begging there. This one of his house servants arrived and informed the illustrious Bishop Rabbula of the same city of Edessa concerning the details about this holy man. But not only did the servant not find him, he was not believed because his account was so out of the ordinary. Finally, being unable to find him, he departed and went to search for him in other regions.

The holy man had indeed recognized his house servants, when they entered and left the church. These, however, when he appeared before them begging, had no suspicion that it was he, not even for a second, because he was so indigent and showed not a trace of [his former] dignity. For how could they recognize this man dressed in rags and begging? In fact, it is even likely that he received alms from them.

Then, a long time later, a sacristan, one who was chaste and worthy of enlightenment, left one night to see whether it was time for the service. When he left, he found this humble man with his arms extended in the form of a cross, praying, while every one else was asleep. This man did not see him once or twice, but innumerable times throughout the length of the night. On one of these nights, this sacristan went and stood before him, asking him: "Where are you from and what do you do?" At first the blessed did not utter a word to the sacristan when he questioned him. Then finally, out of dismay because of this man's forceful entreaty, he responded to him, saying: "Why indeed do you address me about these matters? Ask those who are before you and you will learn who I am and from where I am. For I am one of them." The sacristan, however, was not able to bring himself to leave without [further] exploring such a strange case as this. For his mind was filled with curiosity. He swore an oath and put himself under the threat of a curse that he would not leave, until he had learned the truth about him.

Then this Man of God felt compelled [to speak], because of fear for the oaths and the curse and also because of his dislike for disputes. He agreed to reveal the truth to the sacristan. But he also exacted oaths from the sacristan not to reveal anything while he was alive. Then he revealed everything about himself, saying: "O Christian, the one who came here earlier in search for a man was a member of my household. It was I whom he was searching for." Then when the sacristan heard this, he tried mightily to persuade him, asking him to live with him. But being unable to persuade him, he left him. Then from this time on, this sacristan, although already practiced in his good deeds, gave himself over to a harsh ascetic life and made battle against the members of his body more than before, until his very appearance also gave witness to his harsh penances. He said to himself: "If this man, raised in magnificent splendor, performs such acts, what must we miserable beings not do to attain our salvation?"

Then a long time after this, the humble and godlike blessed fell sick and lay between the columns [of the church]. When the sacristan was passing here and there and did not see the holy man as he was accustomed to, he inquired about him solicitously. When he found him, he asked him forcefully to come with him to his home, so that he might be cared for in his sickness. But he did not want to. He also said to him: "After your cure, I will let you return to your habitual way of acting." But he did not consent. Then the sacristan said to him: "Let me take you then to the hospital." He consented to do what was asked but [only] after an intense [inner] struggle and putting the sacristan under an oath not to do more for him than he would for [other] strangers. This man took the oath, led him away [to the hospital], and visited him constantly.

But God who always watches over those who serve Him brought the holy man's way of life to a close and confirmed his crown and, even after his death, preserved [knowledge of] his humility [for posterity]. For on that day that he was about to depart from this world for a heavenly dwelling, the sacristan ran into a difficulty and was not able, as he usually was, to go and visit the humble one. But when the blessed died, those in the hospital, as was their custom, immediately carried him in the ordinary way on a stretcher to where strangers are hastily buried. After those who were burying him had set out and were at some distance, then the sacristan came and inquired about him. And when he learned that he had died and they had already left to bury him, he immediately began to weep and groan mightily.

The sacristan ran to the holy Bishop Rabbula and fell at his feet, imploring him thus: "I beg of you, my lord, be mindful of me and take pity on me." Then Bishop Rabbula, whose bodily eyesight was almost unimpaired, sought together with his entourage to calm the bereaved sacristan and asked him what is the cause of his crying? He then told everything that had happened and earnestly sought that this man's pure and sinless body be honored in a great and solemn ceremony and be placed in a known location.

When he had heard these words, the bishop was filled with amazement and inflamed, as it were, by a passionate fire, because he was zealous for noble causes. He immediately decided to go to where they had borne the saint for burial. While they were on the way, behold, they met the porters who interred him, as they were returning from where they had buried the heroic one. After they inquired: "Where have you buried him?" they said: "With the strangers, his companions." Then the bishop and his entourage took the porters with them, so that they might show them the grave. When they arrived at the grave, the bishop ordered that it be reopened. He and his entourage, together with the porters, entered so that they might see the corpse and begin to honor it. They then looked and saw in the place where the holy man had been set only his rags. His body, however, was not there. Astonished, these then searched for the corpse in every grave. They found not it, but only his rags. Amazement and profound apprehension seized them for a long period of time.

When the bishop regained his composure, he said: "Let us pray!" Then after he prayed, the holy Rabbula wept and said: "Henceforth far be it from me, my Lord, that there be any other work for me, but only a diligent care of strangers! For who knows how many others there are similar to this holy man who delight in humility and other works pleasing in themselves to God, but not known to us humans because of their humble nature." From then on, the holy Mar Rabbula engaged in and ordered many things to be done for strangers. He continuously poured out his gifts with tremendous zeal upon the poor and strangers and exhorted others by his word to a love for strangers. He ceased his mighty building projects and turned away from a burdensome care for things that are transitory. He attended only to orphans and widows and was solicitous for the misfortunate and strangers. Likewise he was no longer concerned about and provident for only his city, but also cared responsibly for strangers of remote cities and distant countries by supporting them with his gifts, in order that he might be near to God by his sharing in the beatitude promised to the merciful. This is how the blessed Rabbula began and how he brought to fulfillment his love for strangers.

This life, therefore, that we have just narrated above about the Man of God, has been publicly proclaimed by the sacristan, who was a friend of the blessed, and written down by him for our recording. For he was careful to question the holy man under the threat of a curse and under oaths. And this one explained his whole former life of grandeur and his later days of abasement, and he has hidden nothing from him.

The end of the life of the Man of God.

4

THE STRANGER WITHIN, THE STRANGER WITHOUT

Ascetical Withdrawal and the Second Letter

of Basil the Great

Richard Valantasis

There is a certain poetic justice to linking asceticism and strangeness.[1] Asceticism is a strange subject, an arena of behavior and theology difficult to comprehend, a set of attitudes strangely peculiar, unusually renunciative, weirdly denunciatory of other ways of living, peculiarly estranged from the dominant culture from which the ascetic withdraws.[2] Strangeness and asceticism go hand in hand; indeed, asceticism defines a set of systems marked by both becoming a stranger within oneself and becoming a stranger within society. This essay explores the ascetic's creation of the stranger within and the stranger without, the interior stranger constructed of withdrawal from the normative personality within a culture, the exterior stranger created

[1]This essay grew out of two lectures given at two different times. The original lecture was presented to the Modern Greek Literature section of the Center for Literary and Cultural Studies at Harvard University under the graceful leadership of Professor Margaret Alexiou. The final form of the lecture was presented at Mary Washington University where Professor James Goehring and many students debated with me about the implications of these theories. The final form here, unfortunately, may not always reflect the valuable criticism I received at both institutions, but I gratefully acknowledge their intellectual hospitality.

[2]Recently many scholars have turned their attention to the study of asceticism. This present study emerges from collaborative work on Asceticism in Greco-Roman Society Group of the Society for Biblical Literature. That group has published the following significant works: *Ascetic Behavior in Greco-Roman Antiquity: A Sourcebook*, ed. Vincent L. Wimbush, Studies in Antiquity and Christianity (Minneapolis: Fortress, 1990); volumes 57 and 58 (1992) of *Semeia* whose general theme was *Discursive Formations, Ascetic Piety and the Interpretation of Early Christian Literature*; and *Asceticism*, ed. Vincent Wimbush and Richard Valantasis (New York: Oxford UP, forthcoming).

by withdrawal from the normative relationships of the dominant society.

I would like to pursue this stranger within and stranger without in a number of different ways. First, by telling a true story about a pilgrim monk who stayed in the same place, an estranged person by culture and vocation whose estrangement was manifest and clear. Second, I will analyze the stranger within and the stranger without through a brief discussion of a theory of asceticism. Third, I would like to explore the development of ascetical theology as a theology of the stranger from a letter of *the* ascetical theologian of the Eastern Church, Basil the Great, Bishop of Caesarea (c.330-79). Fourth, and finally, I would like to draw some conclusions (both historical and theological) from this construction of asceticism.

The Estranged Monk Who Stayed in One Place

While travelling on one of the Greek islands recently, I heard of a monk, Jacob, who was a former Anglican priest now living as a monk in an Orthodox cenobitic community. Being interested in monastic asceticism in the Christian East, I went to see him. When I arrived at the monastery to ask about him, however, the guestmaster pointed in another direction, to either a church near the cemetery, or to what seemed to be an abandoned monastery on the next mountain. I searched for him first at the cemetery, knowing that in monastic tradition there would be no reason that a person could not pray and live there. Not finding him, I began the long trek in the morning heat to the next mountain.

When I finally made it to the small church complex, I knocked at the door. No one answered. I knocked again. Still silence. Then at the third knock, the monk poked his head out the window above the door and asked what I wanted. When I asked for him by name, he said that he would allow me to enter, explaining that normally he does not admit visitors except those who seem to have serious business, and since I knew his name, I must have had a serious intent. He looked very much like an Orthodox monk, dressed as he was in a monastic habit dirty from manual labor, face bearded and head covered with a small cap. His Greek pronunciation, however, betrayed his British origins.

After showing me to his chapel to pray, and after giving me a short tour of the monastery where he lived as a hermit, we settled in his common room and the monk began, in response to my initial questions about him, to relate the story of his life. His spiritual pilgrimage began at a theological school of a British university during the First World War. He was part of a small movement within the Anglican communion which sought union with the Roman Catholic Church and acknowledgment of the Catholic basis of Anglican holy orders, because the Anglican communion could not (according to followers of this movement at least) provide the connection to the primitive Church, either in purity of doctrine, continuity of orders, or catholicity of orientation. After his ordination to the priesthood in the Church of England, the young priest took up his first parochial position and continued intensive study of Roman Catholic dogma and practice, ostensibly to institute Roman Catholic practice, ritual, and doctrine into his local parish, but, in actuality, in anticipation of being received into the Roman Catholic Church. During this curacy, he visited a Benedictine monastery in France, for he was also interested in exploring his vocation as a monk in the Roman Catholic Church.

While in France, however, he met some people newly converted to Greek Orthodox Christianity who introduced him to the liturgy and theology of the Orthodox Church. His long fascination with the Roman Catholic Church began to wane. He was no longer convinced that the Roman Catholic Church retained the pure and clear apostolic doctrine and practice which he sought. What he yearned for seemed to be fully present only in Eastern Orthodox Christianity. Gradually he was drawn more and more into the Orthodox Church. Eventually he was chrismated, and then received as a novice into the monastery where he ultimately took on the great and holy schema (vesture) of a monk.

The monastery into which he was received as a novice had a reputation for strict observance of the monastic life, for significant intellectual and spiritual work by the abbot and the monks, and for receptivity to non-Greeks and non-Orthodox for theological dialogue and debate. It was an obvious place for him to be.

In this illustrious monastery, the monk, after rigorous training in the religious life and detailed study of Orthodox faith and practice, became disillusioned with the manner of life there. After many years of complaint to the abbot and his fellow monks about their manner of life and their liturgical practice, the monk could no longer contain his dismay. His desire for purity and literal observance of the monastic rules needed to be addressed.

Some background about Orthodox ascetical practice is necessary here. Fasting in the Eastern Orthodox Church, and especially in monasteries, consists of limiting both the quantity and the kinds of food which can be eaten.[3] On days of strict fasting, the monk (and other devout Orthodox Christians) do not eat anything until after Vespers (late afternoon, usually about 3:30 p.m.). On normal fasting days, meals may be taken at the normal times. Orthodox fasting rules have various levels of restriction. Most days restrict meat and dairy products; other days restrict meat, dairy products, fish, and wine; some days there is also a restriction of oil, or of oil and wine. Each day of the year is graded as to the manner of observing the fast. Monasteries regularly observe the strict fast as a norm, while devout Orthodox lay people restrict the fast to Wednesdays and Fridays throughout the year, the fast before the Nativity of the Lord (from about November 29 until Christmas), the fast of Great Lent (the forty days before Easter), the fast of the Dormition of the Theotokos (August 1 through 14), and other specified days throughout the year.

Since meals are connected with the monastic horarium, that is, since the breaking of the fast is determined by the singing of Vespers, the monks at this monastery, and at many other Orthodox monasteries including Mount Athos, have adjusted their monastic horarium so that all of the offices are sung at one time throughout the night.[4] Arising at about 2:30 a.m., the monks chant the Night Office, Matins, Lauds, the Little Hours (Prime, Terce, Sext, and None), and Vespers so that the entire sequence of offices is usually completed by sunrise or a little later. This means that, Vespers having been completed, the monks may eat their meal, and then proceed to a full day of work and solitary prayer until Compline and sleep. This practice meant that the correlation between the actual setting of the sun and the monastic

---

[3] These directions are given to Orthodox Christians in the ecclesiastical calendar. See *The Church Kalendar*, ed. Fedor S. Kovalchuk (South Canaan, PA: St. Tikhon's Seminary P, 1947).

[4] These adjustments are not necessarily accepted by all Orthodox parishes and monasteries. The Russian tradition, at least, gathers the offices into three "aggregates" to be recited at sunset, sunrise, and midday. See *Abridged Typicon*, 2nd ed., ed. Feodor S. Kovalchuk (South Canaan, PA: St. Tikhon's Seminary P, 1985) 36-74.

office of vespers to be sung as the sun was setting was disrupted. No longer was there a correlation between the hours of the day and the monastic office.

The monk living at the hermitage did not like the disruption. He preferred to have the symbolism of the office match the actual time of day. He wanted the offices to correlate to the actual rising of the sun and the hours of the day, Vespers to follow at its proper time in the late afternoon, and to break the fast only at the appointed time after Vespers. So he asked for permission to live alone as a hermit in order to fulfill the full complement of monastic offices in their chronological sequence and to fulfill the monastic fast strictly according to the ancient monastic traditions. This withdrawal was the only way he could imagine coming to the true life of a monk living according to the ancient and pure monastic way. Living alone and chanting the monastic offices alone, he could insure that they would be done properly and in accordance with the ancient monastic ways.

A Theory of Asceticism

This story serves as the basis for exploring a theory of asceticism,[5] through which I wish to interpret Jacob and his relationship to his monastic community. Asceticism revolves about the creation of a new identity. A person begins ascetical practices precisely in order to become someone else, to become a different kind or quality of person. Newness of personality marks the ascetic impulse. Jacob was searching for a new identity, first in his vocation as an Anglican priest, then through his interest in Roman Catholicism, subsequently in his reception into the Greek Orthodox Church and his acceptance into the monastic life, and eventually in his life as a hermit. In each one of these situations, Jacob sought to become a new person, a more authentic person, a more enlivened person.

This new personality, however, does not operate in a vacuum. In

[5]The following is an early articulation of my theory of asceticism. For continuing work, see my "A Theory of the Social Function of Asceticism" in *Asceticism*; and my "Constructions of Power in Asceticism," *Journal of the American Academy of Religion* (forthcoming). The most significant available theoretical analysis of asceticism is that of Geoffrey Galt Harpham, *The Ascetic Imperative in Culture and Criticism* (Chicago: U of Chicago P, 1987).

order to become a new person through ascetical practices, the person must also restructure social relations and recreate the cultural universe in which the person lives. In other words, the ascetic must leave behind the old person in order to become a new person, and that leaving behind includes the intricate social relationships that support the old way of life in favor of new social relations which support the new way of life.[6] The ascetic, as well, must put aside the old way of looking at the world, the old culture, and create a new culture. Jacob did both of these things. In leaving England, in visiting France, in rejecting Western society, Jacob created a free space in which Eastern monks and Eastern culture would support and enhance his new personality. But the monks of the monastery, although culturally connected to the Greek people living outside the monastery, had also left the normative social relationships of their families, villages, and nation in order to enter the monastery. They too left the mundane world of their Greek culture to enter a cultural world defined by the centrality of their religious vocations.

So asceticism may be defined as practices intended to inaugurate a new personality, to develop new social relationships, and to support these by the articulation of a new culture, a new world-view.[7] The foundation of all ascetical practice revolves about a series of withdrawals, from old conditioning of personality, from old, intricate, social relations, from an old understanding of the world. In other words, there can be no asceticism, no new personality, no new social relations, no newly articulated world view, without first becoming a stranger to the old. Becoming a stranger, therefore, stands at the heart of ascetic activity. The stranger within defines the person who withdraws from the familiarity of an already defined personality to move toward a new definition of personality. The stranger without defines the person who has withdrawn from society in order to create a different sort of society, and withdrawn from the world as normally

---

[6]This observation is based upon the primary insight of Max Weber. As an historian of economics and as a sociologist, Weber has opened the ascetical to its social and economic implications. See *The Protestant Ethic and the Spirit of Capitalism*, trans. Talcott Parsons (London: Unwyn Hyman, 1930) and his *The Sociology of Religion*, trans. Ephraim Fischoff (Boston: Beacon, 1963).

[7]The contours of this discussion may be (naively) dependent upon the anthropologist Clifford Geertz, *The Interpretation of Cultures* (New York: Basic Books, 1973) 144.

understood in order to enter a new world.

The complex interaction of these elements of my theory, however, becomes clearer in a further exploration of Jacob's relationship with his community. At each level of these descriptions (personal, social, cultural) our hermit monk had become proficient at the cultural practices without becoming fully acculturated. Jacob entered the monastic life while never really becoming a part of it—he remained a stranger. He clearly had mastered the theology and literary tradition of Orthodox monks both through reading and through intellectual training; these traditions defined the cultural world of the Eastern Orthodox monks. He had also become proficient at the monastic discipline (prayer, fasting, reading, manual labor, corporate prayer) through his own training as a monk and through many years of practice. In short, the monk had become proficient in and a master of the practices and social relationships of the monk, without fully assimilating some of their cultural elements. Jacob's estrangement from the community articulates this.

The difference between this monk and his brothers did not relate to questions of proper actions or proper ascetical practice—for they agreed about the form and content of those activities—but rather to questions of the construction of the monastic culture. The hermit monk Jacob needed and valued a literal correlation between the hours of the day and the times of the monastic hours. Lauds was to be chanted as the sun rose, Vespers was chanted toward the end of the day. The other brothers neither needed or valued such a literal correlation. Their world and its time were constructed of the liturgies which determined them, not by the course of the sun through the day. One world view was literal, the other figurative.[8] They were differently constructed understandings, and, therefore, different religious cultures, for at the basis of the division were elements essential to the interpretation of all other monastic activity—ascetical, liturgical, spiritual, and secular. Since the cultural perspectives differed, the practices which make such a plan of life emotionally accessible and satisfying was not correlative. The emotional appropriation could not happen for the hermit monk. The cultural transfer had not been complete and the hermit monk never

---

[8]This difference is fully explored in the metaphor theory of George Lakoff and Mark Johnson, *Metaphors We Live By* (Chicago: U of Chicago P, 1962). See especially pages 3-10.

was able to fully enter his brothers' culture. Jacob, at many levels, would always remain a stranger to his community.

Jacob, however, was not at a disadvantage in his remaining a stranger, because even the community defined itself as a stranger to the wider culture, the wider world, in which the community found itself and from which the community withdrew. The center of ascetic behavior embraces a series of estrangements signified by a series of withdrawals.[9] Jacob withdrew from his world to join the monastic world. Then he withdrew from the monastic community to become a hermit. The rest of the community would view this series of withdrawals as a deepening conversion, as a calling toward more sanctified living. To the community's eyes, Jacob was simply progressing normally, even though his personal estrangement began in a different culture and centered on different kinds of issues. To become a monk means precisely to become a stranger, first to the world at large, and then even to other monastic practitioners. To understand this process of continually becoming a stranger within oneself and from society we turn now to Orthodox ascetical theology.

The Case of Basil's Second Letter

Basil of Caesarea plays a central and critical role in the discussion of religious formation through asceticism, and his influence persists today. His writings belong to the foundational documents of Christian asceticism and of Orthodox monasticism. His famous second letter to his friend and fellow bishop Gregory of Nazianzus (329-89), written about 358,[10] provides a concise summary of Basil's ascetical theology and encapsulates the ascetical culture which Basil wished to promulgate. For this essay Basil's letter provides a testing site for the dynamics of ascetical theory presented above.

---

[9]For a fuller account of this process, see my "Daemons and the Perfecting of the Monk's Body: Monastic Anthropology, Daemonology, and Asceticism," *Semeia* 58 (1992) 47-79.

[10]The text and most of the following translations from this letter (unless otherwise noted) are found in *St. Basil: The Letters*, 1:6-25, trans. Roy J. Deferrari, Loeb Classical Library 190 (Cambridge, MA: Harvard UP, 1972).

Cultural Level

At the basis of Basil's ascetical theology rests the preference of a new world over the common world. Basil posits a blissful or blessed state "which counts all the things of this earth as nothing compared with the promised bliss which is in store for us,"[11] and which, he submits, is the norm of human life. This blissful world or state contrasts negatively with the problematized world that only leads to mental and spiritual distraction, because "man's mind when distracted by his countless worldly cares cannot focus itself distinctly on the truth."[12] The blessed state may be characterized in a number of different ways: entrance into the heavenly court,[13] transformation into a living temple of God,[14] filling the memory with God.[15] These all relate to the existence of another world, a more blessed world which is the destiny for human beings. As destiny, however, that blessed world does not naturally reveal itself to the common world which is filled with trouble, distractions, disturbances, and the remnants of distraction and the distracted self.[16] Escape from this world, and withdrawal from society, and the recreation of the self constitute the means of entering this blissful world.[17]

Entrance into this world requires withdrawal from city, society, and from self. The goal of withdrawal is to contemplate God. A myth informs both the withdrawal and the contemplation of God. The soul, when it is undistracted by worldly cares, naturally ascends toward contemplation of God, and receives an illumination which enables the soul to forget its own nature and thus no longer able to be drawn away from contemplation and illumination; this contemplation and

---

[11]"τῆς πάντα τὰ τῆδε μηδὲν τιθεμένης πρὸς τὴν ἐν ἐπαγγελίαις ἡμῖν ἀποκειμένην μακαριότητα" ibid. 1:6-8.

[12]"οὕτω καὶ νοῦν ἀνθρώπου ὑπὸ μυρίων τῶν κατὰ τὸν κόσμον φροντίδων περιελκόμενον ἀμήχανον ἐναργῶς ἐνατενίσαι τῇ ἀληθείᾳ" ibid. 1:8-9.

[13]"τί οὖν μακαριώτερον τοῦ τὴν ἀγγέλων χορείαν ἐν γῇ μιμεῖσθαι" ibid. 1:12.

[14]"οὕτω γινόμεθα ναὸς Θεοῦ" ibid. 1:18.

[15]"καὶ τοῦτό ἐστι Θεοῦ ἐνοίκησις, τὸ διὰ τῆς μνήμης ἐνιδρυμένον ἔχειν ἐν ἑαυτῷ τὸν Θεὸν" ibid. 1:16.

[16]"κατέλιπον μὲν γὰρ τὰς ἐν ἄστει διατριβὰς ὡς μυρίων κακῶν ἀφορμάς" ibid. 1:8.

[17]"Τούτων δὲ μία φυγή, ὁ χωρισμὸς ἀπὸ τοῦ κόσμου παντός" ibid. 1:10.

illumination orient the soul to the development of virtuous living.[18] Prayer, scripture study, pious asceticism, create this tranquility of mind which characterizes both the illuminated state and the goal of withdrawal. This transformation of the soul by contemplation and illumination reconstructs and reconstitutes the soul—a soul no longer distracted and weighed down by the lower nature, but one oriented toward the memory of God and the tranquility of contemplation. By becoming a stranger to the common and normative world, the ascetic begins the process of self-transformation and renewal.

Social Level

Social relations are at once problematized and idealized. The positive goal of "withdrawal" finds its definition in a series of privations which characterize the ascetic's estrangement.

> The withdrawal from the world is not somatically to be outside it, but rather to sever the sympathy of the soul towards the body and to become cityless, homeless, possessionless, friendless, propertyless, without means of living, without business activity, without converse with other humans, and ignorant of human teaching.[19]

The marking of this "withdrawal" is (as the Greek text indicates) through the privative. This withdrawal also means the reception into the heart of "impressions of the divine teaching."

Involvement in social and business relations hinders the activity of the ascetic and impedes progress toward the supernatural goal by implicating the soul in distracting and complicating systems. Only by

---

[18]"νοῦς μὲν γὰρ μὴ σκεδαννύμενος ἐπὶ τὰ ἔξω μηδὲ ὑπὸ τῶν αἰσθητηρίων ἐπὶ τὸν κόσμον διαχεόμενος ἐπάνεισι μὲν πρὸς ἑαυτόν, δι᾽ ἑαυτοῦ δὲ πρὸς τὴν περὶ Θεοῦ ἔννοιαν ἀναβαίνει· κἀκείνῳ τῷ κάλλει περιλαμπόμενός τε καὶ ἐλλαμπόμενος καὶ αὐτῆς τῆς φύσεως λήθην λαμβάνει· μήτε πρὸς τροφῆς φροντίδα μήτε πρὸς περιβολαίων μέριμναν τὴν ψυχὴν καθελκόμενος, ἀλλὰ σχολὴν ἀπὸ τῶν γηΐνων φροντίδων ἄγων, τὴν πᾶσαν ἑαυτοῦ σπουδὴν ἐπὶ τὴν κτῆσιν τῶν αἰωνίων ἀγαθῶν μετατίθησι" ibid. 1:12-14.

[19]"κόσμου δὲ ἀναχώρησις, οὐ τὸ ἔξω αὐτοῦ γενέσθαι σωματικῶς, ἀλλὰ τῆς πρὸς τὸ σῶμα συμπαθείας τὴν ψυχὴν ἀπορρῆξαι καὶ γενέσθαι ἄπολιν, ἄοικον, ἀνίδιον, ἀφιλέταιρον, ἀκτήμονα, ἄβιον, ἀπράγμονα, ἀσυνάλλακτον, ἀμαθῆ τῶν ἀνθρωπίνων διδαγμάτων, ἕτοιμον ὑποδέξασθαι τῇ καρδίᾳ τὰς ἐκ τῆς θείας διδασκαλίας ἐγγινομένας διατυπώσεις" ibid. 1:10. Translation mine.

becoming a stranger to family, friends, business, wisdom, and all other socially normative activities may the ascetic achieve the highest teaching, the divine state.

Consistent with this problematization of social relationships, marital and familial relationships present particular problems. Both in the desire for marriage, children, and a household in which to nurture a family, and in the actual marriage relationship, rearing of children and management of a household, family destroys tranquility.[20] Such relationships bind the ascetic to the matters of the lower nature of human being and prevent the soul from its natural ascent to God and toward contemplation. The ascetic, therefore, must become a stranger to family and even the desire for family.

The ascetic develops a different set of relationships to replace the old, rejected relations. These idealized relationships encouraged in Basil's system revolve about the culturally defined higher or spiritual aspect of human existence. Ascetics form spiritual community. This is the intent, after all, of the letter to Gregory so that he might be persuaded to live the ascetic life in community. The community, oriented toward tranquility and the contemplation of God, structures relationships so as to assist the soul in its ascent. This community also includes the society of scriptural models. One by one, the masters of the religious life (Jesus, Joseph the lover of chastity, Job the teacher of fortitude, David the warrior and hymnodist, Moses the strong advocate against idolatry) become active members of the community through meditation, imitation, and godly converse. And, of course, there are the angels and the heavenly chorus with whom the ascetic sings the divine hymns. These relationships with other human beings, with biblical archetypes, and with heavenly beings reformulate the nature of society and reconstitute society now only in relation to ascetical goals. While becoming a stranger to normative social relations, the ascetic becomes friends of biblical figures, angels, and

---

[20]"ἀλλὰ τὸν μὲν οὔπω τοῖς δεσμοῖς τοῦ γάμου συνεζευγμένον λυσσώδεις ἐπιθυμίαι καὶ ὁρμαὶ δυσκάθεκτοι καὶ ἔρωτές τινες δυσέρωτες ἐκταράσσουσι· τὸν δὲ ἤδη συγκατειλημμένον ὁμοζύγῳ ἕτερος θόρυβος φροντίδων ἐκδέχεται· ἐν ἀπαιδίᾳ, παίδων ἐπιθυμία· ἐν τῇ κτήσει τῶν παίδων, παιδοτροφίας μέριμνα, γυναικὸς φυλακή, οἴκου ἐπιμέλεια, οἰκετῶν προστασίαι, αἱ κατὰ τὰ συμβόλαια βλάβαι, οἱ πρὸς τοὺς γείτονας διαπληκτισμοί, αἱ ἐν τοῖς δικαστηρίοις συμπλοκαί, τῆς ἐμπορίας οἱ κίνδυνοι, αἱ τῆς γεωργίας διαπονήσεις" ibid. 1:8-10.

God. The new society implicates the ascetic in the same way that the negative relationships of the old society did, but now in relation to the proper goal and higher aspect of human being.

Again, at the social level, the ascetic recreates and redefines the self. The self created in social solitude, unlearns habits acquired in the world for relating, and learns a manner of conversation consistent with the new divine and heavenly society in which the ascetic lives.[21] The physical location of the ascetic mirrors the new self. It is far from social intercourse, far from distractions and interruptions, conducive to contemplation, and peopled only with sympathetic others of similar bent.

Personal Level

The seriousness of becoming a stranger within and a stranger without is most evident at the personal level. The negative aspects of estrangement are most pronounced at the level of personal integration and behavior. Asceticism appears as mostly negative behavioral injunctions, the negative aspects of becoming a stranger. Despite leaving the city, Basil describes himself as unable to leave his own self, since even in his solitude he carries about with him the interior disorders and disturbances which were present in the city. Even though he is a stranger without, Basil finds the creation of the interior stranger to be the most difficult. This is the central behavioral problem: to still this interior dialogue and to fill the mind rather with the memory of God. This quietude emerges from a retraining of the mind and the self, like the training of the eye not to shift its gaze sporadically, but to focus its attention on only one thing.[22] The mind, like the eye, needs to be focussed. The interior stranger emerges from the intense concentration on God alone.

---

[21]"ἑτοιμασία δὲ καρδίας ἡ ἀπομάθησις τῶν ἐκ πονηρᾶς συνηθείας προκατασχόντων αὐτὴν διδαγμάτων" ibid. 1:10.

[22]"ὡς γὰρ ὀφθαλμὸν περιαγόμενον συνεχῶς, καὶ νῦν μὲν ἐπὶ τὰ πλάγια περιφερόμενον, νῦν δὲ πρὸς τὰ ἄνω καὶ κάτω πυκνὰ μεταστρεφόμενον, ἰδεῖν ἐναργῶς τὸ ὑποκείμενον οὐχ οἷόν τε, ἀλλὰ χρὴ προσερεισθῆναι τὴν ὄψιν τῷ ὁρωμένῳ, εἰ μέλλοι ἐναργῆ αὐτοῦ ποιεῖσθαι τὴν θέαν· οὕτω καὶ νοῦν ἀνθρώπου ὑπὸ μυρίων τῶν κατὰ τὸν κόσμον φροντίδων περιελκόμενον ἀμήχανον ἐναργῶς ἐνατενίσαι τῇ ἀληθείᾳ" ibid. 1:8.

The beginning of that focussing occurs in the renunciation of marriage, family, and household, and the renunciation as well of the desire for them. This renunciation is mirrored in flight from the world and withdrawal into a life of social privation. In this altered environment, the soul may be reconceptualized and understood anew, so that the old patterns of behavior and reaction may be broken and new patterns inscribed on the ascetic's life. Through solitude, and assisted by liturgical and corporate prayer, the old ways are erased and new ones created. Through solitude and the fellowship of others living this higher life, the tongue, eyes, ears, and lips are turned away from their lower functions and reoriented toward the steady gaze upon God.

This new person, capable of contemplating God, stranger to the world while friend of saints and angels, finds new practices to fill the void created by stillness. The ascetic's new personality orients self toward positive practices which enhance the new personality. The study of scripture opens up the new world.[23] After study of scripture, prayer reënvisions God and orients the ascetic to the new world which emerges as the memory of God fills the mind with nothing but God.[24] Other practices, such as the careful regulation of conversation, attention to simplicity and functional vesture, limited and healthful food, and moderate sleep, assist in the process of ascent by enacting in the body the reorientation toward the spiritual, the modulation of the self, necessary for the vision of God. The stranger within and the stranger without gradually becomes a friend of God.

Two Sets of Conclusions

The story of Jacob the monk, as well as Basil's ascetical theology, have underscored the complex relationship of the familiar and the

---

[23]"Μεγίστη δὲ ὁδὸς πρὸς τὴν τοῦ καθήκοντος εὕρεσιν καὶ ἡ μελέτη τῶν θεοπνεύστων Γραφῶν. ἐν ταύταις γὰρ καὶ αἱ τῶν πράξεων ὑποθῆκαι εὑρίσκονται καὶ οἱ βίοι τῶν μακαρίων ἀνδρῶν ἀνάγραπτοι παραδεδομένοι, οἷον εἰκόνες τινὲς ἔμψυχοι τῆς κατὰ Θεὸν πολιτείας, τῷ μιμήματι τῶν ἀγαθῶν ἔργων πρόκεινται" ibid. 1:14.

[24]"Εὐχαὶ πάλιν τὰς ἀναγνώσεις διαδεχόμεναι νεαρωτέραν τὴν ψυχὴν καὶ ἀκμαιοτέραν τῷ πρὸς Θεὸν πόθῳ κεκινημένην παραλαμβάνουσιν. εὐχὴ δὲ καλή, ἡ ἐναργῆ ἐμποιοῦσα τοῦ Θεοῦ ἔννοιαν τῇ ψυχῇ. καὶ τοῦτό ἐστι Θεοῦ ἐνοίκησις, τὸ διὰ τῆς μνήμης ἐνιδρυμένον ἔχειν ἐν ἑαυτῷ τὸν Θεόν" ibid. 1:16.

strange, the old and the new. The process of becoming a stranger to the normative culture becomes the means of becoming a participant in another world and another society, while also becoming the basis of a new personality. But why become a stranger within and a stranger without? What is the social value of withdrawal? What is the social function of asceticism? This leads to two different kinds of conclusions. The first is about the historical rhetoric of Basil's letter; the second is about the method of remaking modern society.

First, I will address the historical conclusions about Basil's ascetical theology.[25] Basil's letter probably does not address Basil's own biography, nor even that of his fellow bishop Gregory, because they both were actively involved in the life of the Church and in its theological development. Basil promulgates, however, a life which both Hellene and Christian could understand. Although there may be some modeling of the withdrawn philosophical life on that of the monks of the Egyptian and Palestinian deserts, Basil's description does not resonate with the literatures and models developed in desert monasticism.[26] Rather, Basil's monastic culture resonates fully with the sort of philosophically based asceticism found in Greco-Roman philosophical circles.[27] Basil's description of his withdrawn life could provide the rule of living which is implicit in Porphyry's *Life of Plotinus* and the *Order of his Works*; Basil's myth of the soul rising to contemplation parallels that of Plotinus in his *Enneads*. The image of the contemplative life of undistracted attention to God, as well as the vision of the continuous delving into the mysteries of God, find their theoretical explication in Gregory Thaumaturgus' *Oration to Origen.*

[25]Many historians have studied asceticism in historical context. See Peter Brown, *The Body and Society: Men, Women and Sexual Renunciation in Early Christianity* (New York: Columbia UP, 1988), especially pages 210-338; Elizabeth A. Clark, *Ascetic Piety and Women's Faith: Essays in Late Ancient Christianity* (Lewiston, NY: Edwin Mellen, 1986); and Susan Ashbrook Harvey, Asceticism and Society in Crisis: John of Ephesus and the "Lives of the Eastern Saints" (Berkeley: U of California P, 1990).

[26]For a description, see Philip Rousseau, *Pachomius: The Making of a Community in Fourth-Century Egypt*, The Transformation of the Classical Heritage 6 (Berkeley: U of California P, 1985).

[27]Anthony Meredith, "Asceticism—Christian and Greek," *Journal of Theological Studies* n.s. 27 (1976) 312-32. For the Christian perspective alone, see Philip Rousseau, *Ascetics, Authority, and the Church in the Age of Jerome and Cassian* (Oxford: Oxford UP, 1978).

Basil's intertextual field lay primarily with the images of Platonic community refracted through Plotinus and Porphyry, and with the images of Christian gnosticism refracted through Origen's ascetic writings and Gregory Thaumaturgus. These texts, together with the Jewish *On the Contemplative Life* of Philo of Alexandria, provide the primary reference points for Basil's philosophical and ascetical life. Basil applies the pan-religious cultural phenomenon of ascetic withdrawal for contemplation to the ascetical life of the Christian. His strategy was to apply the "Hellenic" or "Roman" to Christian intellectual life. Philosophical and religious movements outside Christianity were, through ascetical practices, integrated into Christian practice. Basil Christianizes foreign practice by creating a Christian philosophical and ascetical life of withdrawal for contemplation, comparable to that of other philosophical and ascetic communities of Late Antiquity.

In the days following the Emperor Constantine, Christianity moved from a persecuted to an imperial religion.[28] The writers of the fourth-century Church, responding to the shift in religious attitudes and religion, consciously began to create a Christian culture.[29] Emperor Julian's attempt to discredit and displace that Christian culture stands as proof of the vitality and speed of this cultivation of a universal culture.[30] Likewise, Julian's attempt to reinstitute the philosophical asceticism of Hellenic culture as the means of displacing Christian influence also speaks of the centrality of asceticism to that cultural agenda.

Patristic religious writing aimed at creating a Christian culture whose theological battles were a screen against which the contours and geography of that Christian culture were projected. Fighting Gnostics, Manichaeans, and other religious organizations which were outside the Church, as well as fighting heretical doctrinal and ascetical movements within the Church, the early writers of the Christian era developed an acceptable cultural milieu through argumentation. These battles were not simply theological arguments, but elements in the construction of

---

[28]For an extensive discussion, see W.H.C. Frend, *The Rise of Christianity* (Philadelphia: Fortress, 1984) 439-517.

[29]See Robin Lane Fox, *Pagans and Christians* (New York: Knopf, 1987), especially pages 21-23.

[30]See G.W. Bowersock, *Julian the Apostate* (Cambridge, MA: Harvard UP, 1978) 55-65.

a world view, the foundation of the new culture.

The creation of this new culture, with its new understanding of human personality, social relations, and cultural dynamics, was a complex ascetical activity. The new Christian culture begins in the estrangement from the old Roman culture. The withdrawal creates the space in which a new culture may be founded. So at first, all the old Roman culture is marked as "stranger" and rejected, but gradually the most effective elements of that society are translated into the Christian culture. The cultural stranger must also become a friend of God. And this is what Basil is doing. The best of the estranged culture is transferred into the Christian faith, reconciling the most prized aspects of the older culture with the new creation in Christianity. By being transferred into Christianity, however, the old cultural systems of contemplation become, like the ascetic, something new. The new context, the new symbolic systems, the new social relations create a different meaning in a different environment. In historical terms, this ascetical project of the early Church became precisely the instrument of cultural, social, and psychological redefinition and reorientation, and simultaneously the means of ascribing new meaning and interpretations to common cultural realities. Historically, asceticism, by claiming the reality of being a stranger to the old cultural way of living, created the means whereby the old could be remade into something new.

This is the historical conclusion to my presentation on the stranger within and the stranger without in ascetical theory and in Basil of Caesarea's second letter. There is also a conclusion regarding contemporary life. I learned a great deal from talking with the monk Jacob—much about him, but even more about myself, American culture, cultural myopia, and frustrations with the world as it exists. Jacob and most ascetics shed light on the world they have left. The ascetic illuminates the dynamics of the world by holding up a light at its edges.

Jacob the ascetic speaks to us, not of becoming a stranger in order to baptize the old culture into the new (as Basil did), but of the possibility, through personal formation, of transforming our own lives, our relationships, our world. Jacob directs our attention to the power of transformation.

At the personal level, Jacob always sought out the strange, the foreign, the different, as the place precisely where he might more directly find God. From the cultured sophistication of English university life, Jacob ended up as an unwashed, bearded, fasting, poorly clothed, monk in a small hermitage on a Greek island. His transformation led him directly into difference, into the strange. We, however, fear the different. We are xenophobic, fearers of the strange. So we learn instead to create homogenous communities of similar people—where the "we" may signify a very diverse set of possibilities: Muslim fundamentalist, Christian liberal, Vietnamese Buddhist, Indian Hindu, American Indian. Our society has yet to be transformed into a society capable of including wide diversity and difference. Ascetics teach us that we are all strangers, we are all strange, we are all on the outside looking in, and, therefore, that we are all called to the performances which bring us into closer contact with the other, the stranger, the different, so that we may be transformed and find our rest, as Jacob did. By embracing the stranger, we become a friend.

Jacob also speaks to us in our modern times about the transformation of society. This British convert to Eastern Orthodox Christianity called the rest of his community (and ours) to task for unfaithfulness to our highest ideals. Although we modern Western people speak of ourselves as peaceable people, yet we continue to construct the normative relationship of people around violence. Our cities are filled with armies of youths, equipped with the weapons of destruction, using them to destroy those perceived as their enemies. Our Churches violently attack each other for disagreement about values. Our government violently enters other countries to inflict upon them a peace to our liking. Our national congress fights and bickers continually, without ending the sort of bureaucratic stalement that our continued progress and corporate health depend on. Our weapons are words, drugs, guns, abusive patterns, slurs, sound-bites, characterizations, dishonest speaking, and disrespect. We are a violent people who speak of ourselves as peaceable, inviting, loving, and kind. The ascetic points a way for each one of us to withdraw from the world of violence, and to construct, through the reformation of each individual life, a society of peace.

And finally, the ascetic points to the transformation of the world. The ascetic points to the universality of the need for transformation, of the movement from estrangement to friendship, of the transformation of violence into peace. Everyone everywhere in the world must undertake an ascetical transformation. Standing on the edge of society, the ascetic shows the rest of us the interconnectedness of all things: ascetic with non-ascetic, rich with poor, Indian with African, American with Bosnian, Muslim with Christian with animist. Everything around us interconnects and forms a unity with everything else. We are both part of the transformation and part of the need for transformation, part of the problem and part of the solution, part of the violence in the cities and part of the poverty in the country, part of the bickering in Washington and part of the peacemaking in Palestine, part of the Hezbollah and part of the Serbian Christians. The ascetic speaks from the edge of society. No matter how we withdraw, no matter how we define ourselves and our social relations and our world, no matter where and who we are, ultimately, we can never be a stranger within or a stranger without. There is no such thing as an estrangement, there is no such person as a stranger. We are all, both within and without, whether we know it or ignore it, ascetics forming ourselves into a new people, into a new society, into a newly understood world.

5

DE VTRAQVE CIVITATE

Strangers in a Foreign Land

Kenneth B. Steinhauser

T he inquiry into the relationship between Jesus and Paul, which
grew out of the "quest for the historical Jesus" preoccupation of
the late nineteenth and early twentieth centuries, remains to this day a
continuing concern of biblical scholars and theologians alike. Paul is
frequently alleged to have been the real founder of Christianity while
Jesus, standing at the beginning of the new messianic sect, is an
elusive figure whose genuine historical identity can never be recovered.
The myth of the gospels inserts the enigmatic sayings of the cynic
philosopher, Jesus, into fictitious scenes created by the community who
believed in him.[1] Paul, the first theologian of the new religion,
developed its theoretical underpinnings and its world view.

In this context, then, the relationship between Jesus and Paul
becomes a burning issue.[2] Most students of the New Testament would
have to agree with the assertion that Jesus preached the kingdom of
God while Paul preached Jesus. This statement, as simple as it may
appear, implies that a tremendous theological transformation had taken
place in the two decades between the ministry of Jesus and the mission
of Paul. The preacher became the preached. The subject of Christianity
became its object. Jesus came preaching the advent of the kingdom of
God while Paul preached the redemptive death and Resurrection of
Jesus: "Jesus Christ is Lord" (Phil 2:11). My purpose here is not to
review the "Jesus-Paul" controversy in its historical details but to

---

[1]On Jesus as a cynic philosopher, see Burton L. Mack, *A Myth of Innocence:
Mark and Christian Origins* (Philadelphia: Fortress, 1988) 67-74.

[2]For an overview and a collection of studies dealing with this problem, see
From Jesus to Paul: Studies in Honor of Francis Wright Beare, eds. Peter
Richardson and John C. Hurd (Waterloo: Wilfrid Laurier UP, 1984).

propose the "Jesus-Paul" controversy as a paradigm for understanding contextual theological development. In other words, I wish to demonstrate that just as Paul adapted the apocalyptic message of Jesus to changing historical circumstances, which led him to consider the concrete salvation of individual human beings, so also Augustine adapted the essentially Pauline soteriology, which he had inherited, to new historical circumstances, which led him to consider human beings in community, society and history.

From Jesus to Paul

Otto Kuss rightly describes the "Jesus-Paul" problem as existing on three levels.[3] First, the question is often raised whether Paul actually knew the earthly Jesus before the Easter event. Due to the lack of historical evidence this question cannot and will never be answered. Second, one may inquire as to the portrait of Jesus which Paul paints in his letters and one may compare this characterization to other portraits found in the gospels and elsewhere. This would insert the writings of Paul into the historical Jesus problem, which is not under consideration here. Third, the relationship of the preaching of Jesus to the preaching of Paul may be investigated. This third aspect of the "Jesus-Paul" problem is the one which concerns us here and now. Both Jesus and Paul have a gospel to proclaim. Both Jesus and Paul explicitly use the word "gospel" in a similar context, leading one to conclude that they are speaking about the same thing. Jesus' good news announces that the kingdom of God is at hand.[4] Paul's good news announces that Jesus died for our sins, was buried, and on the third day was raised according to the scriptures.[5]

Various theories have been developed to explain the transition from Jesus' gospel to Paul's. Early in the present century Wilhelm Wrede and the *Religionsgeschichtliche Schule* held that Paul had transferred a pre-existing salvation myth to Jesus.[6] In other words, the Christianity

---

[3]See Otto Kuss, *Paulus: Die Rolle des Apostels in der theologischen Entwicklung der Urkirche*, Auslegung und Verkündigung 3 (Regensburg: Pustet, 1976) 440-51.

[4]See Mark 1:15.

[5]See 1 Cor 15:3-4.

[6]William Wrede, *Paul* (1907; Lexington: ATLA, 1962) 147-54; on this

of Paul was the result of a religious syncretism involving the amalgamation of Christianity with the mythological pagan mysteries. Wrede was reacting against Adolf von Harnack's theory that Paul represents the change from Palestinian to Hellenistic Christianity.[7] In this case, during the Gentile mission the original message of the Jewish Jesus was Hellenized by Paul. Christianity then is the end result of an Hegelian synthesis, which grew out of the encounter between primitive Jewish Christianity and Hellenistic thought. Neither of these views is in vogue today, especially in the light of the more recent research of Martin Hengel, who has adequately demonstrated that the sharp distinction between Palestinian Judaism and diaspora Judaism is fallacious because Palestine was already thoroughly Hellenized at the time of Jesus.[8] Furthermore, Jesus himself was a Hellenized Jew or in the words of John Dominic Crossan "a Mediterranean peasant."[9] Even when one investigates the "urban" environment of the Pauline mission in order to describe the social milieu of primitive Christian expansion,[10] one discovers that for Paul neither the city nor the village nor the empire becomes an analogy descriptive of a theological reality. Rather, the paradox of Jesus' self-emptying or *kenosis*, his humiliation and his ultimate exaltation dominates Paul's theology of incarnation and atonement. According to the early Christian hymn, which Paul cites in his letter to the Philippians, Jesus emptied himself and was glorified by God the Father.[11]

question, see Hans Rollmann, "*Paulus alienus*: William Wrede on Comparing Jesus and Paul," in *From Jesus to Paul* 23-45.

[7]See Adolf von Harnack, *Die Mission und Ausbreitung des Christentums in den ersten drei Jahrhunderten* (Leipzig: Hinrichs, 1902) 1-60; unfortunately more recent studies, for example E. Glenn Hinson, *The Evangelization of the Roman Empire: Identity and Adaptability* (Macon: Mercer UP, 1987), seem to be overly preoccupied with internal institutional development rather than with the serious issue of theological acculturation.

[8]See Martin Hengel, *Judaism and Hellenism: Studies in their Encounter in Palestine during the Early Hellenistic Period* (Philadelphia: Fortress, 1981) 58-106.

[9]See John Dominic Crossan, *The Historical Jesus: The Life of a Mediterranean Jewish Peasant* (San Francisco: Harper, 1991) 417-26.

[10]See Wayne A. Meeks, *The First Urban Christians: The Social World of the Apostle Paul* (New Haven: Yale UP, 1983) 171-80.

[11]See Phil 2:6-11; also Donald Macpherson Baillie, *God was in Christ: An Essay on Incarnation and Atonement* (London: Faber, 1963) 106-32.

Stephen Wilson has shed further light on the "Jesus-Paul" controversy by highlighting similarities in the preaching of Jesus and Paul.[12] First, the eschatology of both is immediate while still reflecting the tension of "already" but "not yet." The eschatological proclamation of Jesus that "the kingdom of God has come near" (Mark 1:15). is quite similar to the statement of Paul that "the present form of this world is passing away" (1 Cor 7:31). Second, both the preaching of Jesus concerning the law in the Sermon on the Mount and the teaching of Paul concerning the covenant in Galatians show that the law is not salvific "for if justification comes through the law, then Christ died for nothing" (Gal 2:21). Third, the ethical teachings of both Jesus and Paul grow out of their respective eschatologies. For example, as Jesus speaks of eunuchs for the kingdom, Paul states that it would be better not to marry in this time of stress. Fourth, both have a similar concept of Messiahship. Paul's proclamation of Jesus as Messiah is rooted in the teaching of Jesus specifically where Jesus speaks of himself as the Son of Man coming in future glory.

However, Wilson also observes certain differences. In Paul we find a further development. In the light of the strictly theological preaching of Jesus, Paul developed a Christology by dealing with the necessary issues of sin, grace, freedom and salvation. In other words, Paul's Christology logically required the development of an anthropology corresponding to the realities which Paul believed had occurred in the redemptive death and Resurrection of Jesus. Thus, among other human concerns, Paul writes about being baptized into the death and Resurrection of Jesus or, in other words, the receiving side of Jesus' redemptive act.

From Paul to Augustine

In the famous garden scene recorded in his *Confessions*, at the command of a child Augustine picks up Paul's letter to the Romans, reads a section and is thus moved to conversion: "Not in reveling and drunkenness, not in debauchery and licentiousness, not in quarreling and jealousy. Instead, put on the Lord Jesus Christ, and make no

---

[12]See Stephen G. Wilson, "From Jesus to Paul: The Contours and Consequences of a Debate," in *From Jesus to Paul* 1-21.

provision for the flesh, to gratify its desires" (Rom 13:13-14).[13] Since Paul was popular among the Manichaeans, perhaps Augustine had already come to know the letters of Paul during his Manichaean youth. In any event we are certain that the letters of Paul enjoyed an independent circulation in North Africa from the earliest days of Christianity there. A Christian accused before a pagan tribunal in Scillita publicly told a judge that he had with him "books and letters of a just man named Paul."[14]

In the late fourth and early fifth centuries, there was obviously a resurgence of interest in Paul in the West since no less than six authors published commentaries on various Pauline letters. Earlier in Alexandria Origen had already written several commentaries on the letters of the Pauline corpus including Romans, Philippians, Colossians, Thessalonians, Hebrews and Titus. Rufinus translated Origen's Romans commentary into Latin sometime after 378 when he had settled in Jerusalem. Extensive portions of this commentary are extant only in its Latin translation although some fragments survive in Greek. Origen's other Pauline commentaries are lost. Latin theologians were not content to rely exclusively on translations of Origen. Marius Victorinus wrote commentaries on Galatians, Ephesians and Philippians shortly after 362. Ambrosiaster or pseudo-Ambrose wrote a commentary on the thirteen Pauline letters between 363 and 384. Pelagius also wrote a commentary on the thirteen Pauline letters before 410. Neither Ambrosiaster nor Pelagius included Hebrews in their respective lists of Paul's letters, probably because it was not considered Pauline. Jerome commented on Philippians, Galatians, Ephesians and Titus between 387 and 389. Augustine wrote two commentaries on Romans (one incomplete) and a commentary on Galatians between 394 and 396. Furthermore, the elderly priest, friend and confidant of Augustine, Simplician, who had succeeded Ambrose in the bishopric of Milan, wrote to Augustine posing a series of questions on the letter to the Romans and the book of Kings, which Augustine answered with his *De diuersis questionibus ad Simplicianum*, written about 397 shortly after

---

[13]*Confessiones* 8.12.29, Corpus Christianorum Series Latina 27, ed. Luc Verheijen (Turnhout: Brepols, 1981) 131; R.S. Pine-Coffin, trans., *Saint Augustine: "Confessions"* (New York: Penguin, 1961) 178.

[14]"The Acts of the Scillitan Martyrs," trans. Herbert Musurillo [text: J. Armitage Robinson] *The Acts of the Christian Martyrs* (Oxford: Clarendon, 1972) 89.

his own entry into the episcopacy. Tyconius, the maverick Donatist, was also a foremost interpreter of Paul.[15] This is abundantly evident in the third rule of his *Liber regularum*, which deals with the law and justification by faith. In summation, then, toward the end of the fourth century there was an intense interest in and study of Paul among both orthodox and heterodox theologians in the West. In this regard, Augustine was no exception. Although Augustine's questions sprout from his Roman cultural environment, his answers are frequently Pauline.

Galatians 5:17 was an especially significant verse for Augustine: "For what the flesh desires is opposed to the Spirit, and what the Spirit desires is opposed to the flesh." Citing this passage in his *Confessions*, Augustine remarks that he experienced the struggle of good and evil within himself: "So these two wills within me, one old, one new, one the servant of the flesh, the other of the spirit, were in conflict and between them they tore my soul apart."[16] In his *City of God* Augustine draws the social consequences of this teaching:

> The conflict, therefore, that arose between Remus and Romulus showed how the earthly city is divided against itself, but the dispute between Cain and Abel proved that there is enmity between the two cities themselves, the City of God and the city of men. Accordingly, there are battles of wicked against wicked. There are also battles of wicked against good and good against wicked. But the good, if they have achieved perfection, cannot fight among themselves. If, however, they are advancing toward perfection but have not yet attained it, fighting among them is possible to the extent that each good man may fight against another through that part of him with which he also fights against himself. Even in a single person "the desires of the flesh are against the spirit, and the desires of the spirit are against the flesh."[17]

Paul had already shaped the theocentric preaching of Jesus that the kingdom of God is now present into a christocentric anthropology of sin and salvation. Here Augustine now transforms Paul's christocentric anthropology of sin and salvation into a theological understanding of

[15]See William S. Babcock, "Augustine's Interpretation of Romans (A.D. 394-396)," *Augustinian Studies* 10 (1979) 55-74; and "Augustine and Tyconius: A Study in the Latin Appropriation of Paul," *Studia Patristica* 17 (1982) 1209-15.

[16]*Confessiones* 8.5.10, Verheijen 120; Pine-Coffin 164.

[17]*De ciuitate Dei* 15.5, Loeb Classical Library 414, trans. Philip Levine [text: B. Dombart and A. Kalb] (Cambridge: Harvard UP, 1966) 429-31.

history and the human community. The eschatological urgency of Jesus' message precluded the development of a sophisticated soteriology while the eschatological urgency of Paul's preaching precluded the development of a theology of history and society. By the beginning of the fifth century that sense of urgency had waned. Augustine viewed the coming of Christ as a future event. As Paul had to deal with the relationship of the proclaimer to his proclamation, Augustine now had to address a new problem which emerged out of the extension of Christianity through time and space. The eschatological shift from present to future necessitated a paradigmatic shift in interpretation. Basil Studer appropriately points out that the second part of Augustine's *City of God* is a kind of biblical theology, namely an *historia sacra*, based on the Old and New Testaments.[18] Thus, God's present kingdom became God's glorious city.

From Kingdom to City

In his *Retractationes* Augustine makes the following comment regarding his *City of God*: "Although the entire twenty-two books were written on each city (*de utraque ciuitate*), they have received their title from the better one so as to be called only the city of God (*de ciuitate Dei*)."[19] Generally speaking scholars have found four possible sources, which may either individually or in combination account for Augustine's concept of the two cities.

First, according to some, particularly Alfred Adam, Augustine remains forever the Manichaean.[20] Dualistic Manichaeism with its principle of good and principle of evil is the source of the two cities

---

[18]Basil Studer, "Zum Aufbau von Augustins *De Civitate Dei*," in *Collectanea Augustiniana: Mélanges T.J. van Bavel*, Bibliotheca Ephemeridum Theologicarum Lovaniensium 42-B, eds. B. Bruning, M. Lamberigts, J. van Houtem (Leuven: University P, 1990) 948.

[19]*Retractationes* 2.43(69), Corpus Christianorum Series Latina 57, ed. Almut Mutzenbecher (Turnhout: Brepols, 1984) 125; Fathers of the Church 60, trans. Mary Inez Bogan (Washington: Catholic U of Am P, 1968) 209.

[20]See Alfred Adam, "Der manichäische Ursprung der Lehre von den zwei Reichen bei Augustin," *Theologische Literaturzeitung* 77 (1952) 385-90; and "Das Fortwirken des Manichäismus bei Augustin," *Zeitschrift für Kirchengeschichte* 69 (1958) 1-25; rpt. *Sprache und Dogma: Untersuchungen zu Grundproblemen der Kirchengeschichte* (Gütersloh: Mohn, 1969) 133-66.

or two kingdoms which wage war with one another. Augustine had to frequently defend himself against residual Manichaeism and the question remains whether, or to what extent, Augustine actually broke with his Manichaean past.

Second, Prosper Alfaric and many after him have identified the conversion of Augustine as a conversion to Neoplatonic thought which opened for Augustine the possibility of spiritual reality, including a spiritual deity who was not part of the material world but separate from it.[21] Plotinus also refers to a spiritual realm and a physical realm which approximates the two opposing cities.[22]

Third, Tyconius wrote of the Lord's bipartite body in his *Liber regularum*.[23] Heinrich Scholz finds a strong Tyconian influence in Augustine's *City of God* including some significant paraphrases from Tyconius' lost Apocalypse commentary.[24] Very clear and graphic is Tyconius' metaphor of Esau and Jacob who struggled with one another in the womb even before birth.[25] Tyconius likens that struggle to conflict within the Church.

Fourth, Johannes van Oort in his recent dissertation places the origin of Augustine's two cities in the catechetical tradition of the Church.[26] His most compelling evidence is parallel passages in Augustine's *De catechizandis rudibus* which describe the two cities to prospective converts.

Departing from these various opinions, though not necessarily altogether rejecting them, I prefer to consider Augustine primarily an

[21]See Prosper Alfaric, *L'Evolution intellectuelle de saint Augustin: Du Manichéisme au Néoplatonisme* (Paris: Nourry, 1918); also Pierre Courcelle, *Recherches sur les Confessions de saint Augustin* (Paris: Boccard, 1968) 311-82.

[22]See Ulrich Duchrow, *Christenheit und Weltverantwortung: Traditionsgeschichte und systematische Struktur der Zweireichelehre*, Forschungen und Berichte der Evangelischen Studiengemeinschaft im Auftrag des Wissenschaftlichen Kuratoriums 25 (Stuttgart: Klett, 1970) 186-93.

[23]See *Liber regularum* 2, Texts and Translations 31, Early Christian Literature Series 7, trans. William S. Babcock [text: F.C. Burkitt] (Atlanta: Scholars P, 1989) 14-21.

[24]See Heinrich Scholz, *Glaube und Unglaube in der Weltgeschichte: Ein Kommentar zu Augustins* De Civitate Dei (Leipzig: Hinrichs, 1911) 109-17.

[25]See *Liber regularum* 3, Babcock 50-51.

[26]See Johannes van Oort, *Jerusalem and Babylon: A Study into Augustine's "City of God" and the Sources of his Doctrine of the Two Cities* (Leiden: Brill, 1991) 175-98.

interpreter of Paul. Paul's emphasis on an immanent parousia prevented him from drawing the social consequences of his eschatology. For example, Paul tells the community at Thessalonica not to fret about those who have died because, when the Lord comes in glory, the dead will rise first. "Then we who are alive, who are left, will be caught up in the clouds together with them to meet the Lord in the air" (1 Thess 4:17). Clearly Paul expects the Lord to return during his lifetime. Elsewhere when Paul deals with marriage and married life, he makes no effort at all to develop a theology of marriage but interprets marriage in terms of the parousia. His advice is for the married to remain married and for the single to remain single because "the appointed time has grown short" (1 Cor 7:29).

Augustine derives his teaching *de utraque ciuitate* as a unified world view primarily from Paul's teaching concerning spirit and flesh. Augustine simultaneously completes Paul where he found him deficient and expands Pauline teaching on spirit and flesh from an anthropology into a universal theology with an extended theory of society and the state based upon the spiritual city and the earthly city—Jerusalem and Babylon. What was a somewhat theoretical anthropology in Paul becomes a storyline in Augustine. Paul writes abstractly of the conflict between the flesh and the spirit while Augustine writes concretely of human history—Troy, Greece, Carthage, Rome, and the Goths who had recently sacked the city.

Augustine's choice of words is significant. Three specific terms were available to him to describe human socio-political structures, namely *regnum, imperium* and *ciuitas. Regnum Dei* was commonly used to translate *basileia tou theou* of the synoptic gospels. The *imperium* was the worldly power of Rome. The *ciuitas* comes from the *ciues*—namely the citizens.[27] *Urbs* is a geographic term and would not come into question at all as a possible description of people living in society. The *ciuitas* is reminiscent of the *polis*. However, Augustine refers to the *ciuitas Dei*, namely God's city. Two *regna* would have

---

[27]See Wilhelm Kamlah, *Christentum und Selbstbehauptung: Historische und philosophische Untersuchungen zur Entstehung des Christentums und zu Augustins "Bürgerschaft Gottes"* (Frankfurt: Klostermann, 1940) 199-246; Alois Dempf, *Sacrum Imperium: Geschichts- und Staatsphilosophie des Mittelalters und der politischen Renaissance* (Munich: Oldenbourg, 1929) 116-32; and Lidia Storoni Mazzolani, *The Idea of the City in Roman Thought: From Walled City to Spiritual Commonwealth* (Bloomington: Indiana UP, 1970) 242-79.

been blatantly dualistic as also would have two *imperia*. One is reminded of Tyconius' interpretation of Paul *duae sunt partes in ecclesia* and elsewhere *unum corpus et bonum esse et malum.*[28] There are two *ciuitates* because the anthropological basis of the terminology is dichotomous but in no way dualistic. In other words, the image explains both the internal and external conflict without making the negative force an independent and self-sufficient entity.

Perhaps one could compare Augustine's approach to Origen's theory of exegesis as a parallel development. Since the human being, according to Plato and subsequently Philo, is made up of body, soul, and spirit, the word of God too has a corresponding threefold meaning, the literal, moral, and allegorical. Just as Origen's exegesis had an anthropological basis, so also Augustine's teaching on history and society had its foundation in anthropology. According to Paul there is an inner man and an outer man, spirit and flesh, the old man and the new man, in each and every human being. However, some men are spiritual while others are carnal. Thus, according to Augustine there is a spiritual city and fleshly city, where these men dwell. Augustine calls these realms cities because there can be no *ciuitas* without *ciues*, no city without citizens.

Ciues peregrinantes

The paradigm of transition may be considered from three different perspectives, namely history, consciousness, and plot. Each perspective has the net effect of making the Christian a stranger on earth.[29] "I would write about the origin, progress and appointed ends of the two cities, the one of God and the other of this world, in which the former resides as an alien, so far as mankind is concerned."[30]

---

[28]*Liber regularum* 7, Babcock 120-21: "There are two parts in the church"; and *Liber regularum* 2, Babcock 20-21: "The one body is both good and evil."

[29]For an overview of this theme in antiquity, see E. Fascher, "Fremder," in *Reallexikon für Antike und Christentum*, ed. Theodor Klauser (Stuttgart: Hiersemann, 1976) 8:306-47; and Norbert Brox, "Die Fremden und die Anderen im Frühchristentum," *Internationale Zeitschrift für die Praxis der Kirche* 24 (1993) 322-27.

[30]*De ciuitate Dei* 18.1, Loeb Classical Library 415, trans. E.M. Sanford and W.M. Green [text: B. Dombart and A. Kalb] (Cambridge: Harvard UP, 1965)

First, as the spirit and the flesh live in tension with each another in the human person, so also do the spiritual city and the earthly city live in tension with each other in this world. Through his investigation and description of the world's history Augustine exposes the conflict between the two cities as it existed in the events of the past, as it continues in the tumultuous happenings of the present and as it will endure as long as human beings live. Yet, in order to maintain peace God has given precepts to human beings. "This is the way that the citizens of the City of God are nursed while they sojourn here on earth and sigh for the peace of their heavenly fatherland."[31] The true Christian is never at home in this world. The citizens of God's city are strangers on this earth as the events of history continuously unfold leaving them longing for the "eternal Sabbath" which Augustine fittingly describes in the last book of his *Confessions*.[32]

Second, Augustine's description of each city presupposes a communal or perhaps even a tribal self-consciousness which is absent from Paul. In other words, the genuine Christian must be aware of himself or herself as a citizen of God's city by which he or she is distinguished from the rest of humankind. This also may imply membership in the Christian community, the Church, although the city of God cannot be equated with the Church. The mere existence of this self-consciousness is not sufficient. For the authentic Christian, belonging to God's city is the unique source of one's self-consciousness or self-identity.

Third, the city contextualizes the kingdom. Jesus proclaimed the kingdom of God; Paul proclaimed Jesus. In this transition the kingdom of God was personalized by Paul as he found it necessary to describe exactly what happens to human beings who are saved. Paul proclaimed Jesus; Augustine proclaimed the city of God. A kingdom represents the static and stable reign of a monarch or a king while a city, that is the *polis* or the *ciuitas*, represents the political interaction of its citizens among themselves or with the citizens of other cities. In the transition from kingdom to city Augustine gave the history of salvation, which is all of human history, a plot in terms of the two cities. An important and necessary consequence of Augustine's emplotment of the kingdom

---

363; see van Oort 131-42.

[31]*De ciuitate Dei* 15.6, Loeb 414, 433.

[32]See *Confessiones* 13.35.50-13.38.53, Verheijen 272-73; Pine-Coffin 346-47.

as the city was to make all spiritual human beings sojourners in this world and all genuine Christians strangers in a foreign land.

6

WOMEN AS FAMILIAR STRANGERS

IN MEDIEVAL CHURCH LAW

Joan A. Range, A.S.C.

What could the term "familiar stranger" mean? Isn't it an oxymoron? Could there be a human being who is at the same time both familiar and strange? The contention of this article is that, yes, there is such a human being and she is woman in the human family.

Bernhard Asen's earlier essay on the meaning of the term "stranger" in the Hebrew scriptures earlier in this collection presents the many nuances that the term held, the many social and religious conditions that framed the meaning of that term in the biblical world. None of these meanings were gender-related, however. Nevertheless, in a patrilineal, patriarchal society such as Israelite society was, the woman was a stranger. Phyllis Bird describes women's status there as that of "aliens and transients within their family of residence."[1] Woman's most important functions, the "common set of expectations and values that govern the life of every Israelite woman of every period and circumstance," was especially in the sphere of "'reproductive' work," to be the mother of children, above all sons,[2] who would then continue to be faithful to the covenant with the God of the Hebrews, keepers of the law, and inheritors of the promise (Deut 4:13-14).

But the woman herself did not have the same standing as a man did. In her study of women in the Mishnah, Judith Romney Wegner describes the woman as "anomalous," sometimes treated as a person, sometimes as chattel.[3] She was the possession of her father until

[1]Phyllis Bird, "Woman (OT)," *Anchor Bible Dictionary*, 1992 ed.
[2]See 1 Sam 2:5.
[3]Judith Romney Wegner, *Chattel or Person? The Status of Women in the Mishnah* (New York: Oxford UP, 1988) 175. The Misnah, compiled in the 2nd century, C.E., is an interpretation of the Torah, reflects Jewish culture and study,

marriage, when she became the possession of her husband. The law protected her; she was not to be coveted by men who had no right to her (Ex 20:17). Widowed, she needed the protection of her sons.[4] Childless, she considered herself cursed by God (Gen 30:23). Her condition was anomalous, as Wegner asserts; she was a stranger in her own family: blood of her ancestors' blood, bone of her people's bone, but not a member as her brothers were.

At the origin of the Christian movement within Judaism, there seems to have been a breakthrough for women who then seemed to be equal members of the community of the disciples of the Christ. Recent literature has pointed out the extraordinary treatment of women by Jesus during his ministry. He touched women (Mk 1:31), allowed them to touch him (Mk 5:27-31). He instructed them as a rabbi did his male disciples (Lk 10:38-42). There is no reason to believe that he did not send them out as part of his seventy-two to preach the nearness of the Reign of God. Women were among his closest friends (Jn 11:5). They provided for him materially (Lk 8:2-3) and performed the loving acts that women do (Jn 12:1-3). His compassion extended even to women who were sinners (Lk 7:36-40). Most importantly, they were the ones to first experience him as the Risen One and to announce that fact to his male disciples (Mk 16:9-11).

From the texts of the earliest Christian communities, it appears that this revolution in the relations between the genders continued as the disciples were empowered to spread the Gospel, the meaning of Jesus the Christ for all peoples (Acts 1:14; 2:1-4). Paul, whose record is the fullest regarding the social context of the earliest Christian communities, understood that among the disciples, the classic divisions were simply transcended. There were no slaves or free, no Jews or Gentiles, no male or female (Gal 3:28). In Christ all are one. Paul's language fails him as he tries to express the mystery of Christians' relationship to the Christ and so to each other. His analogies are reminiscent of the images in John's gospel (Jn 15:5): organic, vital

---

and so moves beyond the biblical text itself. Its theoretical basis is the logical effort to categorize and settle the various aspects of Jewish life and law, especially in hard cases. The title of Wegner's work suggests the anomalous status of the woman: a hybrid difficult to categorize.

[4]The position of Naomi and Ruth after the death of their husbands as narrated in the Book of Ruth demonstrates the vulnerability of women who lack the legal protection of men.

connections among everyone who is "in Christ" (1 Cor 12:12-13; Rom 12:4-5; Eph 4:25; Col 3:15), without the divisions that keep human beings separated from one another. These divisions were social, economic, racial and gender divisions. In Christ they did not matter, they did not exist; living in Christ erased them all (Col 3:11).

But the early insights of Paul, profound though they were, were also fragile. It seems that outside the assembly of the worshipping community, and even within it, the usual social relationships continued (1 Cor 4:3-6). The wife was to be obedient to her husband; the other household rules which defined the position of the father remained (Eph 5:21-6:9). The liberation of the female disciple of the Christ, did not carry over into the ordinary social structures of those Jews who were followers of the Way. As the Gentiles accepted the Gospel, the position of women was controlled by the norms of the Jewish community, especially if the converts came from permissive pagan religious culture (Rom 1:26-27). What had been acceptable behavior for a pagan woman became unacceptable to a group profoundly shaped by Jewish law and custom, even though it struggled to emerge from a mentality shaped by those legal codes (1 Cor 4:34-35; 11:16).

The later epistles of the Pauline school reflect this retrenchment. Recent scholarship, especially the ground breaking work of Elisabeth Schüssler Fiorenza, has challenged the perception of what emerged in the sub-apostolic Church as normative for Christians.[5] The liberated woman of the liberating Christ vanished as the structure of the Church more and more reflected the civil societies of the world in which it found itself. Recent feminist biblical scholarship has demonstrated that this development was not faithful to the vision of those who knew Jesus during his earthly ministry nor of those who were empowered by his Spirit after his resurrection to spread this vision and power to the ends of the earth.

The task of separating out merely cultural developments from the authentic religious meaning of the Christ for women is the task of feminist theologians. Criticism is at the heart of this task. The origin of this critical work is, ironically, the experience of women liberated by the Christ whose grace has exploded the dictates of patriarchal

---

[5]Elisabeth Schüssler Fiorenza, *In Memory of Her: A Feminist Theological Reconstruction of Christian Origins* (New York: Crossroad, 1983), parts II and III.

tradition. In Christ we are indeed one and the divisions formed by human culture are not determinative among the disciples of the Risen One. The differences among Christians are based on the gifts of the Spirit given according to God's designs, not according to human wisdom. This faith is the origin of Christian critical feminist scholarship.

Women in the Medieval World

Recent studies women in the medieval world have demonstrated very clearly both her familiar place in society, the home, family and Church, and the ambiguous and suspicious perception that males had of women, whatever the male relationship to women may have been.[6]

Penelope Johnson's recent work, *Equal in Monastic Profession*, for example, has shown that, on one hand, the place of the woman in the monastery was both respected and promoted.[7] She benefitted from the social status of monastic women and from both civil and canon law that protected her rights and that of her monastery from the intrusive and ambitious encroachment of others. Furthermore, through the abbess and other monastic officials the monastery entered into the economic and civil systems of the time—one would hope to its own profit and to fulfill the many human needs within its environs in a religious way. The ability or lack of it, in matters of administration and communication on the part of the monastic superiors, worked its

---

[6]Derek Baker, ed., *Medieval Women* (Oxford: Blackwell, 1978); Anne L. Barstowe, *Married Priests and the Reforming Papacy: The Eleventh Century Debates* (New York: Edwin Mellen, 1982); Christopher N.L. Brooke, *The Medieval Idea of Marriage* (New York: Oxford UP, 1989); Penny L. Gold, *The Lady and the Virgin: Image, Attitude, and Experience in Twelfth-Century France* (Chicago: U of Chicago P, 1985); David Herlihy, *Opera Muliebria: Women and Work in Medieval Europe* (New York: McGraw-Hill, 1989); Penelope D. Johnson, *Equal in Monastic Profession: Religious Women in Medieval France* (Chicago: U of Chicago P, 1991); Susan Mosher Stuard, ed., *Women in Medieval Society* (Philadelphia: U of Pennsylvania P, 1976); Susan F. Wemple, *Women in Frankish Society: Marriage and the Cloister, 500-900* (Philadelphia: U of Pennsylvania P, 1981).

[7]"Most nuns were not venerated as saints, but they were still respected as intercessors, valued as relatives, and needed for their many contributions to society. Whether or not a nun achieved holiness, her life of striving won admiration" (P. Johnson 143).

inevitable effects on their community members and their assets. So women enjoyed a certain autonomy, although a limited one, within that female world.[8]

On the other hand, because these monastics were female they suffered from the usual condition of all women, that is, they were expected to be submissive to male authority. Johnson discusses, as an example, the difference between the effects of the rule of enclosure, which bound both genders within monasticism equally, when it was applied to women as compared with how it was applied to male monastics. Some writers used the authority of St. Jerome to justify a call for stricter enclosure for nuns because they believed, as Jerome had, "in the fundamental weakness of female nature."[9] Moreover, as the campaign for priestly celibacy intensified during the Gregorian Reform (1073-85), the rhetoric against women, including female monastics, escalated. Johnson points out that "claustration, intended in theory as protective enclosure for all monastics, evolved into an ambivalent means of attempting to control nuns, whose sexuality threatened the post-Gregorian strict priestly chastity."[10]

The situation of female monastics was replicated in the life of lay women as well. Some were loved and respected within the family environment; others suffered from a lack of both love and respect. Insofar as the laws protected the rights of women, they could win their rights if they were able to initiate a cause before the appropriate tribunal. But, by and large, their condition depended upon their fortuitous connection with males. The anomalous condition of women, which we have noted in the Christian scriptures at the origin of Christianity and as those writings were interpreted through the Christian centuries in commentaries, continued in the medieval centuries of Western Europe as well.

My task as a historian of the canonical tradition of the Western Catholic Church is to point out the distortions that the legal system of the Church incorporated into its belief and practice due to its misogynistic mentality and inherited patriarchal structure. It is important to recognize these laws as distortions of the Christian message. The canonical tradition must be rectified if the Church is to

[8]Ibid. 166-206.
[9]Ibid. 152.
[10]Ibid. 165.

be faithful to the Christ. The woman must not exist as a stranger in her own land, among her own people. The community of Christians must recognize her as equally a sister of the Christ—as the man is a brother—an heir along with her brother to the Reign of God, a God who is our mother as well as our father, whose care for us is nurturing as well as protective, whose reality transcends all our limited categories.[11]

The legal system that the Western Catholic Church finally assumed was based on Roman law. There was a lengthy struggle before the Christian community accepted that legal system as appropriate. The Roman legal model was resisted, first of all, because it was the law of pagans, the law of those who did not recognize the Christ and his Church, and a law which had been a powerful tool for persecution of Christians in the first three centuries of the Christian era.

Moreover, since the fall of the Roman Empire, the culture of the Germanic tribes which overcame the Empire controlled much of the northern parts of the continent. Germanic laws were primarily customary and had greatly influenced the development of Church structures.[12] The Investiture Controversy (late eleventh and twelfth centuries) and its accompanying successful struggle for a stable legal system finally overcame Germanic law and established Roman legal principles as the basis for Church law and the papacy as *the* lawgiver for the Church of the West.[13]

At the beginning of the twelfth century (c.1141), the *Decretum* of Magister Gratian was composed in Bologna where the recovery of Roman law had been carried out in the eleventh century. This document, *Concordantia discordantium canonum*, became the foundation for the development of canon law in the Western Church.[14]

---

[11]Elizabeth Johnson, *She Who Is: The Mystery of God in Feminist Theological Discourse* (New York: Crossroad, 1992). Here Johnson investigates the tradition of God language and its limitations when referring to a reality that can be known only by analogy and for which our concepts are at best more dissimilar than similar. She constructs some possible new uses of language and suggests making language more inclusive than only male terms permit and thus better able to reflect a reality that no language can ever fully capture.

[12]Gerd Tellenbach, *Church, State and Christian Society at the Time of the Investiture Contest*, trans. R.F. Bennett (1940; Toronto: U of Toronto P, 1991) 69-76.

[13]Ibid. 162-68.

[14]*Decretum Magistri Gratiani* in *Corpus iuris canonici: Pars prior*, 2nd

Prior to this work, the legal system of the Western Church was a vast corpus of varying authority that bore witness to the fortunes and misfortunes of the human community within which the Church of Western Europe had developed. The *Decretum* both sums up the corpus of canons, harmonizes them according to theological and legal principles, and provides the basis for future canonical development.[15]

Because this work both reflects and shapes legal tradition, it will be the document that we will examine to show how the ambivalent attitude toward women is present in the laws of the Christian community.[16] Broadly speaking, Gratian's *Decretum* achieved the following victories for the Church: the emergence of the papacy as the locus of supreme power in the Church; of the bishop as the ecclesiastically elected pastor of his portion of the Church; and of the orders of priest, deacon and sub-deacon as celibate ministers to the faithful.[17] They were essential platforms of the reform-minded popes of the Middle Ages. Later history has shown that these victories were more legal than real in many cases, but the patterns, from which the Church has never seriously deviated since, were then set in law.

This pattern reflected and in some ways caused the ambivalent position of women who, on one hand, clearly belonged to the Church, yet, on the other hand, were eliminated from the public arena of Church activity and became more and more restricted even in the private areas of life and learning.[18] Women were prohibited from

---

Leipzig ed., ed. Aemilius Ludwig Richter, with notes by Emil Friedberg (1879; Graz: Akademische Druck- u. Verlagsanstalt, 1959).

[15]Stephan Kuttner, *Harmony from Dissonance* (Latrobe, PA: St. Vincent Abbey P, 1960). Kuttner's lecture, recorded in this book, is a fine summary of Gratian's accomplishment.

[16]While my essay intends to point out the inequities worked against women, I am aware of the benefits of the Gregorian Reform for the good order of the Church. For churchmen to be loyal to the Church rather than a temporal lord, for the property of the Church to be maintained as the sacred space it was intended to be and not as the legacy of wealthy families to sons and their offspring were essential values for late medieval centuries. The Gregorian Reform set the Church on a path toward good organization. Unfortunately, as centralized power became more and more real, the position of women became more and more powerless.

[17]Whether or not the vow of celibacy reached to the sub-diaconate is not clear in Gratian's work. The sources he quotes sometimes indicate sub-deacons are to be celibate, at other times only the order of deacons.

[18]Wemple documents the efforts of the Carolingian Reform to exclude women

participating in the sacred sphere; their role in public life was diminished; and the limited leadership some churchwomen enjoyed and exercised was lost as jurisdiction became exclusively associated with the sacrament of orders.

Strangers in the Family of the Faithful

One of the images that controls Gratian's discussion of the Church and its members is the image of the family. The Church is the *familia fidelium*. Can there be a stranger within this family? Do all the members of the family equally belong? Certainly there are distinctions in every family: children are not parents, daughters are not sons. These distinctions are not in the nature of injustices.

Within the family of the Church, too, there are distinctions just as there is within a natural family. Does the nature of the Church ensure that the distinctions do not become the bases for division and discrimination, as the distinctions within the natural family so frequently do?[19]

Predictably, as all of history witnesses and as the texts of the tradition bear out, the nature of human society, even in the Church, reflects rather than perfects relationships among people. There were strangers within the family of the Church; there were some members who simply and completely belonged, and other members whose belonging was conditional. All were not equally heirs, equally citizens of the city, residents whose right to a home was unquestioned. Adults

from exercising functions that they had previously performed: "Even nuns were forbidden to approach the altar, touch the sacred vessels, and help distribute the body and blood of Christ. If altar linens had to be washed, they were to be removed by clerics and turned over to women at the altar rail. Similarly, offerings brought by women were to be received by priests at the altar rail" (143).

[19]Susan Moller Okin in *Justice, Gender, and the Family* discusses the absence of the virtue of justice and its accompanying legal structures as operative categories in the thought of the political theorists of Western culture regarding the family. The family supposedly operates on the basis of love and altruism; therefore, justice is not the applicable virtue. However, as Okin argues and as history bears out, the result has been that women cannot effectively protect themselves, either within marriage or before the judicial system, when altruistic love fails, as it so often does.

were not all capable of the same acts, laboring under the same obligations, enjoying the same privileges.

Gratian used the image of the *familia fidelium*[20] to establish two basic laws. This image provided him with reasons both for a celibate male clergy and for the prohibition against marrying within certain degrees of blood relationships. The first is to our purpose. Why it is appropriate for clergy within the Christian dispensation to be celibate, especially if members of the Church are understood as belonging to an ecclesial family?

The struggle for a celibate clergy in the Western Church had been going on for centuries.[21] The Gregorian Reform had intensified both the struggle for clerical celibacy and resistance against it, but eventually clerical celibacy became law.[22] Besides eliminating wives for clerics in major orders, Gratian also had to deal with terms that seemed to indicate that women had held clerical office in the Church in the past, as the existence of the terms *presbytera, episcopa* and *deaconissa* in early documents demonstrates. These terms, however, have traditionally been understood as referring to the wives of those who held these offices, except for the office of deaconess.[23] In fact, as

---

[20]The term *familia* is not explicitly used by Gratian, but the image is implied in Gratian's discussion of the Chosen People of Israel and how their progeny (the Christian Church) inherited the promises which Israel had received from God. Thus, the church is described in the same terms as ancient Israel, *mutatis mutandis*. See note 29 below.

[21]Canon thirty-three of the Council of Elvira (c.300-303) required continence of the clergy: "Placuit in totum prohibere episcopis, presbyteris et diaconibus, vel omnibus clericis positis in ministerio, abstinere se a coniugibus suis et non generare filios; quicumque vero fecerit, ab honore clericatus exterminetur. ("It is agreed that bishops, priests, and deacons, and all clerics in the ministry, are to abstain from their wives and are not to procreate children; whoever might do so is to be removed from his clerical position." Translation mine.) (Joannes Dominicus Mansi, ed., *Sacrorum conciliorum nova et amplissima collectio* [1759; facsimile ed. Paris: Welter, 1901] 2:11.)

[22]In his study, *Law and Revolution: The Formation of the Western Legal Tradition* (Cambridge: Harvard UP, 1983), Harold J. Berman notes that "once he became pope, Gregory did not hesitate to use revolutionary tactics to accomplish his objectives. In 1075, for example, he ordered all Christians to boycott priests who were living in concubinage or marriage, and not to accept their offices for the sacraments or other purposes. As a result of opposition to this decree, there were open riots in churches and beating and stoning of those who opposed clerical marriage" (95).

[23]This traditional interpretation is being challenged by recent historical works.

early as the sixth century there was a general prohibition against women as deaconesses in the Western Church.

Removing the clergy from the environment of a natural family, as the law of celibacy in fact did, had two effects. First, it eliminated the natural relationship to a wife and children that marriage entails for a man. Secondly, women were removed from active involvement in parish life. There are, of course, no records of parish responsibilities for the priest's wife, but we can imagine that they existed, given her role as his helpmate.[24] This effect of clerical celibacy had far-reaching political impact. In her study of the Frankish Church Wemple points out the negative effect that this law certainly had on the wives themselves: "Those married to clerks in higher orders suffered the denigration of their virtue and the defamation of their characters if they tried to remain with their husbands."[25] Furthermore, the priest or deacon was no longer susceptible to feminine influence on his duties or on his loyalties. No longer did the ambitions and desires of a spouse to whom and for whom he was responsible enter into his own ambitions and desires or into the fulfillment of his duties. His peer relationships were with men in the public sphere. As a cleric he had no peer relationships in the private sphere.

The responsibilities of children, likewise, no longer bore down upon

Karen Jo Torjesen in her recent book, *When Women Were Priests: Women's Leadership in the Early Church and the Scandal of Their Subordination in the Rise of Christianity* (San Francisco: Harper, 1993), reinterprets the evidence to conclude that women actually were *presbyterae* and *episcopae*.

[24]The wife was certainly housekeeper and cook. These functions, to this day, cause constant communication with the people of the parish. Common concerns among mothers for their children, especially their health, must have involved the priest's wife with other women. Dealing with people who came to the door with different needs would have involved her as well. This exchange, though unrecorded, certainly existed. In later history, the abuse of priests' concubines mirrors the contempt with which these women were treated as a result of the laws requiring celibacy and their effective dissemination and implementation. In her study of women in Frankish society, Wemple contrasts the role of women in the pagan Roman Empire with that of women within Christianity: "Christianity welcomed both men and women to its worship and ritual. Although women were barred from the Christian priesthood, they could share in pastoral care as priests' wives, deaconesses, or virgins and widows dedicated to the service of God" (127). It was these very practices which were eliminated by the Gregorian Reform, of course.

[25]Wemple 191.

the cleric's future. Church property and Church office were rescued from the liability of family entanglement.[26] Priests had no moral responsibility to provide for children; they could not will Church property to heirs; sons could not inherit the office of their fathers. With the law that clerics could not validly marry,[27] there remained no legal responsibility to concubines and illegitimate children. The Second Lateran Council stated in canon seven, "For we do not deem there to be a marriage which, it is agreed, has been contracted against ecclesiastical law."[28]

Both politically and economically, then, the exclusion of women and children from any legitimate, personal relationship with the clergy removed the clergy from the influence that wives and heirs have on husbands and fathers. The feminine and familial were eliminated from the public life of pastoral care and communal worship. The lives of ministers at the altar were radically separated from the community to which they ministered. The woman especially suffered from this separation. A woman could participate in worship only as spectator; she would feel the pastoral touch of the Church only as a recipient.

The requirement of celibacy corrupted the image of the family that Gratian used in describing the Church. There is no family without a woman. This corruption, however, entered Church structures without being noticed. A theology developed in Gratian's process of argumentation which justified this perversion in the Church. It is necessary to trace the origins of this theology because it apparently validated the exclusion of women from being active in the public life of the Church. It rendered them passive and, in one important sense, unnecessary in the Church.

Gratian formulated this quasi-theological argument in the *dictum* he arrived at after a rather extensive argument[29] which deals with whether or not a man can choose to have children from another woman if his

---

[26]Berman notes that "clerical marriage was not only a moral issue, in the narrow sense, but also a social and political and economic issue. Marriage brought the priesthood within the clan and feudal structure. It also involved the inheritance of some church offices by priests' sons and other relatives" (92).

[27]See canons six and seven of the Second Lateran Council (1139) in Norman P. Tanner, ed., *Decrees of the Ecumenical Councils*, vol. 1, *Nicaea to Lateran V* (Washington, D.C.: Georgetown UP, 1990) 198.

[28]Ibid.

[29]*Decretum* Secunda pars, causa 32, q 4, ante c 3 (1127)

wife is sterile. The Old Testament precedents of Abraham, Sarah, and Hagar are invoked and their story would seem to permit this possibility. Gratian argues, however, that the founders of different dispensations established different conditions. By founders he means Abraham in the Old Testament who was the founder of the people whom God chose to be his own; the founders in the New Testament were the Apostles whom God chose from among that people to found a new dispensation. The Apostles are like fathers of the faith then, just as Abraham was for the chosen people. Succession to the promise of the Old Covenant went to the progeny of Abraham: "Succession through blood brought about the continuance of the faith."[30] Marriage of priests was also decreed in the Old Testament because establishment in Levitical office came about through blood relationship.[31] The new dispensation, however, does not rely upon the natural ties of blood, but upon grace, a spiritual reality. Because of this new dispensation, virginity is preferred to fecundity, and so priests of the new dispensation are bound to chastity.[32]

This argument suggests that women are unnecessary in the Church. Gratian did not draw that conclusion, nor could he in terms of membership, but it is a logical conclusion. In fact, it became operative in the life of the Church: women are not needed for grace to be spread to others. What is needed is the office of priest who is appropriately celibate. There are only fathers in the Church; there are no mothers. Women are unnecessary in this family, having nothing to do, no essential role to play—unlike their brothers who are essential in the Church's life. This is a strange family indeed.

Gratian gives another theological reason for excluding women from actively participating in the Church's life. Using the Old Testament's example of a woman who was a public figure, a judge, in the history of Israel, Judith, he concludes that this role for a woman is no longer an acceptable precedent because of the new dispensation.[33] Gratian's understanding of a "new dispensation," introduced in the light of the gospels, leads him to some interesting conclusions. He justifies the

---

[30]"Quia in successione sanguinis erat successio fidei" (ibid).

[31]"Quia in successione familiare successio constabat officii" (ibid).

[32]"Et virginitas fecunditati prefertur, et sacerdotibus continentiae castitas imperatur" (ibid).

[33]*Decretum* Secunda pars, causa 15, q 3, ante c 1 (750).

emergence of important customs and laws which are not in the Christian scriptures nor in the Apostolic Constitutions.[34] These practices developed in the course of the ongoing life of the Church because of "the perfection of grace," a grace which ensured the appropriateness of these changes as surely as the earthly presence of the Lord Christ and the Apostles' presence in the early Church assured the sanctity of the customs of those years. In this way Gratian develops an argument to explain how the Church can introduce laws which were not in the Old Testament, the gospels or the early Church, but which are still completely appropriate, even ecclesiastically perfecting. These new laws improve the Church over time. The developments are three as Gratian classifies them: clerical celibacy, sacramental liturgy and restrictions on marriage within certain degrees of relatedness.

With respect to the Old Testament precedent that we are now considering, especially the example of Judith, Gratian quotes Paul's judgment on women, a view which, in Gratian's opinion, had not been clearly understood under the old dispensation, but which is now clear in the new. In the Old Testament many things were permitted which today are prohibited because of *perfectione gratiae*.[35] This clarification came from the Apostle Paul who says that those who are responsible for sin—of course women, through the sin of Eve, were responsible[36]—are to be ashamed, subject to their husbands, and veiled as a sign of their subjection. Therefore, women can no longer function for the Church in a public way.

In arguing this point, however, Gratian quotes Roman law which similarly did not allow women to function publicly, in the case cited, as accusers before the court, because of their sex and the social order. The Digest of Justinian decreed that this activity on the part of women was "contrary to the modesty in keeping with their sex" and so the law prohibited this role to prevent "women from performing the functions of men."[37] Under some strictly limited circumstances, however, namely, accusations of *lesae maiestatis* (that is, lese majesty) and in the case of corrupt public judges, women were permitted to function

---

[34]Gratian evidently believed that this document derived from apostolic times. Later historical analysis dates it from the latter half of the fourth century.

[35]*Decretum* Secunda pars, causa 15, q 3, ante c 1 (750).

[36]"Quod mulier induxit" (ibid).

[37]Theodore Mommsen and Paul Keuger, eds., *The Digest of Justinian*, trans. Alan Watson (Philadelphia: U of Pennsylvania P, 1985) III.1.1.5 (1:79).

publicly.

As Gratian continues his argument, he finds an accusation, similar in gravity to *lesae maiestatis*, which a woman could bring forward, despite her subordinate nature, even in the Church. These accusations were heresy and simony. In such extreme cases, the woman could legally stand before a Church court to accuse a man, specifically a cleric. However, in the case Gratian had constructed to deal with the question, the hypothetical circumstances included a woman accusing the priest, not of simony, but of fornication. The cleric had sinned with her carnally.

But, Gratian argued, that accusation by a woman is not permitted for two reasons. The first is that a person cannot accuse another if that person could not fulfill the office of the one accused.[38] A woman cannot become a priest; therefore she cannot accuse a priest. The more compelling legal argument, however, is that no one, male or female, can accuse someone of a crime which necessarily implicates themselves.[39] Both of these reasons have their source in Roman law and not in the Church, but Gratian utilizes these legal precedents from Roman law as he resolves this case of ecclesiastical jurisprudence.

Using this complex, constructed case and its argumentation, Gratian developed a strong brief for why the Church can introduce laws which were not in the Old Testament nor the gospels nor directly from the Apostles.[40] The resolution he came to used Old Testament precedents, New Testament correctives to these earlier precedents, principles from Roman law and judgments of Church history to establish the goodness of a practice that, in fact, had no basis in the gospels: namely, excluding women from any public function in the Church.

When dealing with another case, Gratian explicitly stated the capacity of the Church to overturn practices reported in the scriptures in order to perfect salutary discipline for its members. The question specifically refers to "magical" practices such as sooth-saying, fortune-telling, casting lots, and the like. These were all practiced in the Old Testament, some even in the New Testament, such as Zachary's lot to serve in the sanctuary (Lk 1:9) or the choice of

---

[38]This ancient rule of thumb eliminated ambitious and unscrupulous accusers who sought to better themselves at an innocent person's expense.

[39]*Decretum* Secunda pars, causa 15, q 3, post c 4 (752).

[40]Ibid. Secunda pars, causa 26, q 2, post c 1 (1020).

Matthias to replace Judas (Acts 1:26). But today they are, by Church law, prohibited so that the people do not let their attention on the goal of salvation be distracted by vain pursuits. Forbidding women to function publicly in the Church derives from the same source as these prohibitions. That is, the light of the Gospel has shown them to be incompatible with the new dispensation.[41]

Besides prohibiting women from public functions in the Church the laws Gratian quotes constitute a retrenchment from what had formerly been acceptable for women liturgically. Women had taken consecrated bread to the infirm, probably women, in their homes. But according to the source that Gratian quotes, that practice must cease.[42] Women had also participated in the liturgy somewhat like acolytes, preparing and incensing the altar and handling the sacred vessels. Gratian quotes Pope Soter who urged the immediate cessation of this activity which he calls utterly reprehensible.[43] Probably the only area where women could continue to function liturgically was among nuns in choir where they read the sacred texts aloud during the Divine Office. The abbess or prioress would have publicly blessed her congregation as well. But women were legally allowed to perform these functions only among other women. Obviously the prohibition had many irregular exceptions, especially in double monasteries led by abbesses and in monasteries in which the nuns had feudal control over churches and even houses of male clerics.

Litigation, of course, arose and continued regarding the jurisdictional powers of the great abbesses and female monastics, as they struggled to remain free and effective administrators of their subjects and possessions. But as the concept of jurisdiction became more clearly distinguished from and related only to the sacrament of orders, these efforts were less and less successful for women. Although female monastics thrived through these centuries and although the laws of both Church and state protected them in many ways, their public status

---

[41]"Ante, quam evangelium claresceret, multa permittebantur, que tempore perfectioris disciplinae penitus eliminata sunt" (ibid).

[42]Gratian quotes canon two from one of the councils of Rheims, which strictly prohibits the priest from giving permission to a layman or a woman ("laico aut feminae") to deliver the "sacrum corpus domini" to the infirm. See *Decretum* Tertia pars, dist 2, c 29 (1323). The canon begins with the phrase: "It has come to our notice that...."

[43]*Decretum* Prima pars, dist 23, post c 24 (85-86).

was restricted.[44] As centralization of power in the Church became more and more a fact, the local variations of earlier centuries, which had allowed the public functioning of powerful women, were eliminated.[45]

There remained, however, the exceptional activity of women *in extremis*. Gratian quoted canons which allowed women to baptize their own infants as well as any dying person in this circumstance;[46] she, as a lay person, could even hear the confession of someone dying in the absence of a priest and in that situation offer the hope of pardon to a dying person.[47] These exceptional circumstances raise the question of the woman's capacity for public functioning. Obviously, *in extremis* is not public, but the function exercised is valid and the grace extended real. The rule which covered these special cases was *necessitas non habet legem*; one does what must be done for the salvation of the dying person. Gender is not operative in this case.

The question remains, however, what the obstacle to public function for women is in the normal situation. Does the law, in and of itself, render an action radically ineffective in its purpose? Or does the law order a community according to its constitution, thereby only making some actions legal and others illegal? Is that legal procedure equivalent to rendering an activity non-existent in its effects? Lawgivers may use words such as "reprehensible" for the illegal. But could they use words such as "null" for the actions of a baptized member irrespective of her or his gender? Does the use of the legal category "null" certainly imply non-existence?[48]

---

[44]In a letter to an abbess Pope Honorius III forbade her to excommunicate her subjects. Her subjects, however, are bound to obey her. The pope described her subjects as "canicas suas et clericos suae iurisdictioni subiectos" (*Decretales Gregorii IX* in *Corpus iuris canonici, Pars secunda*, 2nd Leipzig ed., ed. Aemilius Ludwig Richter, with notes by Emil Friedberg (1879; Graz: Akademische Druck-u. Verlagsanstalt, 1959) lib 1, tit 33, cap 12 (201).

[45]Wemple 195. She argues throughout her work that centralization of power seems to lead inevitably to the elimination of regional and local creativity and variety. Women's roles suffer suppression in this movement as well.

[46]*Drecretum* Tertia pars, dist 4, post c 20 (1367).

[47]*Decretum* Secunda pars, causa 26, q 6, post c 11 (1039)

[48]This question obviously has considerable theological importance as well as legal significance. The theological basis supports the legal, not the other way around. However, in the Western church, sometimes the canonical status of a specific institution seems to control its theological status. This is a case of the

The Private Sphere of Marriage

The one area where there appears to be equality between men and women is in the area of taking vows. Gratian argues that for marriage, the spouse, male or female, must consent to assume the obligations of the state to which they are vowing themselves.[49] The practice of parents giving their sons and daughters as oblates to monasteries was not perceived as an intrusion on the freedom of their child. Cases were, of course, argued, that if a child, when she or he came of age at twelve years, decided not to accept the monastic life, was he or she free to leave?[50] Gratian argued that a child could not be forced to follow the will of a parent who had given the child to the monastery as a child. However, society assumed that dutiful children would fulfill the ordination of their parents, either to become a monastic or to marry a partner chosen by parents. Gratian's arguments indicate this presumption. However, he also argued that no one could be forced to take a vow; it must be consented to, whether it was a matter of monastic vows or the vows of marriage. In this respect women and men were treated equally when they came of age.

Once married, the mutual obligations of husband and wife to bed and board were strictly upheld in Church law.[51] Spouses must be equally available to each other. Even in the case of taking other vows, consent of the partner was essential. Certainly if a married man or woman wanted to assume the vows of religion, they needed the willing cooperation of the other spouse.[52]

James Brundage's work on the Crusades and Canon law[53] has

---

tail wagging the dog.

[49]In presenting the questions for this case, Gratian quotes St. John Chrysostom among others who state that matrimony is not realized through intercourse but through consent: "Matrimonium quidem non facit coitus, sed voluntas" (*Decretum* Secunda pars, causa 27, q 2, c 1 [1063]). This Roman principle varied, of course, from the Germanic practice which was inclined to hold that intercourse was what accomplished the social union of marriage.

[50]*Decretum* Secunda pars, causa 20, q 1, post c 8 (845).

[51]*Decretum* Secunda pars, causa 33, qq 1-2 (1148-59). See following questions as well.

[52]*Decretum* Secunda pars, causa 27, q 2, c 19 (1068). See also following canons.

[53]James A. Brundage, "The Crusaders Wife: A Canonistic Quandary," in *The*

investigated this aspect of equality within marriage. After the preaching of the first Crusade by Urban II in 1095, the need for crusaders increased as attempts to recover the Holy Land lingered for years. Given the need to have a wife agree to her husband's taking the crusader's vow, or her agreement to also take the vow and accompany him, difficulties multiplied between spouses and so for the Church. From the perspective of the papacy there seems to have been an attempt to diminish the wife's power over her husband in this matter.[54] The concern appears to have been fidelity. If a spouse was not sexually available to the other, the temptation to adultery was considered a grave danger. Marriage was conceived as a "remedy to concupiscence" for both genders from the time of Augustine, and this understanding was still operative in the Middle Ages.

Conclusion

Using the image of family as the framework for organizing Church legislation, but legally excluding women from public activity in this family, places women in a strange position. A family must include both women and men. If women are excluded, the framework cannot be that of family. It must clearly be some other patriarchal structure. The Church, with its laws as Gratian described them, was certainly that kind of structure.

Theologically speaking, the justification for this patriarchal structure came from the understanding that the Apostles and all the disciples were male and that Jesus intended masculine leadership for the Church. Patriarchy is intrinsic to the Church, according to this argument.

Another theological distinction operative in Gratian's laws was the distinction, perhaps implicit, between office and charism. The pursuit of holiness, the following of Christ in consecrated states of life, was

---

Crusades, Holy War and Canon Law (Brookfield, VT: Gower, 1991) 427-41.

[54]He notes two papal bulls allowing this exception: "The papacy found it necessary to permit husbands to contravene what earlier canonists had normally assumed was a natural right of married women, arising out of the very nature of the marriage contract itself. Although none of them denied its validity as law, nevertheless the decretalist commentators appeared to be uncomfortable in dealing with this provision of *Ex multa,* as is evidenced by their chary handling of it" (Brundage 435).

also operative in the *Decretum* and clearly recognized as a normal part of the Church's life. Women were simply accepted as part of the charismatic life of the Church.

The distinction between the sexes in terms of charisms has continued in the legal tradition of the Church to this day. There are now, as there were then, powerful women who are leaders among consecrated women and whose leadership makes them sources of power in both Church life and ministry. Their power, however, is never official in the Church. It is only official within their religious communities, and it relates to the official Church outside only in so far as these women leaders are held accountable for their communities' fulfillment of their charismatic roles in the Church.

The distinction between office and charism is a very old one in ecclesiastical tradition. If one looks carefully, it can be found in some of Paul's letters and in the *Didachē* as well, both first century texts. Whether this distinction followed gender lines, however, is a source of considerable study among biblical and early Church scholars. Historically, however, whatever the end of that scholarly debate may be, it is certainly true that women were later excluded from Church office. Groups that desired their inclusion were regularly labelled heretics by the official Church (Donatists, Waldensians, Albigensians, for example). Finally, as legal categories developed more precisely in the Middle Ages, the concept of jurisdiction and its exercise were limited to clerics, except in rare cases.[55] The structure of the family of the Church had no official place for women, even though they were valued in the charismatic life of the Church.

The chief theological justification for this exclusion, namely, the

---

[55]An exception that proves the rule is that of the great abbesses of the Middle Ages. Into the nineteenth century, for example, the Abbess of the Royal Monastery of Las Huelgas in Spain, a Cistercian monastery, exercised quasi-episcopal jurisdiction. She was an abbess *nullius* and her powers, based on immemorial custom, were safeguarded by papal bulls. Although these rights were periodically contested by local bishops and even by the Abbot of Citeaux, they were never removed. The precise nature of this jurisdiction is still a matter of controversy among theologians and canonists. See Pie de Langogne, "Abbesses" in *Dictionnaire de théologie catholique* 1 (1930) 17-22; J. de Puniet, "Abbesses" in *Dictionnaire de spiritualité* 1 (1937) 57-61; J. Baucher, "Abbesses" in *Dictionnaire de droit canonique* 1 (1935) 62-71; Josemaria Escrivá de Balaguer, *La abadesa de Las Huelgas: Estudio theologico juridico,* 2nd ed. (Madrid: Rialp, 1974).

maleness of Church leaders as in Christian scriptures, has been undermined by recent scholarship. The other source for justifying this exclusion, the responsibility of women for sin, is also untenable both scripturally and morally.

The discipline of clerical celibacy seems to be at the heart of the strange position of women as it emerged from the establishment of the canonical legislation of the Western Church in the Middle Ages. A possible solution to this problem—clerical celibacy marginalizing women—is not so much the elimination of clerical celibacy as it is the inclusion of women among the clergy. Contemporary theology and the practice of many Churches indicate that there are no good reasons for this exclusion and many reasons for women's inclusion. The canonical tradition of the Catholic Church can be changed. Obviously, the appreciation of the complete equality of women as human beings, of her belonging as a member of the Church equally, just as men belong, of her nature as a member of the body of Christ, just as men are, is basic to perceiving the necessity for change. The theological tradition of the inferiority of women has, in fact, already changed. Whatever the bases for that assumption were, they are clearly perceived today to have been false. The arguments that Gratian marshalled for the position he took with respect to women in the Church are untenable today; this is clear. And so the laws can and must be changed.

On what basis, then, can the law continue to exclude women from its official life when there are no religious, theological, moral or legal reasons for the exclusion? If law arises from the life of the Church, from addressing the needs of humanity through the gifts God gives to its members so all can be won for Christ, gender distinction within the family of the Church provides no grounding for law. Therefore, the law must be changed.

The sacrament of marriage, however limited its medieval estimation, turns out to be the whetstone of equality which the Church could not recognize clearly at the time. The availability of the partners to each other because of their relationship within the sacrament of matrimony is the image of the family that the Church should use as its paradigm for membership. The availability of Church members to each other because of their union in Christ—the responsibility to the other members of the family, new or old, because of their need for life, for food and drink, for comfort and healing—fits the image of men and women as equal family members very well. At different times chronologically the gifts of men and women are called upon differently. But the gifts are necessary and desirable all the time. The role of law must be to recognize the mutuality of membership, the needs of humanity, and the gifts of different members to meet those needs. Everyone in the family is completely engaged in developing its life; everyone is necessary and belongs to the family fully. There are no strangers in the family of the Church. The Church's laws must recognize this fact and order its life accordingly.

7

RICHARD SIMON

Faith and Modernity

Francis W. Nichols

R ichard Simon (1638-1712) is universally recognized as one of the founders of critical biblical studies. Here I will argue that he was a creator of modern or even post-modern mentalities as well.[1] Born in Dieppe, Simon studied theology in Paris and learned Hebrew and other Oriental languages on the side. A member of the French Oratory from 1662 to 1678, he passed much of this time working in the library of the main Oratorian house in Paris. Expelled from the Oratory in 1678 as a political liability for the order, he had to continue his intellectual work independently. His vast scholarly output included translations and commentaries on works which explained Judaism and Oriental Christianity to the Christian West. His principal critical studies of the

---

[1]Most histories of biblical criticism put Simon prominently at the beginning of modern studies, as for example, Alexa Suelzer and John S. Kselman, "Modern Old Testament Criticism," in *The New Jerome Biblical Commentary*, eds. Raymond E. Brown, Joseph A. Fitzmyer, and Roland E. Murphy (Englewood Cliffs, NJ: Prentice Hall), 1115. Paul Hazard, in his classic study, *The European Mind: The Critical Years (1680-1715)* (1935; New Haven: Yale UP, 1953) 180-97, regards Simon as an important force in the construction of modern consciousness. Richard Popkin insists even more strongly on the importance of Simon for the rise of modernity in "Bible Criticism and Social Science," in *Methodological and Historical Essays in the Natural and Social Sciences*, eds. Robert S. Cohen and Marx W. Wartofsky, Boston Studies in the Philosophy of Science 14 (Boston: Reidel, 1974) 340-60, and "Cartesianism and Biblical Criticism," in *Problems of Cartesiansism*, eds. Thomas M. Lennon, John M. Nicholas, and John W. Davis (Kingston: McGill-Queen's UP, 1982) 61-81. James A. Sanders is inclined to "nominate Simon as the godfather of canonical criticism" ("Hebrew Bible *and* Old Testament: Textual Criticism in Service of Biblical Studies," in *Hebrew Bible or Old Testament? Studying the Bible in Judaism and Christianity*, eds. Roger Brooks and John J. Collins [Notre Dame, IN: U of Notre Dame P, 1990] 51).

Old and New Testaments led to extensive controversy with Protestants. Above all, his critical approaches to the Bible, its text and commentators, and his lack of due respect for the opinions of the Church Fathers on such questions, especially his criticism of St. Augustine, got him into trouble with Jacques Bénigne Bossuet (1627-1704). Consequently, many of his books had to be published in Holland, England and elsewhere. He died piously in his native Dieppe in 1712, without disciples or obvious successors.[2]

All his life, Simon was a prodigious worker, author of some thirty-six works of daunting erudition and immense scope, touching on all areas of biblical criticism (texts, versions, commentaries) and what we would call today the history of religion, ethnography, linguistics and the like, in so far as they bear on biblical and interconfessional studies.[3] His oeuvre encompasses well over seventeen thousand pages. The 1685 edition of his great *Histoire critique du Vieux Testament* came to more than seven hundred quarto pages. His *Histoires critiques* of the text of the New Testament (1689) ran to 430 pages, of the versions of the New Testament (1692) to 539 pages, of New Testament commentators (1693) to 928 pages. Two years later (1695) he had a few more things to say about the New Testament, and his *Nouvelles observations sur le texte et les versions du Nouveau Testament* amounted to another 599 pages. His 1702 translation of the New Testament alone, with abundant notes and comments in four volumes, added up to another 1,340 pages. And this is not to mention his considerable works on Judaism, Oriental Christianity, his collected

[2]The principal contemporary studies of Simon are Jean Steinmann's brilliant but perhaps overly enthusiastic essay, *Richard Simon et les origines de l'exégèse biblique* (Paris: Desclée de Brouwer, 1960), and Paul Auvray's more sober work, *Richard Simon (1638-1712): Étude bio-bibliographique avec des textes inédits* (Paris: Presses Universitaires de France, 1974). Both are indebted to the excellent nineteenth century study of Simon's Old Testament period by Auguste Bernus, *Richard Simon et son Histoire critique du Vieux Testament: La critique biblique au siècle de Louis XIV* (Thesis presented to the Faculté de Théologie de l'Église Libre de Vaud, Lausanne, 1869; reprint, Geneva: Slatkine, 1969), and the impressive bibliography, also by Bernus, "Richard Simon," in A.-M.-P. Ingold, *Essai de bibliographie oratorienne* (Paris: A. Sauton and Poussielgue Frères, 1880-1882) 121-63.

[3]Simon's works have a complicated publishing history. See the carefully sorted out list in Auvray 181-89.

letters and controversial works.[4] As a recently noted manuscript in the Bibliothèque National which reports Paris salon gossip of 1670-71 informs us, even as a young scholar in his early thirties Simon's opinion on Augustine, Jerome, Bernard of Clairvaux, the Septuagint, Greek Orthodox theology, Erasmus and so on, were listened to with interest. Already the observer could say, "He has read through practically all the Church Fathers. He is very competent in languages and wishes to critique all the Bibles done in the last two hundred years, Critica et Criticorum."[5] Jean Steinmann (1911-63) sums him up. "He is the greatest biblical critic of ancient France. His importance equals that of Erasmus of Rotterdam [1469-1536] or Baruch Spinoza [1632-77].... From the Renaissance to the end of the nineteenth century his genius dominates biblical exegesis."[6]

And yet, he was a virtual pariah in his own age and remains in many ways a conundrum to this very day. He was personally eccentric, he was regarded with suspicion by Protestants and fellow Catholics alike, his works were mostly proscribed by the French government and condemned by the Roman *Index* (where many of his books remained right up to the *Index*'s abolition in 1966).[7] He had no disciples[8] and

---

[4]See Auvray for bibliographical details. These figures are approximate as pagination for these works pose all sorts of problems, usually detailed by Auvray.

[5]Jacques Le Brun and John D. Woodbridge, eds., *Richard Simon, Additions aux "Recherches curieuses sur la diversité des langues et religions d'Edward Brerewood"* (Paris: Presses Universitaires de France, 1983) 19.

[6]Steinmann 7.

[7]The 1948 edition, *Index librorum prohibitorum* (Rome: Typis Polyglottis Vaticanis), listed five works under "Simon, Richard," and five others under the pseudonyms "Bolleville," "Costa," "Le Camus," and "Moni."

[8]Steinmann (page 7), following Renan, emphasizes this, though recent studies have shown that Simon was influential in the eighteenth and nineteenth centuries, a fact seldom acknowledged by authors before the end of the nineteenth century. See Bertram Eugene Schwarzbach, "La fortune de Richard Simon au XVIIIe siècle," *Revue des études juives* 146 (1987) 225-39, and John D. Woodbridge, "German Responses to the Biblical Critic Richard Simon: From Leibniz to J.S. Semler," in *Historische Kritik und biblischer Kanon in der deutschen Aufklärung*, eds. Henning Graf Reventlow, Walter Sparn and John Woodbridge (Wiesbaden: Otto Harrassowitz, 1988) 65-87; and "Richard Simon le 'père de la critique biblique,'" in *Le grand siècle et la bible*, ed. Jean Robert Armogathe (Paris: Beauchesne, 1989). Marie-Hélène Cotoni mentions many eighteenth century French scholars who knew the writings of Simon well (*L'Exégèse du Nouveau Testament dans la philosophie française du XVIIIe siècle* [Oxford: The Voltaire

his works were not reprinted until the appearance of a number of facsimile editions in recent years.[9] What made Simon so unwelcome? Why did he strike so many as strange? This question is the focus of the present essay. It is clear that Simon was in certain ways a somewhat eccentric person. His close associations with Judaism also made him suspicious. In fact, he struck both Protestants and Catholics as clearly dangerous to the faith. But the real reason he seemed so strange, I am arguing here, is that he was announcing, even creating, the modern and even the post-modern sensibility. I will take all this up one point at a time.

Simon's Personality

Physically, he seems to have been unimpressive. His nephew's *Eloge historique,* which generally presents a very positive picture of Simon, describes him as follows.

> Monsieur Simon was small and physically somewhat unattractive. It could not be said of him, as it might of others, that nature had composed a letter of recommendation on his visage. When he spoke, it was difficult to see that he was as gifted as he in fact was.[10]

As for his voice, even Simon himself, in filling out a questionnaire from his Oratorian superiors, responded to an inquiry about his knowledge of liturgical music and singing that "he had studied music from the age of fourteen, though he has since forgotten it, his voice having unfortunately changed to a pitiable falsetto."[11] No portrait has

---

Foundation, 1984]), and Bernus observes that Germany was the country where the *Histoire Critique du Vieux Testament* was read with the greatest care and exercised the greatest influence (*Richard Simon et son Histoire Critique du Vieux Testament* 140).

[9] Since 1967, eleven works have been reprinted by Minerva in Germany, some of these eleven also by Johnson Reprints (five) in the United States and by Slakine (one) in Switzerland.

[10] Bruzen de La Martinière, *Eloge historique de Richard Simon, prêtre,* in *Lettres choisies où l'on trouve un grand nombre de faits anecdotes de littérature. Nouvelle édition, revüe, corrigée et augmentée d'un volume, et de la Vie de l'auteur par M. Bruzen la Marinière* (Amsterdam: Pierre Mortier, 1730) 1:15.

[11] Quoted by Auvray 201, from an otherwise unpublished manuscript.

survived.[12]

His work habits too were singular.

> He ordinarily studied seated on a thick carpet with several cushions. About him on the floor he had a writing desk, paper, and the books he wanted to consult. He rarely ate in the evening and lived in great sobriety, taking hardly enough food to keep himself alive.[13]

During one period of especially intense work, while he was hastening to compose a major response to Jean Le Clerc (1657-1736), he was trying to live on

> nothing but coffee and chocolate, a diet which so enfeebled his stomach and so overheated him that he became completely deformed by the rashes and boils which covered his whole body. His doctor, Monsieur Mauger, found no better remedy to restore his health than reducing him to eating fish alone.[14]

Whatever about his physical appearance and his work habits, Simon was also an unusual figure for his age because of his social roots. He came out of a lower class background. His father is generally described as a blacksmith or some sort of artisan who worked with edge tools. His relatives included a hatter, a cooper, and a shoemaker. On the other hand, a few members of the family were moving up. In the sixteenth century there was a notary, younger relatives included a lawyer and Jacques Simon, his nephew, who became a priest. Another nephew, Antoine-Augustin Bruzen de La Martinière (1683-1749), the one who composed his *Éloge historique*, was a well known geographer.[15] But for all that Richard Simon led a precarious economic existence all his life. His early education was subsidized by his parish priest who evidently recognized his gifts. Simon was the only son of an artisan and the only scholarship student in his first novitiate class.[16] When he left the Oratorians after this first attempt at

[12]Bernus, *Richard Simon et son Histoire critique du Vieux Testament* 118.

[13]Bruzen de La Martinière, *Éloge historique,* in *Lettres choisies* 1:99-100.

[14]*Notice sur les hommes célèbres de Normandie*, composed anonymously between 1714 and 1720, and published by l'abbé Cochet, in *Gallerie dieppoise* (Dieppe, 1862) 351, and quoted by Auvray 83.

[15]Auvray 10.

[16]Ibid. 14.

a novitiate and returned to his native Dieppe in 1658, he was only subsequently able to continue theological studies in Paris because of the generosity of a Dieppe friend, Hyacinthe de La Roque-Hue (c.1636-1728), later a canon at Rouen, who also wanted to study in Paris and who paid Simon's way too.[17]

Oratorians were something between a traditional religious order and secular priests. That is, those who could afford to do so supported themselves. Simon, in all his time with the Oratory, had to depend on the generosity of the order. This obviously bothered him.[18] Though Simon personally wanted to continue his studies in Paris, he asked to be sent to the Oratorian's main college in Juilly so he could earn his keep. Later in the 1670s, when he was negotiating with Protestants about a translation of the Bible, one of his motivations seemed to have been a desire to make some money out of the deal, an aspect of the affair that Bossuet and others used to discredit his motives.[19] Later he was given the very modest income from the tiny parish of Bolleville in the diocese of Rouen. This support enabled him to survive in the years just after his expulsion from the Oratory. But he resigned even that source of security after just a few years, for the rest of his life apparently making do on the income from his books, a sum which couldn't have been enormous. In an age when ecclesiastical contemporaries who had reputations comparable with Simon's enjoyed security and leisure to work, either on the basis of their family's wealth or from the various benefices attached to largely nominal offices, Simon received no preferment.

But it wasn't so much his appearance or his behavior or even his poverty which made Simon unusual but something more to do with his fierce independence. When he went to Paris to study theology in 1659, he did the regular theological studies, but along with studying at the Sorbonne, he also followed lectures at the Jesuit college in Paris,

---

[17]Zéphirin Sanson, "Mémoires pour servir à l'histoire de la vie et des ouvrages de feu M. Simon," *Journal littéraire de La Haye* 3 (January-February 1714) 614, quoted in Auvray 15.

[18]Auvray 29.

[19]Bossuet, for example, later tried to make hay of an accusation raised by Le Clerc in his controversies with Simon. Le Clerc said that Simon was supposed to get paid handsomely for his work on this translations. See *Instructions sur la version du Nouveau Testament imprimée à Trévoux* in *Oeuvres complètes de Bossuet* (Paris: Louis Vivès, 1863) 3:476.

worked at Hebrew, and read enormously on his own. He never pursued a doctorate in theology, very likely because he had little respect for the scholastic theology then still in vogue.

> I admit that I never enjoyed the method which consists in composing big volumes with little content, where one often reasons more as a metaphysician than as a theologian. You know that theology, especially when it is a question of facts, ought to be developed using documents and not by simple reasonings.[20]

In the midst of the fiery theological debates of the latter part of *le grand siècle*, everyone was assigned to some party or another. Were you for or against the Jansenists, for or against the Jesuits, for or against the king or the pope on the question of controlling Church affairs, Cartesian or scholastic? Particularly among the Oratorians in the 1770s there were cliques of pro and contra Jansenist groups. Simon would have none of this.

> In all my work I have tried to belong to the party of truth and not to tie myself to any special master. A true Christian, who professes the Catholic faith, should not be a disciple of St. Augustine rather than of St. Jerome or of any other Church Father, because his faith is founded on the word of Jesus Christ, contained in the writings of the Apostles and in the constant tradition of the Catholic Churches.... Since I have no special interest which binds me to what one might call a party—the very name party is odious to me—I protest that I had no other purpose in view in composing this work than to be useful to the Church, supporting what it holds most sacred and divine.[21]

Simon was sometimes suspected of having Jesuit sympathies. As a youth he spent a year at the Jesuit college in Rouen just after Pascal's *Lettres écrites à un provincial* had appeared and where Jean de Brisacier (1592-1668), S.J., the director of the college, was very active in the anti-Jansenist crusade.[22] When he studied theology, he also attended lectures by Étienne Dechamps (1613-1701), S.J., likewise an

---

[20]*Lettres choisies* 2:56-57.

[21]*Histoire critique du texte du Nouveau Testament, où l'on établit la vérité des actes sur lesquels la Religion chrétienne est fondée, par Richard Simon, prêtre* (Rotterdam: Reinier Leers, 1689), Preface [viii]. Simon describes himself, in his usual modest manner, as "un homme doux, dégagé de préjugés, impartial et éclairé" (*Additions* 44). At least this was his ideal.

[22]Auvray 12.

author of many anti-Jansenist works, at the Jesuit college in Paris. When Simon was criticized for his excessively intellectual pursuits during his novitiate, he apparently seriously considered joining the Jesuits instead of the Oratory.[23] When he was criticized for heterodox opinions on critical matters, he often cited earlier Jesuits famous in biblical and historical theology, figures like Juan Maldonado (1533-1583), Cornelius a Lapide (1567-1637), and Dionysius Petavius (1583-1652). On the other hand, he also wrote a whole work against a Jesuit named Dominique Bouhours (1628-1702) who had translated the New Testament into French, but not well, according to Simon.[24] In the course of these letters against Bouhours' work, Simon indicated that he felt attacked by Jesuits. And, according to Bruzen de La Martinière, Jesuits reported Simon to civil authorities shortly before his death, and out of fear that his files would be confiscated and handed over to the Jesuits for censure, Simon is supposed to have filled several large barrels with his papers, rolled them during the night to the Dieppe city walls and burned them.[25] There are questions about the facts of this colorful story, but at least the supposition that Jesuits might be after Simon was apparently plausible.[26]

If he wasn't really close to Jesuits, his distance from Jansenists was even more evident. One of Simon's earliest works[27] was an attempt to supplement and improve on a huge Jansenist work, *Perpétuité de la foy à l'Eucharistie*, by Pierre Nicole (1625-95) and, to some extent, by Antoine Arnauld (1612-94). Since, in effect, Simon was showing these very famous Jansenist scholars the right way to do a defense of Catholic belief, his help was not appreciated. As we shall see, Simon regarded Jansenists as enemies his whole life, and had good reason to suspect that they were behind many of the troubles he had getting his

[23]Sanson 186, as quoted in Auvray 17.

[24]*Difficultéz proposées au Révérend Père Bouhours de la Compagnie de Jésus, sur sa traduction françoise des quatre Evangélistes* (Amsterdam: Adrian Braakmann, 1697).

[25]Bruzen de La Martinière, *Eloge historique*, in *Lettres choisies* 1:99.

[26]Auvray 150-52.

[27]*Fides Ecclesiae Orientalis seu Gabrielis Metropolitae Philadelphiensis opuscula, nunc primum de graecis conserva, cum notis uberioribus quibus nationum orientalium persuasio maxime de rebus eucharisticis ex libris praesertim manuscriptis vel nondum latio donatis illustratur, adversus Claudii Responsum ad Perpetuitatem Fidei Ecclesiae catholicae, opera et studio Richardi Simonis e Congregatione Oratorii...* (Paris: G. Meturas, 1674).

work published in Paris.

Simon's independence and exotic tastes also come out in the range of his scholarly interests. *"Ce savant, ce grand liseur,"* Le Brun and Woodbridge call him.[28] For example, when asked about his intellectual background before he had entered the Oratory, he bragged about all the studies he had done and the books he had read during his student days in Paris and back at Dieppe before his entry into the novitiate the second time. Not only did he follow the theological lectures at the Sorbonne, and those by Etienne Dechamps, S.J., at the Jesuit college in Paris, he also pursued independent studies of Hebrew and Syriac. As for books, he lists a huge hodgepodge:

> The *Summa* of Saint Thomas [Aquinas, (1225-74), O.P.], along with the Master of the *Sentences* [Peter Lombard, 1100-60], all the theology of [N.] Isambert..., [Philippe de] Gamaches [1568-1625], and something of [Francisco de] Suarez [(1548-1617), S.J.] and [Martin] Becanus [(1563-1624), S.J.], also some commentaries on the Bible, several heretical works..., the summary of [Cesare] Baronius [1538-1607] by [Henri de] Sponde [1568-1643], [Isaac] Casaubon [1559-1614] against Baronius, six centuries of the history by the Magdeburg Centuriators [1559-74], the Bible of [John Immanuel] Tremellius [1510-80] and [Franciscus] Junius [1545-1602] with notes, the New Testament with the paraphrase by [Desiderius] Erasmus [1469-1536], the commentary of [Juan] Maldonado [(1533-83), S.J.], the major notes by [Theodore] Beza [1519-1605], something from [Robert] Bellarmine [(1542-1621), S.J.] and the heretics who wrote against him, the summary of the councils by Coriolan, and so on, plus some secular studies.[29]

His monumental translations of and commentaries on works which explained Judaism and Oriental Christianity led him into studies of religious customs and beliefs in every direction, including Islam. In fact Arnauld, for example, accused Simon of having judged Islam too favorably and to have, by implication, promoted indifference in matters of religion.[30] Simon responded:

> There is nothing in the works of the wisest pagans that can be compared with what Arab writers say about the unity of God, his perfections, the

---

[28]Page 18.

[29]From the "Notice autobiographique" of 1673, reproduced in Auvray 200. N. Isambert was a professor in the faculty of theology at Paris, and Cariolan is presumably another late sixteenth or early seventeenth century theologian.

[30]Steinmann 163.

worship due him, and the charity one ought to have for one's neighbor. Is Monsieur Arnauld angry that they have borrowed all these insights from Jews and Christians?[31]

His interest in and command of Oriental Christianity was not superficial. When a Chaldean priest came to Paris in 1770, Simon acted as deacon for him when he said Mass in the Oratorian chapel. In the course of the Mass Simon noticed that the priest mixed Latin, Maronite and Chaldean liturgies and that the name Nestorius had been scratched out in his Chaldean missal. Simon even gave the Chaldean priest a lesson on the consecration and the epiclesis.[32]

This independence and catholicity of tastes was one more thing that raised Bossuet's hackles. He accused Simon of using "all kinds of authors, Catholic or Protestant indifferently," picking out all sorts of things, especially "the most singular and bizarre."[33] Of course, Bossuet reproached Simon for much more, but I will return to all that later. Another prominent seventeenth century scholar bishop, Pierre-Daniel Huet (1630-1721), in a handwritten note in his copy of the *Histoire critique du Vieux Testament*, said that Simon, "admiring no one and blaspheming everyone, merited the fact that everyone blasphemed him."[34]

For Simon, his intense independence, also meant that he criticized everyone. As Huet points out, that behavior did not win friends. Simon himself seemed to be puzzled by others' resentment. Simon always believed he was just being a critic, which for him meant trying to get things straight. He seemed to think that others should be grateful when he corrected them. Of course, he himself did not take criticism lying down. But there was something else in all this about Simon's personality that raised suspicions. There was the matter of his pseudonyms, his publications outside France (sometimes with false imprints), his posing in various works as a Protestant, as a professor of theology at the Sorbonne, and even as a group of Amsterdam rabbis, farcically thanking one of his opponents. Furthermore, he denied writing works that he clearly did write. What are we to make of all this?

[31]*Lettres choisies* 3:257.
[32]Steinmann 49.
[33]*Instructions* 3:472.
[34]Bernus, *Richard Simon et son Histoire critique du Vieux Testament* 43 note.

One must remember that publishing something regarded as heretical or as injurious to the crown could be very dangerous in seventeenth century France.[35] Simon's fellow Oratorian and his Paris superior, Claude Séguenot (1596-1676), for example, had been "bastilized" by Richelieu for five years for remarks about attrition attached to his translation of St. Augustine's *De virginitate*.[36] A novitiate confrere of Simon, Bernard Lamy (1640-1715), was exiled to Grenoble for having taught Cartesian ideas. Another confrere, this time not his friend, Pierre Faydit (1644-1703), spent time in a mental institution where authorities hoped to correct his theological ideas. Another Oratorian friend, even though a Jansenist, J. B. du Breuil (1611-1699), spent the last fourteen years of his life in a series of prisons for trafficking in forbidden books.[37] In fact, Simon is remarkable for having survived largely unscathed. He often had to publish in this unorthodox way to save his own skin. Of course, some of his works ended up on the Roman *Index*. But he was never excommunicated, never banished or imprisoned, and he died in good standing as a Catholic priest. Many other controversial figures of his age could not say the same. Almost all the prominent Jansenists of his day died in exile outside France. Consequently, much of this so-called duplicity on Simon's part should be taken as understandable caution. Even at that, many of his pseudonyms were immediately transparent. Recared Sçimeon, R. Schimeon ben Joacim, le Prieur de Bolleville, Jean Reuchlin, for example, were more humorous than real pseudonyms and fooled few for long. On the other hand, some pseudonyms were harder to figure out, but in most cases, even here, there was some joke hidden behind the name: Sieur de Mony, Sieur de Simonville, Richard de Lisle,

[35]See, for example, Patrick J. Lambe, "Biblical Criticism and Censorship in Ancien Régime France: The Case of Richard Simon," *Harvard Theological Review* 78 (1985) 149-77.

[36]Séguenot said that penance is not assured in the absence of true contrition while Richelieu had maintained in his *Catéchisme* that "attrition," moved merely by the fear of punishment, was sufficient. There was probably more to Richelieu's action. He had been incited by the Capuchin *éminence grise* Joseph du Tremblay; imprisoning Séguenot was aimed as much at Saint-Simon and the whole devout party who opposed Richelieu's international politics and his associates in the devout party. See A. Molien, "Séguenot, Claude," in *Dictionnaire de théologie catholique* 14 (1941) 1775-80; and Michel Join-Lambert, "Séguenot (Claude)," in *Dictionnaire de spiritualité* 14 (1960) 524-25.

[37]Auvray 22, 24, 167-68.

Origenes Adamantius, Jérôme de Costa, Hieronymus le Camus, Pierre Ambrun, Ambrosius, Jérôme de Sainte-Foi.

Richard Simon was a bit strange then. His appearance, the fact he was an intellectual loner, his use of pseudonyms and deception in his writing all contributed to that image. But it was more especially his independence from all contemporary power bases and his assumption that everything was up for criticism, even in religious matters, which earned him this reputation as a stranger in the intellectual world of his day. And then too, he seemed to some far too sympathetic to other strangers, to religious outsiders, for example, to Jews.

Simon and the Jews

Jews in seventeenth century France enjoyed only marginal tolerance. Henry II (1547-1559) had allowed Maranos to settle in France, a permission renewed by Louis XIV in 1656, but they were not permitted to practice Judaism. Only in eastern France were Jews tolerated as such.[38] Individual Jews, however, were given permission to reside in France for specific reasons and for limited periods of time. Among these was Jonah Salvador, an Italian Jew in France as a tobacco merchant, who became Simon's Hebrew tutor.[39] Salvador is not known outside of his relationship with Simon, but it is obvious from everything Simon says about him that Salvador was quite sophisticated in rabbinic studies.[40] During the 1670s they used to get together on Saturdays in the Oratorian library to study Jewish texts together. Evidently their relationship was a warm one. For example, Simon chided Salvador for carrying heavy rabbinic commentaries around the library on the Sabbath day, and Salvador invited Simon to work with him on a Latin translation of the Talmud.

In fact, it was through Salvador that Simon learned about the execution in Metz of a certain Raphael Levy (c.1612-1670) for ritual murder, the old blood libel against Jews. In his first formal writing,

---

[38]Jacqueline Hall, "'Ceremonies et coutumes qui s'observent aujourd'hui parmi les juifs': An Important but Little-Known Work by Richard Simon," *Nottingham French Studies* 18 (1979) 14-27.

[39]Steinmann 58-63; Auvray 26-27.

[40]Myriam Yardeni, "La vision des juifs et judaisme dans l'Oeuvre de Richard Simon," *Revue des études juives* 129 (1970) 179-03.

Simon took up the defense of Jews against this accusation, and he was proud to claim that his *Factum* had been influential in the decision of the Royal Council to reverse the judgment of the parlement of Metz against the Jewish community there.[41] Myriam Yardeni, a modern Jewish scholar, maintains that Simon's rehearsal of the calumnies committed against Jews throughout Christian history and his defense of Jews "in its main lines" remains "still valuable today."[42]

Simon flaunted his familiarity with Jewish tradition,[43] although he knew that Christian scholars and other leaders held Jews in contempt and suspected them of all sorts of scholarly misconduct. But Simon signed the Oratorian questionnaire mentioned earlier "R. Schimeon ben Joacim." Simon, in all his critical writings displayed a rare command of rabbinic tradition which he regarded as indispensable for a Christian understanding of the Bible, an opinion that, as Schwartzbach observes, "other French Hebraists of the period refused to admit."[44] One of the main things Simon was doing in his use of the exegetical theories of David Kimchi (1165-1235), Isaac Abrabanel (1437-1508) and others was taking their methods of commenting on the Prophets and the Writings, less sacred parts of the Bible, and applying them to the whole of scripture, because these Jewish critics could not use truly critical principles on the Torah itself. These theories, "reformulated, generalized, applied and historicized, became, and rightly so, the biblical criticism which was the glory and the scandal of Richard Simon."[45]

Simon thought a study of Judaism was important not only for biblical studies but also for understanding the origins of Christianity and the inner meaning of many Christian rituals and traditions. It was

---

[41]*Factum servant de réponse à un livre intitulé "Abrégé du procès fait aux Juifs de Metz,"* in *Bibliothèque critique ou Recüeil de diverses pièces critiques dont la plûpart ne sont point imprimées ou ne se trouvent que très difficilement. Publiées par Mr de Sainjore qui y a ajouté quelques notes* (Amsterdam: Jn. Ls. de Lormes, 1708) 1:109-131. See Simon's comments on this affair in *Lettres choisies* 2:60.

[42]Yardeni, "La vision des juifs" 183.

[43]"He acquired a rare mastery of Hebrew language and literature" (Yardeni 181).

[44]Bertram Eugene Schwarzbach, "Les sources rabbiniques de la critique biblique de Richard Simon," in *Le grand siècle de la bible*, ed. Jean Robert Armogathe (Paris: Beauchesne, 1989) 211.

[45]Schwartzbach 231.

for this reason that he undertook the translation of Leone Modena's (1571-1648) explanation of Jewish customs and ceremonies, to which he attached a long preface and, at the end, his own disquisitions on the Karaites and Samaritans.[46] In fact, the Karaites—an eighth century Jewish sect still alive in the Middle East, Turkey, and Russia in the seventeenth century—were favorites of Simon since he saw in their emphasis on the Torah alone and on the literal sense of scripture some of his own preferences.[47] Simon, like the Karaites, often deplored excessive use of allegorical senses of scripture. It even turned out, Yosef Kaplan claims, that certain Jews in Amsterdam in the early eighteenth century who claimed to be Karaites got their notion of Karaism from Simon's presentation of them as "purified Jews."[48] On the other hand, Simon occasionally identified Protestants with Karaites and Catholics with the rabbis since Protestantism, again like the Karaites, professed to be based on the Bible alone, whereas Catholicism in addition accepted tradition as normative, as the rabbis did. Simon often addressed his Protestant friend Jean de Frémont d'Ablancourt (1621-96) as "Mon cher Caraïte" and signed his letters to him "le Rabbaniste."[49] However, he insisted with Frémond that "there is not as great a distance as you imagine between Karaism and true rabbinism."[50]

As we shall see, Simon was not without his own prejudices against Jews, but he also loyally defended them against the accusation of having falsified the text of the Bible. Though Simon admitted that many errors had crept into the biblical text, "He does not, however, accuse Jews of having deliberately corrupted this text. On the contrary, he continually emphasizes the injustice of this accusation."[51] He also

---

[46]*Cérémonies et coustumes qui s'observent ajouurd'huy parmi les Juifs. Traduites de l'italien de Léon de Modène, rabin de Venise. Avec un supplément touchant les sectes des Caraïtes et des Samaritains de nostre temps, par Don Recared Sçiméon*, 2 vols. (Paris: L. Billaine, 1674).

[47]Georges Tavard, *La tradition au XVIIe siècle en France et en Angleterre* (Paris: Éditions du Cerf, 1969) 126.

[48]"'Karaites' in Early Eighteenth-Century Amsterdam," in *Sceptics, Millenarians and Jews*, eds. David S. Katz and Jonathan I. Israel (Leiden: Brill, 1990) 221.

[49]Steinmann 215.

[50]*Lettres choisies* 3:118.

[51]*Réponse à la lettre de M. Spanheim où* [sic] *Lettre d'un théologien de la Faculté de Paris qui rend compte à un de ses amis de l'Histoire critique du*

defended the so-called usury of Jews, supporting in his *Factum* modern economic principles and pointing out the disabilities of Jews who had few other options. In fact, he says, "Jews by this means bring many Christians out of misery every day."[52]

Furthermore, Simon recognized specifically Jewish virtues, especially their charity and piety. "One can hardly admire enough the modesty and interior recollection of Jews when they go to prayer in the morning." And again:

> Jews not only excel at prayer but also in charity. It shines out in the compassion they have for the poor, an image of the charity the first Christians had for their brethren. They [the first Christians] were following what was done in synagogues and the practices and customs which Jews have retained, while today we [Christians] barely preserve the memory.[53]

It would be hard to find a contemporary who could speak so positively about Jews. As Yardeni says,

> He is among the rare Christians of this period for whom Jews after Jesus are not just a people left in existence as an eternal warning to the whole of humanity, but a living people, endowed with exceptional creative and adaptive power with respect to their civilization.[54]

So Simon was an exception, he was even strange for his age, in his ability to grant Jews and their religion respect and even a certain admiration. But he was also a prisoner of the prejudices of his time. He could stoop to commenting on Jews as "this miserable nation which hates us mortally,"[55] or even, "It appears to me that the majority of Jews today don't have any religion, although exteriorly they observe their ceremonies. All their efforts aim at making money."[56] Yardeni has collected a whole series of similar negative comments from Simon

---

Vieux Testament, attribuée au P. Simon de l'Oratoire (Amsterdam: D. Elzevier, 1680) 23. After 1685 this text was printed at the end of *HCVT*.

[52]*Factum* [pour les] *Juifs de Metz* 9, as quoted in Yardeni, "La vision des juifs" 185.

[53]*Cérémonies [des] Juifs, Préface*, as quoted in Yardeni, "La vision des juifs" 202 note.

[54]Myriam Yardeni, "La vision des juifs" 196.

[55]*Lettres choisies* 2:60.

[56]*Lettres choisies* 2:16.

about Jews.[57] Their allegorical works on scripture are useless, their chronologies and histories are poor, they have contributed little to grammar and science. How does he explain these faults, given the virtues and talents of Jews that he celebrates elsewhere? Simon thinks these failures were due to the fact that Jews were not open to influence from outside. They were not allowed to read the philosophers. That is, they lacked openness to the sort of foreign influences, even strange and exotic ones, that Simon himself was so willing to consider.

Of course, Simon ultimately just wasn't consistent here. He could at times be very daring and positive in his approach to Judaism, but he was also a captive of prevailing prejudices. After the 1670s, as he moved from work on the Old Testament to concentrate more exclusively on the New, he also seems to have spent less time on rabbinical sources. In 1685 he told his Protestant friend Henri Justel (1620-93), "I completely stopped reading the rabbis a long time ago, and, to tell you the truth, they never much pleased me."[58] As in the case of his personality, here too Simon comes across as ambiguous. He was a forerunner of modern comparative religion, of modern openness to the goodness inherent in diverse cultures, but he was also unable to fully escape the limits of his historical setting, and so he also foreshadowed later erudite contempt for Jews. Consequently, he was strange to contemporaries, and he remains strange today, even to modern Jews. Yardeni again:

> Two stereotypes of Richard Simon prevail in Jewish historical literature. According to the first, Richard Simon is a true champion of tolerance and a sincere friend of Jews. The other stereotype presents Simon to us as a precursor of Voltaire, to whom he provided a good part of his anti-Semitic arsenal. ...
>
> A strange mixture which justifies the two stereotypes of Simon and at the same time characterizes, many centuries later, numerous traits of Western mentality regarding Jews.[59]

But if Simon was strange on the subject of Jews, he was equally so when it came to Protestants.

---

[57]Yardeni, "La vision des juifs" 197-201.
[58]*Lettres choisies* 2:187.
[59]Yardeni, "La vision des juifs" 179, 203.

Simon and Protestants

Simon never felt any need to keep his distance from Protestants. Growing up in Dieppe he must have met many. Henri Justel and Jean de Frémont d'Ablancourt, prominent Protestant scholars and civic figures in the Paris of the 1670s, were close friends.[60] He admitted in his *Notice autobiographique* that during his student days he read many heretical works "in order to dispute with Calvinists."[61] Simon commonly covered himself with this excuse, but he actually entertained a certain sincere respect for some aspects of Protestant theology and biblical study.[62] He told Abbé de Bussy de Lameth that during his student period he read Calvin and found that much of what Calvin said satisfied him more than what Catholics wrote.[63] In his scientific work Simon habitually critiqued Catholic, Protestant, and Socinian commentaries, as well as other biblical and historical books, without any distinctions. He praised and found fault where he thought it was deserved, irrespective of confessional allegiances. This attitude scandalized Protestants and Catholics alike.

Simon's most intimate association with Protestants was during the period 1667-1677 when he was seriously proposed by the Reformed theologians of Charenton as a collaborator for a new translation of the Bible. Simon gave advice about the principles that ought to govern this new translation and supplied samples of how he would go about doing it. The money and much of the impetus for this undertaking came from Geneva, but eventually nothing came of the plan. Some claim that Simon's translations were inadequate, others that he was asking for too

---

[60]"Although he [Simon] was intensely Catholic, he distinguished between the writings and the persons of Protestants; and although he contested their opinions fiercely, he did not cease to have illustrious friends among them with whom he communicated by letter and in person with a very lively cordiality" (Bruzen de La Martinière, *Eloge historique*, in *Lettres choisies* 1:100).

[61]Auvray 200.

[62]Or as Simon puts it, "Not everything in the bibles of the heretics are heretical" (*Histoire critique des principaux commentateurs du Nouveau Testament, depuis le commencement du christianisme jusqu'à nôtre tems, avec une Dissertation critique sur les principaux actes manuscrits qui ont été cités dans les trois parties de cet ouvrage, par Richard Simon, prêtre* [Rotterdam: Reinier Leers, 1693] 877).

[63]*Lettres choisies* 2:45.

much money, still others that suspicions between the more conservative Geneva Calvinists and the more liberal French ones accounted for the failure of the venture.[64] During this period there also were questions connected with Simon's editing and adding remarks to a work by the English antiquarian Edward Brerewood (1565-1613) on various languages and religions of the Near East, a work these same Protestants wanted republished in French. That project also came to naught.[65] But the point is, especially during this period, Simon worked closely with Protestants, was obviously trusted by some of them, and Simon himself was even able to envision some sort of ecumenical Bible. Even as late as 1684 Simon published, in Utrecht and largely for a Protestant audience, a short synopsis of a proposal to put out a new polyglot biblical text that would be less expensive than the ones currently available.[66] Of course, all of Simon's works published outside France, whether in England or in the Netherlands, were put out by Protestant publishing houses, especially by Reinier Leers in Rotterdam. This fact too implies good relations between some Protestants and Simon.

Serious controversy with Protestants began gently with Simon's effort to improve Nicole's and Arnauld's argument against Protestant eucharistic theology in their *Perpétuité de la foy à l'Eucharistie*. They had cited Orthodox theologians in support of Catholic views on Eucharist against the Reformed theologian Jean Claude (1619-87). Simon's *Fides ecclesiae orientalis* then, in addition, presented the

[64]Bossuet used just the very fact that Simon cooperated with Protestants on a translation of the bible against him. Worse, Bossuet quoted Le Clerc's description of the plan intended to produce a bible that "*would favor neither party* [Bossuet's emphasis], and which would be useful to both Protestants and Catholics." Bossuet continued, "That's doubtless a fine project for a Catholic priest: producing a bible to satisfy all parties, that is to say, one suited to promote indifference in religion.... The plan and the model for this fine work was provided by Monsieur Simon, and the job was shared with a [Protestant] minister." Of course the bible was to be accompanied by notes, the same sort of notes that Simon had provided for his own translation of the New Testament in 1702, notes which maintain the same "perfect neutrality that was promised between the Church and heresy, between Jesus Christ and Belial" (*Instructions sur la version du Nouveau Testament imprimée à Trévoux*, in *Oeuvres complètes de Bossuet* 3:475-76).

[65]Auvray 36-38; Le Brun and Woodbridge 9-39.

[66]*Novorum Bibliorum polyglottorum synopsis* (Utrecht: Frederici Arnoldi, 1684).

original Greek texts of Gabriel of Philadelphia, along with extended commentary, all supporting Catholic eucharistic doctrine. In the course of some unpleasantness with the Jansenists over this work, Simon also had contacts with Claude through their mutual friend Henri Justel. Claude was an important Protestant theologian of the time who engaged in extended conversations and controversies with Bossuet as well. Though Simon was clearly opposed to Claude's theology, one suspects that Simon had a certain sympathy with him, a sympathy that Simon didn't feel for the Jansenists. Claude and Simon exchanged their respective books relating to this debate with the Jansenists, and Simon invited Claude to rejoin the Catholic Church where, Simon said, Claude could argue his views from within as others do. "Reënter the bosom of her whom your confreres have so often called the great Babylon. There you can then cry out like Clemangis and many other scholars in our communion who believe that there is something to reform regarding discipline."[67] Simon often found it hard to understand why Protestants he knew didn't become Catholics. He certainly felt that way about his friends Justel and Frémont d'Ablancourt. At one point he told the latter, "Let your ministers preach whatever they like and come with us to Mass."[68]

The real fireworks with Protestants, however, began with the publication—or almost publication (since it was suppressed in France and only subsequently published in London and Rotterdam)—of Simon's *Histoire critique du Vieux Testament* [*HCVT*] in 1778. For the next eleven years Simon engaged in a running battle over his critical principles with Protestants of every stripe—Anglicans, Lutherans, Calvinists, Arminians. It would be tedious to rehearse these controversies in detail, but some account is worthwhile. In effect, Simon's responses constitute an ample appendix to his work on the Old Testament since they provided opportunities to clarify and expand his original presentation.[69]

Even before the *HCVT* was finished, Simon sent a copy to Claude for comment, which the latter apparently provided. The Preface

---

[67]*Lettres choisies* 2:98.

[68]Ibid. 1:84.

[69]The intricacies of the publications of this period are admirably sorted out by Bernus, *Richard Simon et son Histoire critique du Vieux Testament* 96-117, and especially in his amazing bibliography—"un peu touffue," as he says—in Ingold's *Essai de bibliographie oratorienne* 125-34.

responded to Claude's reservations without mentioning him by name. Then, while the government, instigated by Bossuet, was making up its mind to proscribe the work and pulp copies already printed, Simon sent several samples to England, one to the bishop of London, Henry Compton (1632-1713), whom Simon had met in Paris in 1673 through his friend Justel. Subsequently, the *HCVT* was translated into English (probably by John Hampden [1656-96], also a friend of Simon) in 1682. The first English reaction was a letter attacking Simon by Charles-Marie de Veil (d.1700), a curious but scholarly figure, originally Jewish, converted by Bossuet, subsequently an Augustinian monk, a canon regular of St. Genevieve, doctor and professor of theology at Angers, curé at Melun, but at the time of his letter (1678) an Anglican minister in England, though he ended up an Anabaptist in the Netherlands. To this letter Simon composed a response in the same year, but it was only published in 1685, inserted at the end of the new edition of the *HCVT*, to which response de Veil replied in the same year. Ezechiel Spanheim (1629-1710), also a serious scholar, in London as the ambassador of the Elector Palatine during this period, likewise published a mostly positive, explanatory summary of the *HCVT* in 1679, but including some mild criticism as well. Simon, who could almost never leave well enough alone, composed a reply to Spanheim too, apparently only publishing it along with the one to de Veil in 1685, also attached to the end of the *HCVT*. Simon added a second response to Spanheim the following year, itself only reaching print in 1704 when it was attached to the second volume of Simon's *Lettres choisies*.

A more extensive debate went on between Simon and Isaac Vossius (1618-89), then canon of Windsor though he was born in Leyden and had served for some years as librarian for Queen Christina of Sweden. Their exchanges, which were very intemperate on both sides, began in 1680 and ended in 1686. Vossius was very big on the absolute importance of the Septuagint, and Simon demonstrated quite convincingly that the Massoretic text had very serious claims as well, often being superior to the Septuagint.

These were the principal Protestant responses to the *HCVT* from England. The most important other ones came from the Netherlands, or from French Protestants who eventually ended up there. The first of these was from Jacques Basnage (1653-1723), originally a pastor at Rouen, but after the revocation of the Edict of Nantes in 1685, pastor at Rotterdam, then at La Haye. Though this aside against Simon appeared in Basnage's first publication (1684), he later became a quite famous historian. Simon responded in 1685, and Basnage replied in 1687. Of course, every Protestant scholar had to leave France in 1685 at the time of the revocation of the Edict of Nantes, so French Protestant responses were inevitably handicapped, given their economic and scholarly dislocation.

Then there was the very substantial debate between Simon and Jean Le Clerc. Le Clerc was a very different sort of Protestant and a very distinguished biblical critic, as his later work demonstrates. In fact, he and Simon remain the most important biblical critics of their age. But at the time of their conflict, Le Clerc was still relatively unknown. Le Clerc began with a response to Simon's request for comments on his proposal for a polyglot Bible in 1684. Simon didn't take Le Clerc's suggestions well, and answered him briefly in Flemish. Le Clerc took up the challenge, publishing in 1685 a 457 page tome called *Sentimens de quelques theologiens de Hollande...*, in the form of a discussion of Simon's *HCVT* among three Protestant theologians. Simon produced a 256 page response the following year. Then Le Clerc replied with a *Défense des Sentimens...* in 459 pages the same year, to which Simon responded with 170 pages, to end the debate, in 1687. This famous exchange was the most unfortunate of Simon's fights during this period. Le Clerc was born in Geneva, but he had developed unorthodox Protestant views and had moved to Holland in search of greater religious liberty. At the time of these events he had recently (1684) been appointed professor of philosophy, Hebrew and literature at the Arminian college in Amsterdam. In fact, he subscribed to many of the basic principles of Simon's critical agenda. In some ways he showed himself even freer of conventional ecclesiastical assumptions than Simon did. His basic criticism of the *HVCT*—that Simon had spent too much time on questions of text and canon and not enough on trying to uncover the authorship, date, and purpose of the various books of the Old Testament—sound very sensible. But Simon, as usual, could not take criticism well. And, in fact, Simon had his own good points over against Le Clerc, but he couldn't refrain from the sort of biting raillery which was his basic controversial mode. On matters of civility Le Clerc came off better.

Finally, there is the case of Pierre Jurieu (1637-1713). (His enemies often called him *"Injurieu"* because of the violence of his polemical works.) He was a famous French Protestant controversialist, having crossed swords with Bossuet and Arnauld, for example. Among his many books was *L'Accomplissement des prophéties, ou la délivrance de l'Église* (1686) which predicted the triumph of Protestantism for the year 1689 and identified the pope with the beast of Babylon in the Book of Revelation. In the course of his debate with Le Clerc, Simon took a swipe at Jurieu, who in turn attacked Simon because Jurieu believed that Simon was the most effective defender of the Catholic claim that tradition was essential for understanding and preserving Christian faith, not the Bible alone as Protestants maintained. But Simon hardly took Jurieu seriously. Simon notes:

> It is an admirable work of Providence that the name M. Jurieu *contains in the sacred language, according to the numerical value of Hebrew letters*, the number 666. Hence it appears that God has desired that the whole earth would know that the beast of Revelation is none other than Monsieur Jurieu, dwelling *in the midst of the waters of Rotterdam*.[70]

In addition to these principal challenges to Simon's ideas, there were many others which he never heard about or declined to contest. Auguste Bernus lists some forty seventeenth and eighteenth century works which attacked Simon, most of them Protestant.[71] But in all this controversy what was the nub of the argument? Of course there were many details, far too many to discuss here. But behind them all were two claims made by Simon which outraged Protestants. According to Simon the text of the Bible itself was never absolutely certain, and the interpretations of the text were open to a great variety of possible explanations. But for Protestants the Bible was the one certain source of Christian truth. Its validity was guaranteed by God himself, and its plain meaning was clear and open to any honest reader. There was no need for any outside authority, any divinely guided tradition, to interpret the text and then pass revelation on down through history, as Simon claimed was necessary. Simon insisted that there was no one, perfect Old Testament text. One had to consider not only the

---

[70]*Réponse au livre intitulé Sentimens de quelques théologiens de Hollande sur l'Histoire critique du Vieux Testament, par le Prieur de Bolleville. Outre la réponse aux Théologiens de Hollande on trouvera dans cet ouvrage de nouvelles preuves et de nouveaux éclaircissemens pour servir de supplément à cette Histoire critique* (Rotterdam: Reinier Leers, 1686) 188-89.

[71]Bernus, "Richard Simon" 125-34.

Massoretic text, but also the Septuagint, the Samaritan Pentateuch, and all the other ancient versions, Syriac, Greek, Latin, in order to arrive at a reasonably secure judgment about the text for a given passage. And even then one was only talking about levels of probability, not any absolute certainty. But worse than that, Simon maintained in the *HCVT* that the Pentateuch, as presently preserved, was not composed by Moses himself. Rather, there had been, Simon hypothesized, a body of scribes in the "Hebrew Republic" who composed the Pentateuch and the other books of the Old Testament, drawing on royal records, some of which went back to Moses himself, though not all did. This process, Simon claimed, was the only way to explain the doublets, gaps, repetitions and other inconsistencies in the biblical text as we have it. In other words, granted the guidance of the Holy Spirit, the Bible had been composed just like other books. The process itself was natural, even if there was a supernatural, though perhaps unconscious, guidance in the process. Therefore, biblical books could and must be analyzed or criticized just as one would analyze any other ancient book.

But that wasn't all. Not only was the text of the Bible open to constant emendation, determining what the text meant was not a simple process either. To understand it one had to know the world from which the text came. One had to know the customs and assumptions of biblical times in order to situate and ultimately understand the message of the Bible. This conviction explains Simon's enthusiasm for study of Jewish and other Oriental customs and beliefs,[72] as well as his special interest in Jewish commentators down through history. Simon believed that Jews had preserved some of the mentalities of Bible times, and their intimate familiarity with the Hebrew language though long study

---

[72]Besides his early *Fides Ecclesiae Orientalis* and *Cérémonies [des] Juifs* (both of 1674) and *Voyage du Mont Liban, traduit de l'italien du R. P. Jérôme Dandini, nonce en ce pays-là, où il est traité tant de la créance et des coûtumes des Maronites que de plusieurs particularitez touchant les Turcs, et de quelques lieux considérables de l'Orient, avec des remarques sur la théologie des Chrétiens du Levant et sur celle des Mahométans. Par R.S.P.* (Paris: Louis Billaine, 1675), there are also his *Antiquitates Ecclesiae Orientalis, clarissimorum virorum, Card. Barberini, L. Allatii,...desertationibus epistolicis enucleatae, nunc ex ipsis autographis editae, quibus praefixa est Jo. Morini Congr. Orat. Paris. PP. vita* (London: Geo. Wells, 1682), and the *Histoire critique de la créance et des coûtumes des nations du levant, publiée par le Sr de Moni* (Frankfurt: Fred. Arnaud, 1684), not to mention all sorts of lengthy historical and anthropological asides in his other works.

and use gave them a certain special insight into the meaning of the Bible. In other words, there are uncertainties on all sides. Criticism alone can never come to final decisions about the ultimate meaning of Christian revelation. Hence, Christianity needs a divinely guided teaching tradition which guarantees the essential Christian message down through time.

It was this critical relativism which so unsettled Protestants, especially the more rigid among them. They might be willing to argue about some small point here and there in the text of the Bible or about the exact interpretation of some passage, but the massive doubt that Simon's huge work cast over the whole body of biblical tradition seemed absolutely abominable to them.[73] As even Le Clerc, who was quite free from ecclesiastical restraints himself, observed, Simon sometimes appeared to be *"un Réformé"* because he used their methods, he praised some of their authors, and he was so free about how he used the Church Fathers. Or you might think he was a Jew, maybe from Spain or Portugal, because he was so favorable to the rabbis, perhaps a Jew who pretends to be a Christian. Or you might think that he was a hidden Spinozist because he seemed to favor some of Spinoza's ideas, and his rules for interpreting scripture were better suited to destroying it than defending it.[74] In fact, many Protestants doubted Simon's religious sincerity. Henry Compton, bishop of London, whom Simon regarded as a friend, remarked, "This man has no religion," and John Hampden, who had cooperated in some of Simon's English publications, eventually concluded that Simon's ideas "tend directly to the rejection of Christian faith in scripture."[75] The most famous Englishman who felt corrupted by Simon was John Dryden (1631-1700) who, in his poem *Religio Laici* of 1682, referred to Simon as one of the main sources of contemporary religious doubt. Dryden was also a friend of John Hampden.

---

[73]"Simon, with a deft touch and with incredible erudition, drowned his opponents in learning and in a sea of problems" (Richard Popkin, "Bible Criticism and Social Science" 349). Even as famous a Protestant skeptic as Pierre Bayle (1647-1706) tended to regard Simon as an unbeliever (Steinmann 418).

[74]Jean Le Clerc, *Sentimens de quelques theologiens de Hollande sur l'Histoire critique Du Vieux Testament, composée par le P. Richard Simon de l'Oratoire. Où en remarquant les fautes de cet Auteur, on donne divers Principes utiles pour l'intelligence de l'Ecriture Sainte* (Amsterdam: Henri Desbordes, 1685) 93-94.

[75]Auvray 168-69.

For some, who have his secret meaning ghes'd,
Have found our Authour not too *much* a *Priest*:
For *Fashion-sake* he seems to have recourse
To *Pope*, and *Councils*, and *Traditions* force....
If *written words* from time are not secur'd,
How can we think have *oral Sounds* endur'd?[76]

So Protestants too found Simon very strange. At times he seemed to favor Protestants and Protestant scholarly pursuits and was accepted by them as a friend. More frequently Protestants thought Simon was not only opposed to their vision of Christian biblical scholarship, but even that he was a hypocritical and deceptive enemy of Christian faith in any form. But it isn't just Jews today, or Protestants then, who found Simon strange. Catholics too, of many varieties, found Simon impossible to understand or trust.

Simon and Catholics

Though suspicion has been cast on the sincerity of Simon's Catholicism by both Protestants and Catholics in his own day as well as today, there really doesn't seem to be any serious reasons for doubting his honest commitment to the Catholic faith.[77] Other Catholics close to him in one way or another did pass over to Protestantism and were rewarded for doing so. There is even reason to suspect that discrete invitations in that direction were extended to him in the days when financial pressures and official Catholic disapproval were at their height. Simon apparently never considered this option. He had been baptized, raised and he was finally buried in his parish church of Saint-Jacques in Dieppe. On his tombstone the epitaph begins, "Here lies M. Richard Simon, priest, great glory of the Church

[76]John Dryden, "Religio Laici," in *The Works of John Dryden* (Berkeley: U of California P, 1972) 2:117, lines 252-53, 270-71.

[77]"Pourtant une chose est certaine: il resta fidèle envers et contre tout" (Auvray 171). The suspicion about Simon's interior motives has been especially promoted in the English speaking world through the translation of the very influential study by Paul Hazard, *The European Mind*. For example, "To know what kind of faith was really his, we should need to know something of those voluminous notes which, in a cautious moment, he himself committed to the flames.... What Simon believed in his innermost soul He from whom no secrets are hid alone can tell" (195-96).

of this city." No moral scandal ever touched his memory, he remained a priest in good standing, saying Mass regularly,[78] and, in spite of all the turmoil which surrounded his scholarly work, he was never personally excommunicated or subject to any ecclesiastical censure.

Of course, his closest Catholic associations were with the Congregation of the Oratory. He had been educated in an Oratorian school in Dieppe, and though he had some initial hesitations, he joined the Oratory himself at the age of twenty-four. Oratorians had subsidized his education, and he was supported by the congregation even later on, as noted earlier. Oratorians in those days represented a new sort of religious organization. They were not as tied to conventional religious life, and their educational and religious experiments were especially enlightened.[79] There were many outstanding seventeenth century Oratorians, beginning with the founder of the French Oratory and spiritual father of the French School of Spirituality, Pierre de Bérulle (1575-1629). A list of other famous Oratorians of the day would include the patristics and biblical scholar Jean Morin (1591-1659), the translator of the official French version of the New Testament Denis Amelotte (1609-78), the very influential theologian Louis Thomassin (1619-95), the brilliant Cartesian Nicolas Malebranche (1638-1715)—Simon tried to get him to study Hebrew and the rabbis—and the later famous Jansenist spiritual writer and biblical commentator, a novitiate companion of Simon, Pasquier Quesnel (1634-1719), among many others. The Oratorians gave Simon opportunity to study and a secure niche in Paris, not far from its main libraries, bookstores, and intellectual salons. There is little doubt that the years from 1662 till 1678 were the happiest of his life. All that ended abruptly with the appearance of his *HCVT* in 1678. He had been working on this his most famous work for more than ten years, and the scholarly world of Paris eagerly awaited its appearance early that year. The syndic or dean of the University of Paris, Edme Pirot (1635-1713), and the superior of the Oratorians, Abel de Sainte-Marthe (1620-1697), had both given their permissions to publish, and Simon

---

[78]"Up to his death, he said Mass every day early in the morning. He had always scrupulously observed all the rules of the church" (Steinmann 418).

[79]As Bossuet himself put it, "There a holy liberty produced a holy commitment; one obeyed without dependency, one governed without commanding." Or as Simon himself said, "It is a body where everyone obeys and no one commands" (Auvray 19).

was waiting for Jesuit friends to ask the king, presently in Ypres, for permission to dedicate the work to His Majesty, when on Holy Thursday, April 7, Bossuet got wind of the imminent appearance of his book and rushed to the chancellor Michel Le Tellier (1603-85) demanding that the book be banned. On April 9 the police lieutenant La Reynie commanded the book's confiscation. Thirty copies were seized that day, 600 more on April 30, and an additional 700 on May 28. On June 19 the King's Council decided to formally ban the book, and the destruction of the confiscated copies took place on July 18, 20 and 22.

Meanwhile, Simon was drummed out of the Oratory. He had had two personal talks with Bossuet in the days after the initial confiscations of his book, in the hope of coming to some sort of an accommodation. The Oratorians, however, were terrified because the congregation was already in trouble with the crown and with some Church authorities because of accusations of Jansenist sympathies among them. The superior general sent off two letters, one to the chancellor Le Tellier, the other to Bossuet, protesting the orthodoxy of the order and explaining that his permission for Simon's book was all a big mistake. He had been misled by Pirot's approbation into thinking the book was orthodox. At the same time, Pirot too backed out, claiming that Simon had not made corrections he had required and that Simon had made further additions to the text which Pirot had originally examined. Apparently without any warning, the Oratorian council decided on May 18 to expel Simon from the congregation. The decision was registered on May 20 and Simon was informed on May 21. Notice that these events took place shortly after the first confiscation of his book and well before its formal banning by the government.

Simon never quite seemed to get over this rejection, and all his life he presented his exit from the Oratory as voluntary. The truth of his expulsion has only come to light through the investigations of Bernus, published in 1869, and the account by Louis Batterel (c.1679-1752) which only became public in 1905.[80] Simon retained close friends

---

[80]For Bernus see note 2. Batterel's memoire appeared as "Richard Simon," in *Mémoires domestiques pour servir à l'histoire de la congrégation de l'Oratoire*, published by A. Ingold and E. Bonnardet (Paris: 1905) 4:233-95. See Auvray 50 note.

among the Oratorians. For some time he continued to identify himself as an Oratorian, and in later life, in 1697, he seemed to entertain a vague hope of returning. Addressing the Jesuit Bouhours, Simon described himself as follows: "Having always been a lover of peace, he will in the future be *cor unum et animam unam* with them. He will return to the land of Israel, which he had only left for a time."[81] Initially, however, Simon apparently expressed his resentment in his own way. For some time he had been preparing the correspondence of Jean Morin for publication. Morin was a very distinguished Oratorian who died shortly before Simon entered the congregation. These letters finally appeared in London in 1682, but in a very defective edition, prefaced by a 117 page life of Morin.[82] In this life Simon went out of his way to discredit Morin as a scholar and even as an honest person, and to picture the Paris Oratorians as nothing but lazy mediocrities. Later Oratorians returned the favor, especially, for example, in the quite hostile entry on Simon in the 1912 *Dictionnaire de la Bible* written by the Oratorian Auguste-Marie-Pierre Ingold (1852-1923) who accused Simon of "lacking a Catholic sense" and harboring an "anti-Christian spirit," as well as other intellectual vices and errors.[83] On the other hand, recent Oratorian scholarship has tended to claim Simon as one of their own, and one should especially recognize the excellent

---

[81]*Difficultéz proposées au Révérend Père Bouhours de la Compagnie de Jésus, sur sa traduction françoise des quatre Evangélistes* (Amsterdam: Adrian Braakmann, 1697) 214.

[82]*Antiquitates Ecclesiae Orientalis*, see note 71 above.

[83]Or at greater length: "R. Simon was attacked, not only by the savants and critics of his time, Jesuits as well as Jansenists, by Bossuet, Huet, and Mabillon as well as by orthodox Protestants and 'by almost all the authors who wrote on the Old Testament at the end of the seventeenth and the first half of the eighteenth century,' says Pastor Bernus, *Richard Simon*, 1869, p. 132. Now, how can this fact be explained if R. Simon had been right? Blaming it on his bad character, his mischievous satire, his constant lies, his vanity, all this does not sufficiently explain why all these authors were united against him. If he can be regarded as a precursor of Modernism 'by his habitual way of disguising the revolting temerity of his criticism, his tricks and bad faith, his diatribes against the Holy Fathers' (expressions from the *Biographie Michaud*), he is all the more so by his whole rationalist tendency, of which Renan has given an account, by his lack of a Catholic sense, and perhaps one can even say by his anti-Christian spirit" (A. Ingold, "Simon," in *Dictionnaire de la bible*, ed. F. Vigouroux [Paris: Letouzey et Ané, 1912] 5:1744-45). My whole purpose here is to uncover just why Simon was so objectionable. Ingold is probably right in noting that it wasn't just Simon's character and personality.

study of Simon by the Oratorian Paul Auvray, to which I frequently refer in this essay. But, all in all, here again with the Oratory, Simon comes across as ambiguous. Devoted though he was to the congregation, he guarded his independence and his vision of authentic Catholic biblical scholarship against all compromise.

His connection with other religious orders was also complicated. Earlier I pointed out his connections with Jesuits, his secondary school education with them, his personal attraction to the order, and his admiration for its independence and for its historical scholars. On the other hand, Simon had controversies with some Jesuits[84] and suspected towards the end of his life that they were out to get him.

But it was the Benedictines who were the particular object of his complaints. At first blush this hostility is hard to understand. One would think that Simon would have been drawn to the historical and patristic studies of the famous Benedictines of Saint Maur. Several circumstances partially explain his antipathy. First, Simon had been asked in 1675 by an Oratorian confrère named François Verjus (1633-1710)—who had a Jesuit brother, which didn't help matters—to prepare a *factum*, a defense, of the rights of the Prince of Neubourg as commendatory abbot of the Benedictine monastery of Fécamp (Verjus was also the prince's grand vicar). This Simon did,[85] and, in the process, took extra swipes at Benedictines generally whom he thought guilty of all sorts of forgeries over the centuries. This somewhat minor research project also led to his work a decade later on the history of ecclesiastical benefices which also attacked Benedictines along the way.[86] Off and on in his correspondence Simon continued to criticize

---

[84]Simon particularly attacked the translation of the gospels by Bouhours, S.J., on various grounds, but particularly for its awkward French and its slavish attachment to the Vulgate. In the process Simon even praised the French of the Jansenist *Nouveau Testament de Mons*. Since the Jesuits never publicly attacked him (up to this point), Simon says the Jansenists accused him of having sold out to the Jesuits. But, he adds, this doctor (Arnauld) and his friends "have never been able to show in what money he had been paid. One thing is sure. He has suffered much from them *propter nomen Jesu*" (*Difficultéz proposées au Révérend Père Bouhours de la Compagnie de Jésus, sur sa traduction françoise des quatre Evangélistes* [Amsterdam: Adrian Braakmann, 1697] 211).

[85]*Factum pour le prince de Neubourg abbé commandataire de Fécamp contre les Religieux bénédictins de la congrégation de Saint-Maur*, in *Bibliothèque critique* 3:2-33.

[86]*Histoire de l'origine et des progrès des revenus ecclésiastiques, où il est*

Benedictines living and long dead, but a more public controversy broke out between Jean Martianay (1647-1717), O.S.B., and Simon. In 1690 Martianay announced a new edition of the works of St. Jerome, provided a prospectus and asked for suggestions from scholars. In this *Prodomus* Martianay pointed out that Simon had blundered when, on the first pages of his *HCVT*, he had identified Sunnia and Fretela, the recipients of two letters from Jerome, as "*dames de qualité*," when, in fact, they were Goth males. Then, when Martianay's first volume came out, there were further criticisms of Simon. Meanwhile, Simon prepared three letters, supposedly written by his nephew, answering Martianay and criticizing his work, though they weren't immediately published. Next, in 1697, Martianay published a standard introduction to the Bible in which he defended the Mosaic authorship of the Pentateuch and Matthew's composition of the gospel attributed to him. In the process, Martianay included Simon, though not by name, in association with a series of clearly disreputable biblical scholars: Isaac de La Peyrère's (c.1596-1676) and his claims about "preadamites," Thomas Hobbes (1588-1679) and the "*fameux Spinoza*." Certain Catholic scholars (really meaning just Simon) "bear the name Catholic but cannot set aside books as dangerous as those of heretics and libertines."[87] Just before Martianay's second volume came out, Simon published his replies in Holland and Basel.[88] Martianay reacted violently, saying he was tired of dealing with Simon's insults and calumnies. Simon can take his "*ordures*," Martianay said, "tie them to a dog's tail and run after them through the streets for the entertainment of idiots and ignoramuses."[89] Simon replied in still other letters

---

traité selon l'ancien et le nouveau droit de tout ce qui regarde les matières bénéficiales, de la régale, des nominations et des autres droits attribués aux Princes, par Jérôme a Costa, docteur en droit et protonotaire apostolique (Frankfurt: Fred. Arnaud, 1684).

[87]*Traitez de la vérité et de la connaissance des livres de la Sainte Ecriture par dom Jean Martianay* (Paris: Huart, 1697) 223.

[88]*Critique du livre publié par les moines bénédictins de la Congrégation de S. Maur, sous le titre de Bibliothèque divine de S. Jérôme* (Cologne: Pierre Marteau, 1699), and *Lettres critiques où l'on voit les sentimens de Monsieur Simon sur plusieurs ouvrages nouveaux, publiées par un gentilhomme allemand* (Basel: Pierre Marteau, 1699). The place of publication of the first (Holland) and the authorship of both are disguised.

[89]*Continuation du I. Traité des Ecritures où l'on répond aux difficultés qu'on a faites contre ce même traité et où l'on défend la Bible de s. Jérôme contre les*

published somewhat later. Though in a 1700 letter to Cardinal Louis Antoine de Noailles (1651-1729), Simon claimed that he "had no intention of offending these religious [the Benedictines], still less did he wish to sully the special public reputation they rightly enjoyed," but he had been attacked and had to defend his reputation.[90] The sniping continued when Simon's papers were published as the years passed.

What was this controversy with Martianay really all about? Of course there was the purely personal animosity. But, in fact, Simon had made valid observations and Martianay had actually corrected himself. The same for Simon. But Martianay was, as Auvray puts it, a "conservative critic." He was "courageous about gathering and comparing manuscripts," but refused "to go beyond this and judge the historical import of texts. Furthermore, he belonged to a school with its own traditions and esprit de corps. All that was intolerable for R. Simon."[91]

Besides his contretemps with Oratorians, Jesuits and Benedictines, the other great Catholic party opposed to Simon was the Jansenists, as I've already pointed out. It all began with Simon's very modest 1669 comments on *Perpétuité de la foy à l'Eucharistie* of Nicole and Arnauld and his 1674 documentary improvement on that in his *Fides Ecclesiae Orientalis*. Through his Oratorian superiors Simon found out that the Jansenists were not pleased. On the other hand, in 1677 the Jansenists tried to get Simon to go to Rome to be their intercessor there, either to get him out of the way in France, or to involve him in intrigues little calculated to enhance his reputation as a scholar. Simon, it turned out, wasn't interested in helping Jansenists and declined the doubtful honor. When Simon's *HCVT* came out in 1678 and was so quickly suppressed, Simon always suspected Jansenists behind Bossuet's moves.[92] He probably wasn't wrong about their general attitude toward him. A letter of 1678 or 1680 by Nicole to Arnauld gives the picture.

I recently read the *Histoire critique* of Father Simon. There has never been

critiques de M. Simon (Paris: Huart, 1699) 180.

[90]Published by Pierre Coustant (1654-1721), O.S.B., in *Vidiciae veterum codicum confirmatae...auctore P. Coustant* (Paris: 1715) 678ff., as quoted in Auvray 119-20.

[91]Auvray 120.

[92]See *Lettres choisies* 4:53-56.

a person more full of himself who filled me less. He is a person of great memory and great reading but little judgment, who delves into great matters for the smallest reasons in the world, and who has the incredible audacity to propose his fantasies without bothering about the harm they might do religion. Ultimately, I am the absolute opposite of this author. He makes me hate books and study. For, in truth, it is just such people of whom it can be said that it would have been better if they knew nothing: *His ut fuerit nil didicisse melius....*[93]

By 1684 Simon was willing to openly oppose Arnauld with an attack on the latter's defense of transubstantiation in Simon's *Histoire critique de la créance*. In Simon's 1690 *Histoire critique des versions du Nouveau Testament* almost one hundred pages were devoted to a detailed critique of the Jansenist *Nouveau Testament de Mons*. Then in Simon's 1693 *Histoire critique des principaux commentateurs du Nouveau Testament*, not only was Augustine's biblical commentary sharply criticized—irreverence toward Augustine was never acceptable to the Jansenists—but there was also a hundred page appendix on New Testament manuscripts principally attacking Arnauld. Meanwhile, besides the biblical controversy with Jansenists, Simon published a thirty-six page denunciation of Arnauld's plan for a *Nouvelle Bibliothèque janséniste*, to which Arnauld promptly replied. Finally, in his *Nouvelles observations sur le texte et les versions du Nouveau Testament* Simon returned to all these affairs. Unfortunately, Arnauld himself died in 1694 before Simon could get back into print, a circumstance Simon regretted, though, he observed, Arnauld's "erudition always seemed quite limited, only excelling in declamation."[94] Thus, it turned out that Arnauld, "an opponent of the first hour"..., "remained so to the end."[95] To appreciate Simon's *lèse-majesté* in all this, one must remember the towering scholarly reputations of Nicole and especially of *le grand Arnauld* in the seventeenth century.

Another figure with close Jansenist attachments was Louis-Ellies Dupin (1657-1719) who, beginning in 1686, published a vast survey

---

[93]Cited by Arnauld in the *Sixième partie des Difficultés proposées à M. Steyaert sur le Nouveau Testament de Mons* (Cologne, 1691) 4; presented as from Nicole to Bossuet in the *Correspondance de Bossuet*, nouvelle édition par Ch. Urbain et E. Lévesque (1909; reprint, Vaduz: Kraus, 1965) 2:72-73.

[94]From a letter to Turettini as quoted in Auvray 109-10.

[95]Auvray 106.

of religious literature from the second century to the seventeenth, *Nouvelle Bibliothèque des auteurs ecclesiastiques*, which eventually came to fifty octavo volumes. Though one might have thought that Dupin's independent judgment and the persecution he suffered because of it might have ingratiated him with Simon, this was not the case. Rather, Simon used Dupin's work to comment once more on the whole history of Christianity and on the whole range of questions touching biblical study and his own contemporaries' scholarly work. Of course the fact that Dupin began his first volume with a criticism of Hobbes, La Peyrère, Spinoza, and the *HCVT*, all in one breath, so to speak, was not the way to win over Simon. He responded in 1687 with a fifty page *Lettre à Monsieur l'Abbé P D et P en Th touchant l'inspiration des livres sacrés*. Then Simon expanded his argument to 125 pages in his *Dissertation critique sur la nouvelle Bibliothèque des autheurs ecclésiastiques* of 1688. The *Lettres critiques* of 1699 had still more criticism. Finally, all Simon's subsequent commentary on the whole work of Dupin up to 1708 was gathered together in the huge four volume *Critique de la Bibliothèque des auteurs ecclésiastiques et des Prolégomèmes de la Bible publiéz par M. Ellies Du-Pin*, published posthumously in 1730 with extensive commentary by Etienne Souciet (1671-1744), S.J.

What was the root of all this controversy with Jansenists? Of course, there was the fact that Simon was something of a Molinist all his life. So he had little patience for Jansenist Augustinianism or the party spirit that went with it. But beyond that, Simon couldn't tolerate what he regarded as an indifference to historical fact and exact textual criticism among the Jansenist leaders. Their reliance on an airy authoritarian traditionalism infuriated Simon, just as his own constant nitpicking and lack of obeisance toward Augustine and conventional critical assumptions generally outraged Nicole and Arnauld. But they weren't the only Catholics scandalized by Simon. There was also the great nemesis of Simon's life, the principal author of his equivocal reputation in Catholic circles to this day, and the greatest ecclesiastical figure of *le grand siècle*, Jacques Bénigne Bossuet.[96]

---

[96]For the most recent and accurate account of details of the controversies between Simon and Bossuet see Auvray, especially pages 77-79, 124-41.

Simon and Bossuet

On April 7, 1678, Nicolas Toinard (1629-1706), a friend of Bossuet, came across a copy of the table of contents of Simon's *HCVT* which by this time had all necessary approvals and was already in print awaiting royal acceptance of its dedication to the crown, before actual distribution. Apparently the printer, perhaps with Simon's encouragement, was circulating copies of the table of contents to promote future sales. The fact that Simon's book was in the works was common knowledge for a long time. But when Bossuet, who very likely already had his suspicions about Simon, read, among other things, the resume of Book I, Chapter V: "Moses couldn't be the author of everything in the books attributed to him,"[97] he immediately rushed to the chancellor, Le Tellier, demanding that publication be stopped. Bossuet recalled his first reaction: "This book was a mass of impiety and a rampart of libertinage."[98] By May 21 Simon had been expelled from the Oratory and by July 22 all available copies of the *HCVT* had been destroyed.[99] Though there were discussions between Bossuet and Simon, and though for a time Simon seemed to think that certain corrections could be made to save the book, the issue was really never in doubt. Bossuet was at the height of his power, and, while there were all sorts of details he objected to, the fact was that the basic orientation of Simon's work horrified him. Bossuet in a letter to Sainte-Marthe, superior of the Oratorians, remarked about Simon, "I am afraid that he hasn't seen the consequences of the doctrines he teaches."[100] Bossuet's only scruple was what to do with Simon. He recognized Simon's technical expertise and, for a while, seemed to cast about for a suitable scholarly task for him, one that would keep Simon busy but steer him away from theological issues. Given Simon's basic critical posture and tenacity, and given Bossuet's rigid orthodoxy, compromise just wasn't possible.

In fact, conversations with Bossuet continued off and on for several years, and when Simon published a new edition of his *Cérémonies et*

[97]*HCVT* 31.

[98]Bossuet, *Correspondance de Bossuet* 13:309.

[99]The whole issue of government censorship of books in pre-Revolutionary France is discussed by Patrick J. Lambe in relationship with the suppression of Simon's *HCVT*. See note 33.

[100]*Correspondance de Bossuet* 2:65.

coustumes qui s'observent ajouurd'huy parmi les Juifs in 1681, it was embellished with a lavish dedication to Bossuet, apparently actually composed by Simon's Protestant friend Frémont d'Ablancourt. As Simon then began to republish his *HCVT*, various other works of controversy with Protestants, and his successive volumes on the text, versions and commentators of the New Testament in Holland, Bossuet kept his eye on him. What Bossuet thought about Simon's vast critical publications during this period, as well as what Bossuet thought of Simon himself at all stages of his relationships with him, comes out in the letter Bossuet wrote to Nicole in 1691.

> A dangerous and libertine criticism is taking shape among us. Some Catholic authors let themselves be infected with it, and the one who imagines that he is the primary critic of our day [Richard Simon] labors secretly at this task. He was recently repulsed as he deserved, but I don't know if his strategies are evident enough. I know that he finds protection in all sorts of places and by various means, and, without mentioning other reasons, it is true that many do not see the consequences. They swallow the poison hidden in his principles without noticing it. As for me, I have never been tricked, and I have never opened any of his books without immediately sensing a secret plan to undermine the foundations of religion. I say "secretly" in relation to those who are not skilled in such matters, but nevertheless evident enough to those who take the trouble to look more carefully.[101]

No matter how polite Bossuet was to Simon officially, Bossuet himself, and rather secretly, constantly attacked him. Just what Bossuet's point was, I will take up a bit later. In any case, of the works of this period, Simon's 1693 *Histoire critique des principaux commentateurs du Nouveau Testament* especially incensed Bossuet. Here Simon openly criticized the exegetical practice of St. Augustine. Bossuet, besides being a traditionalist on all matters biblical and theological, was a very devout disciple of St. Augustine. So it was in this year that Bossuet began work on what became a massive refutation of Simon and all his works and pomps, his *Défense de la tradition et des saints pères*, which was only published a half century later, in 1753.

The next open confrontation with Bossuet came over Simon's translation of the New Testament. This work was the culmination of

---

[101]Bernus, *Richard Simon et son Histoire critique du Vieux Testament* 127 note.

more than a decade's labors on New Testament questions. Simon decided to do his translation from the Vulgate to appease Catholic critics and to acknowledge the importance of the Vulgate in the liturgy and in Catholic tradition generally. But he annotated the text with alternative readings from other ancient versions and supplied abundant notes. In this way he felt he could respond both to scholarly concerns and ecclesiastical scruples. Furthermore, he arranged to have the work first published at Trévoux, a tiny independent principality in Burgundy. There it received all necessary ecclesiastical and civil approvals and was published on February 13, 1702. This was a considerable work in four substantial octavo volumes. Simon immediately proceeded to get permissions for publication of the book in Paris. By March 26 everything seemed ready to go. Bossuet, of course, had not been consulted. Early in the year, however, he got wind of the project and by March 19 he had a copy. Immediately he found all sorts of problems. Though, for some unknown reason, it took a while for his letters to get out, by late May he had written to Cardinal Noailles of Paris and a variety of theologians to see that the *Nouveau Testament de Trévoux* did not get republished in Paris and become official in France.

As Bossuet himself observed, it was the story of the *HCVT* all over again. Bossuet sent notebooks full of corrections to a theologian in contact with Simon, and seemed once again willing to talk about corrections as he had done in the earlier controversy. Only this time Bossuet was not quite as powerful at court as he had been in 1678. Negotiations dragged on and Simon's New Testament was being sold openly in Paris. Finally, on July 23, Cardinal Noailles agreed that the work should be banned, and an *Ordonnance* was drawn up and was to be read in churches on September 24, condemning the reading or possession of the *Nouveau Testament de Trévoux* and excommunicating *ipso facto* "priests, pastors, vicars, confessors and spiritual directors who permit or recommend the same."[102] But then a new difficulty appeared. The royal chancellor, Louis Phélypeaux de Pontchartrain (1643-1727), maintained that Bossuet himself must get government permission to publish his own *Instruction* outlawing the book in his own diocese.[103] Bossuet was beside himself. The government, he

---

[102]The *Ordonnance* is reproduced in Simon, *Lettres choisies* 2:333-44.

[103]John D. Woodbridge analyzes this episcopal-royal conflict over censorship

maintained, could not dictate to bishops on matters of doctrine. But Bossuet had a problem. If he fought this case, the whole matter would be delayed further and Simon's book would continue to be distributed. Meanwhile, Simon drew up his own thirty-two page *Remonstrance* defending himself which was published at Trévoux on October 12. Ultimately, however, Bossuet prevailed. He, Noailles and Pontchartrain came to an agreement on November 25, and an *Ordonnance* was published by the end of the year banning Simon's work. Bossuet's *Instruction* with *Additions,* responding to Simon's *Remonstrance,* appeared December 2.

It is, in fact, remarkable that it took Bossuet so long to get his way. François Ledieu (1640-1713), Bossuet's secretary, who reported on the details of this controversy, noted that Simon acted like a person who "felt supported"[104] by someone higher up. Bossuet suspected Jean-Paul Bignon (1662-1743), a nephew of Pontchartrain and a former Oratorian as well, who was working at the court. Auvray suggests that Simon defended himself better this time around. Certainly Simon's language in his *Remonstrance*, while always respectful, was still quite bold. Simon also replied to the banning with a couple of letters published much later, but for all practical matters this was the end of Simon's creative work. Some wonder what might have happened if Simon had presented this translation just a couple of years later, after Bossuet died in 1704. Of course, there is no way to know. Even at the time though, people wondered about what would happen to Simon after Bossuet was gone. Louis Dufour de Longuerue (1652-1733) in a letter of 1704 to Jean-Alphonse Turretini (1671-1734), the Swiss Protestant theologian, commented, "You have heard about the death of the famous bishop of Meaux, Bossuet. I don't know if Monsieur Simon, liberated from this terrible enemy, can come out of his cave."[105] In fact, Simon never really did recover. He published all sorts of letters and notes in the last ten years of his life, but nothing really new. Bossuet, and Bossuet's version of Simon, triumphed.

---

rights in "Censure royale et censure épiscopale: le conflit de 1702," *Dix-huitième sciècle* 8 (1976) 333-55.

[104]*Les dernières années de Bossuet. Journal de Ledieu.* Nouvelle édition par Ch. Urbain et E. Lévesque (Paris: Desclées de Brouwer, 1928) 1:340.

[105]*Lettres inédites adressées de 1686 à 1737 à J.-A. Turretini, théologien genevois, publiées et annotées par E. de Budé* (Paris and Geneva, 1887) 3:272, as quoted in Auvray 132.

These then are the basic details of the struggle between Simon and Bossuet, but what was the substance of their disagreement? There are three phases of Bossuet's attack on Simon, each corresponding to the three levels of his objections. In truth however, as we shall see, they all boil down to one basic problem.

First, there was Bossuet's suppression of the *HCVT* in 1678. Here his basic objection was Simon's treatment of the composition and text of the Bible. Above all, Simon had questioned the Mosaic authorship of the Pentateuch. The problems of doublets, contradictions and all sorts of historical inconsistencies, so dramatically emphasized by scandalous skeptics like Spinoza, were all calmly dismissed by Simon as a product of the fact that, while Moses might be back somewhere behind the original elements of the text, the present Bible is the result of the editing and supplementing of scribes in the offices of the Hebrew republic, as he called it. Simon assumed that the gift of prophecy or inspiration applied to these redactors too, so the question of just where Moses exactly came in, where his work might have started or stopped, was not really very interesting to Simon. But for Bossuet, and for that matter for most Protestants who had attacked Simon, this account of the origin of the Bible was totally unacceptable. According to Bossuet, the inspiration of the Old Testament was based on the claim that God had spoken to Moses and that Moses had faithfully transmitted this revelation. This understanding, moreover, had been the constant conviction of Christian tradition. How would anyone know where inspiration started and stopped if one could say that all sorts of additions and transformations had taken place in the revelation once delivered to Moses? And if the inspiration of the Bible was so slippery and if the convictions of tradition could be so flippantly dismissed, how then could the whole edifice of Christian faith endure when its very foundations in sacred scripture would be so uncertain?

Nor was that all. Simon regarded the text itself of the Bible, as the Church now receives it, as open to all sorts of questions. That is, Simon treated the Bible like any other ancient book. The Vulgate, certified by the Council of Trent, may be worthy of respect and a certain practical trust, but everywhere it must be subject to critique on the basis of the ancient texts and translations, Hebrew, Greek, Samaritan and so on. None of these early texts is necessarily perfect. For various books and individual passages all must be weighed and measured. Again, Bossuet would have none of this. If the Holy Spirit has not guided the Church in the selection and preservation of the biblical text intact down through the centuries, what then, again, is certain in religious faith? If Simon can dismiss any one passage as a corruption, where would this doubt stop? No, the Bible is not like any other book. What the Church has received, what the Church Fathers and the constant tradition of the Church have preserved, must be accepted as God's very word.

The sort of doubts Simon cast on the origins of the Bible and the authenticity of the received text were just exactly the doubts raised by all freethinkers, whom Bossuet habitually called the Socians.[106] Hence, Bossuet constantly accused Simon of being a secret unbeliever. "How happy Socians, how happy Protestants will be with Monsieur Simon! How agreeably he knows how to flatter their tastes and this satirical spirit which has driven them into schism! Nevertheless, this malevolent satirist takes this bite in play!"[107] Simon is always doing this, "insinuating the sentiments of the Socians." He raises "an infinity of difficulties, which he is neither able to nor interested in solving." All this only "raises doubts about religion. And this is one more charm for freethinkers."[108] But Simon was not impressed with this sort of attack. For Simon, even Spinoza was not all bad. "Spinoza could propose in his book many true things and he could even take them from our authors; but he drew false and impious consequences, and it is this which principally needs to be examined."[109] So the skeptics can present valid arguments, as when they point out the inconsistencies in the Pentateuch. But they conclude from these inconsistencies that the Bible was not inspired. Just what Bossuet thinks the conclusion would have to be. But Simon disagreed. Inspiration covers not only Moses

---

[106]The term was commonly used in the seventeenth century to refer to those who doubted basic Christian tenets like the divinity of Jesus or the inspiration of the Bible. It derives from the Latinized name of two Italian scholars, uncle and nephew, Lelio Francesco Maria Sozini (1525-62) and Fausto Paolo Sozzini (1539-1604), who held liberal and unitarian views. See *The Oxford Dictionary of the Christian Church*, 2nd ed., eds. F. L. Cross and E. A. Livingstone (Oxford: Oxford UP, 1983).

[107]*Oeuvres complètes de Bossuet* 4:105-06.

[108]*Défense de la tradition et des saints pères*, in *Oeuvres complètes de Bossuet* 4:xi.

[109]*Lettre à Monsieur l'abbé P[irot], D[octeur] et P[rofesseur] en Th[éologie], touchant l'inspiration des livres sacrés* (Rotterdam: Reinier Leers, 1687) 43.

but the whole process of producing the Bible. In fact, the difficulties the skeptics mention have often been noticed by Catholic scholars, Simon says. "If the censor [Bossuet] had been as curious about investigating Catholic commentators as he has been about consulting those of Socians, he would without doubt have found what he calls suspect not so at all."[110]

Furthermore, Simon insisted that Catholics know the Pentateuch is inspired and know what revelation teaches, not because Catholics know that Moses wrote it, but because Christian tradition assures the Church that the Bible is inspired and teaches what God's revelation really is. That is why Protestants are in trouble when there are doubts about the Bible, but not Catholics, because Catholics believe that revelation is contained not only in scripture but also in tradition.

And here we come to Bossuet's second big objection, one that became especially acute at the appearance of Simon's *Histoire critique des principaux commentateurs du Nouveau Testament* in 1693. Though Simon was generally careful to speak respectfully of St. Augustine, he nevertheless criticized Augustine's extravagant allegorical interpretations of scripture, his lack of knowledge of the original biblical languages, and his excessive rigorism on questions of grace as compared with some of the Greek Church Fathers. Bossuet, as I have noted earlier, was a committed Augustinian. Any denigration of the Doctor of Grace was an attack on the Church which revered him as one of its principal teachers. And more seriously, to question the scriptural interpretation of the Church Fathers was to question the reliability of the tradition that Simon claimed was a guarantee of fidelity to divine revelation in the face of his critical questioning of both scripture and tradition. Bossuet began his *Défense de la tradition et des saints pères* in 1693, immediately after seeing Simon's history of New Testament commentaries. Bossuet's attack was only published posthumously in 1753 and runs to some 634 pages in the 1862 edition of *Oeuvres complètes de Bossuet*, all directed at Simon and his errors. His name is reviled on every page. It is worthwhile to cite Bossuet's opening paragraph at length since it conveys both the violence of his attack and the rhetorical majesty that always accompanied Bossuet's discourse.

[110]Cited in Tavard 141.

We must not abandon the teaching of the Church Fathers and the tradition of the Church to the new critics any longer. If it were only heretics who rose up against such a holy authority, we would fear the seduction less, since we know their error. But when Catholics and priests, priests, I say, and I say it with sadness, enter into their sentiment and raise up in the Church the same standard of rebellion against the Church Fathers; when they take the part of innovators against the Church under innocent appearance, then we must fear that the faithful, having been deceived, might say like the Jews of old when the false Alcimus insinuated himself among them: "A priest of the line of Aaron," of this ancient succession, of this apostolic order to which Jesus Christ has promised that it will last forever, "has come...and will not do us any wrong" (1 Mac 7:14); and if those who stand watch over the house of Israel do not sound the trumpet, God will demand of their hand the blood of their brethren who have been deceived for not having been warned.[111]

Of course, Bossuet knew that Simon defended himself by saying he revered tradition. In fact, he knew that Simon used this argument against Protestants who claimed that the Bible was sufficient in itself. Simon pointed out all the problems of the biblical text, and then insisted that these difficulties were no threat to Catholic faith because the truths of Christianity were preserved in Church tradition. But then, Bossuet pointed out, Simon raised the very same criticism against the teachings of tradition, against the teachings of the Church Fathers, even of St. Augustine. Not only was the Bible uncertain, but so were the teachings of the Church Fathers.

Wait a minute, he answers us, you are attacking me on tradition which I celebrate in my whole book. He celebrates it, I admit, and he seems to want to give it his wholehearted support; but I have known for a long time how he celebrates good things. When through his criticism of the Old Testament he overthrows the authenticity of all the books he treats, even those of Moses, he pretends to want to strengthen the role of tradition and force heretics to recognize it, while at the same time he overthrows the essence and the foundation of the authenticity of these sacred books.[112]

But Simon countered that Bossuet was too quick about identifying his own interpretation of tradition with tradition itself, or too quick about making his selections from the Church Fathers the norm for tradition, and to make all that "pass too lightly for tradition, which it really

---

[111]*Défense de la tradition et des saints pères*, in *Oeuvres complètes de Bossuet* 2:x.
[112]Ibid. 2:15.

isn't."[113] Simon believed in Church tradition as a norm, but the various specific utterances of Church Fathers, who of course form part of the tradition, have themselves to be subject to criticism, especially when it comes to their interpretations of scripture. Bossuet not only had a certain naive innocence about the interpretation of the Bible, but he had the same sort of uncritical attitude about the Church Fathers.

Finally, the third confrontation between Bossuet and Simon took place over Simon's translation of the New Testament in 1702. Of course, all the same objections reappeared. But this time the emphasis was on how Simon departed from the Vulgate or from traditional French translations of the Bible. A good example is the way Simon discussed the adoration of the magi in Matthew chapter two. Simon pointed out that "adoration" here means to prostrate oneself before someone. "It is the way to greet a person which was in use in a good part of the Orient, and many people still observe this practice with respect to their kings today."[114] This is a typical example of Simon's work. He tried to fix the literal sense of scripture taking into account the use of words in their historical setting and making use of insights from contemporary ethnography. But what did Bossuet think of this sort of interpretation? His *Instruction* forbidding use of Simon's translation explained.

> I base the adoration of Jesus Christ as God on an incontestable tradition. It is clear in the collect for Epiphany, for one reads there these words, "O God, who has today revealed your only Son to the Gentiles under the guidance of a star!" Whoever says "only Son" says he is God of the same nature as his Father; and if Monsieur Simon does not want to believe it, the Church confounds him by the ordinary conclusion of the collect which runs "that this same only Son Jesus Christ is one God, who lives and reigns with his Father in the unity of the Holy Spirit." ... The Church will not for the love of Monsieur Simon change the maxim of St. Augustine which assures us that "the faith of the Church is found in its prayers."[115]

The point is, Simon took the adoration of the magi as an example of a typical Oriental act of respect paid to a distinguished personage,

---

[113]*Lettres choisies* 4:383.

[114]*Le Nouveau Testament de nôtre Seigneur Jésus-Christ, traduit sur l'ancienne édition latine, avec des remarques litérales et critiques sur les principales difficultez* (Trévoux: Etienne Ganeau, 1702) 1:5-6.

[115]*Instructions* 3:446.

whereas for Bossuet the adoration of the magi was an acknowledgement and proof of the divinity of Jesus. Simon interpreted the gesture in the light of the culture of the ancient Near East. Bossuet interpreted the same biblical passage in the light of how the liturgy used the text many centuries later. Simon had no difficulty believing in the divinity of Jesus, nor did he have any problem with the Church's proclaiming that doctrine, nor did he think it wrong for the Church to see in the biblical passage a suitable occasion for presenting this aspect of Christian faith. But the task of the exegete, according to Simon, was to determine what the text meant in its own time and place.

Whether it was question of the origin and text of the Bible, the traditional interpretations of the Bible, or contemporary translations, Bossuet had fundamental objections to Simon's work. Bossuet approached religious faith out of a basically static mind-set. Though he prided himself as a historian, in his *Discours sur l'histoire universelle* (1681) he followed biblical history literally and traced the evolution of later history along lines which simply demonstrated the obvious providential path of Catholic faith. His famous history of Protestantism, *Histoire des variations des Églises protestantes* (1688), had as its principal thesis that the Catholic Church was true because it had never changed and the Protestant Churches were false because they had obviously changed.[116] Simon, on the other hand, simply couldn't see what Bossuet's problem was. Criticism was one thing, faith another. The Church, taken in a large sense, was the guarantor of faith. Criticism was only concerned with getting the facts straight. Of course, that attitude too was somewhat naive. Pierre Magnard explains.

> Simon gave himself to the fight like a trapeze artist who performs without a net. He has no sense of a philosophy that might help him. ... The man has so much faith that, whatever criticism he proposes, it could do nothing against the truth and so he could in all serenity, in all freedom of spirit, without any afterthought, without any worry, freely give himself to his critical work. And I don't know if Bossuet's faith was as whole as that.[117]

[116]The evolution of modern Christian theology from the static world view of Bossuet to Newman's understanding of the development of dogma is, of course, the main theme of Owen Chadwick's *From Bossuet to Newman*, 2nd ed. (Cambridge: Cambridge UP, 1987).

[117]Pierre Magnard, "La tradition chez Bossuet et chez Richard Simon," in *Journées Bossuet: La prédication au XVIIe siècle* (Paris: A.-G. Nizet, 1980) 387.

But of course that was Simon's problem. He intuited but he didn't explain how the sort of criticism he engaged in did not destroy faith. Bossuet at least had a philosophy to explain why his position was necessary. Bossuet had a philosophy of tradition, "a perfectly coherent and logical one," whether we today accept it or not, and "in contrast, you find nothing of the kind in Simon."[118]

So Simon remained forever strange for Bossuet. Here was a priest, who seemed to all the world to be a faithful Catholic, who even attacked Protestants, who spent all his life laboring at biblical studies, and yet, in Bossuet's eyes, everything he wrote only served to undermine the faith. Simon, on his side, seemed to think that he could just modify a few of his interpretations, or present his work in Latin, or explain how his critique didn't really weaken faith, and then Bossuet would approve. It was not to be. Bossuet, without being able to prove Simon was a heretic, tainted his memory for Catholic history almost to the present day.

> No matter how much display he makes of his vain science and how much he exalts his critical work, he can never be forgiven, I don't say for not having known, with all his Greek and Hebrew, the basic elements of theology (for he couldn't have been ignorant of truths so common one learns them in the catechism), but I say he can never be forgiven for overturning the foundations of faith and, in the character of a priest, for having played the role of an enemy of the Church.[119]

It is clear then, that Simon was strange to his age on all sorts of counts. He was eccentric, irascible, irreverent, mischievous. His scholarly tastes were cosmopolitan, ecumenical, omnivorous. He was interested in Jews of various stripes, Christians of all hues, even skeptics and doubters. He seemed to question the absolute character of the Bible and deliverances of Church Fathers, but, then again, he also continued to claim to be and to live as a faithful Catholic. But unbelievers, Jews, Protestants, both liberal and conservative, as well as Catholics couldn't, and to some extent still can't, figure him out. Granted all those personality problems and granted the specific objections various figures in his day had against Simon, just what was the root of Simon's fundamental strangeness? I have suggested all

[118]Magnard 386.
[119]*Défense* 2:8.

along, and especially with respect to Bossuet, what the problem was. Simon was one of the principal enunciators of modern mentalities. Furthermore, he thought these mentalities could be reconciled with Christian faith. This claim needs further explanation.

Simon and Modernity

If anything exemplifies the spirit of modernity it is the critical mentality, the claim that everything must be subject to rational analysis. Simon was first and last the critic. Le Brun and Woodbridge put it well.

> He never ceased writing on the margins of others' works, correcting, adding, judging, exercising critical intelligence stimulated by reading. In this sense he is less an erudite scholar (like [Athanasius] Kircher [1601-80, S.J.], [Samuel] Bochard [1599-1667] or Huet, so different from his style) than one of those curious scholars among whom [Pierre] Bayle [1647-1706] would soon provide one of the best examples.[120]

Of course, criticism had been around for a long time, first in the form of textual criticism of the Bible, then in the critique of all sorts of ecclesiastical and classical texts. But in the case of Simon, criticism was not so much a matter of finding and comparing documents, though to some degree he did the latter. Rather it was a matter of the analysis of what texts mean, how they were composed, what their historical, linguistic and cultural settings were. "Beyond the inquiries of textual criticism, he invents and elaborates literary criticism."[121] In fact, the very French terms *"critique"* and *"critiquer,"* in the sense of the analysis of works of literature, were just coming into use in the latter part of the seventeenth century[122] and Simon was one of the first practitioners of literary criticism in this sense. To be sure, Louis Cappel (1585-1658) had entitled his analysis of the Bible *Critica sacra* in 1650, but that was in Latin and he was a Protestant. Simon's title *Histoire critique du Vieux Testament* shocked people because the word

[120]Le Brun and Woodbridge 35.

[121]Auvray 58.

[122]See *"critique"* and *"critiquer"* in Alan Rey, ed., *Dictionnaire historique de la langue française* (Paris: Dictionnaires Le Robert, 1992), and *Grand Larousse de la langue française* (Paris: Librairie Larousse, 1972).

"*critique*" had then, as it does today, a pejorative sense as well. Simon was not intimidated. His criticism of the Old Testament was followed by his *Histoires critiques* of the text, of the versions, of the commentators of the New Testament, and by all sorts of books with the term critical in the title. As Bernus said, "The essential merit of the work of Simon is to have created a science which did not yet exist...that of a *history* of the Bible."[123] The biblical text is not something that simply lies there before the reader. It is not merely a question of comparing manuscripts and translating the words. One must enter the world of the text. "With Simon the biblical text takes on consistency as text. It organizes itself into an autonomous field were the critic assumes the right to exercise the rules of his art."[124] Beyond textual criticism he envisioned a semantic and literary criticism, an organization of meaning. "Simon's originality lay in his having attached as much importance to literary criticism as to textual criticism, and to having combined them."[125]

But it was precisely this attitude toward the biblical text which terrified Simon's opponents. Not only the verbal text, that too, but even its very sense, trembles under the critic's scrutiny. Certeau puts it dramatically. "His work unfolds entirely *within* loss and *within* uncertainty. He never escapes from either the one or the other. Renouncing a primitive 'purity,' he progresses into the interior of 'corruption.'" Or again: "He multiplies the probable within a field limited by the impossible. At its limit, translation becomes a workshop of the probable, a space open to a calculation of probabilities."[126] This unavoidable uncertainty which attaches to the establishment and interpretation of the biblical text is precisely the modern, or even the post-modern, conviction about every text. Simon can even say that "there is so far no perfect version of sacred scripture. It even seems that it would be impossible once one thinks about all the difficulties."[127] It is easy to see why Bossuet was upset. Here a whole new mentality appears, a world where uncertainty reigns.

---

[123]Bernus, *Richard Simon et son Histoire critique du Vieux Testament* 124.
[124]Beaude 75.
[125]Michel de Certeau, "L'idée de traduction de la bible au XVIIème siècle: Sacy et Simon," *Recherches de science religieuse* 66 (1978) 87.
[126]Ibid. 88, 90.
[127]*HCVT* 352.

Probability was not the sort of thing that believers were accustomed to associate with Christian faith and with interpreting the Bible. Le Brun explains,

> The critic attains to what is "judicious," to what "seems" true, to what is "probable" or "more probable," to what has "the mark," to what is "believable," all of which expressions are to be found on every page of Richard Simon's works. The critic, he endlessly asserts, is not "infallible." Criticism opens an avenue of approach, a way toward an approximation of what is true.... Richard Simon deserves our attention for having been one of the first to understand what the situation of the religions of the Book would be in the modern world.[128]

By this time the scholarly world had become accustomed to textual criticism. Still, in the case of sacred scriptures, religious figures were convinced that the Holy Spirit preserved the Bible from all serious corruption, though some opted for the Septuagint and others for the received Hebrew text. Besides, hadn't the Council of Trent asserted that the Vulgate was reliable? If it were not, where was the Holy Spirit this past millennium and a half and more, if not guarding the sacred scriptures? But, as Beaude puts it, "A definitive loss lies beneath critical work. Erasmus doubtless thought he could overcome it. Simon did not. He managed it."[129] That is, textual critics like Erasmus thought that by a patient sifting of manuscripts one would eventually reach a point of relative certainty about the presumed original text. But Simon saw all kinds of difficulties, and for that matter opportunities, beyond mere textual problems. On one side there was the origin of text itself, to the extent one can even speak of "the" text. There were the stages of composition, the editing which preceded, and the inevitable corruption which followed that creation, down to what we call the text of the Bible today. Then there were the subsequent questions about what the text means after the words had been more or less established.

It was at this point that Simon launched into various levels of linguistics and ethnology. Hence, we have his inclusion of rabbinical commentators in his biblical surveys, as well as his studies of the ceremonies and customs of Jews, Muslims and Oriental Christians. To

---

[128]Jacques Le Brun, "Meaning and Scope of the Return to Origins in Richard Simon's Work," *Trinity Journal* 3 NS (1982) 55-56.

[129]Pierre-Marie Beaude, "Richard Simon: Critique et théologie," in *"Kecharitomene": Mélanges René Laurentin* (Paris: Desclées, 1990) 74.

understand the biblical text one must understand how words were used in the past, how societies were structured and operated. Thus, a whole new science, ethnology, was founded. "Richard Simon...is one of the ancestors of the ethnographic method."[130] In this work one can see today how Simon began to think in terms of "a history of mentalities." One finds in his work "very modern pages, strikingly sympathetic, on Muslim morality, on the social factors which influence mentalities, on Oriental sensibility."[131] His curiosity about everything, his openness to the study of cultures very different from his own in order to enter into the worlds of biblical texts, mark Simon out as a precursor of modern biblical studies and of modern intercultural awareness. His impatience with Bossuet's absolute categories, his contempt for Bossuet's presumption that whatever social and religious structures obtained in seventeenth century Catholicism were what had always been the case, as well his scorn for the deductive scholasticism of the Sorbonne were all typically modern mentalities. Simon always insisted that it was essential to know the "stuff" of language and culture, to learn the facts of history, before one could come to conclusions about what the Bible meant or about the real nature of Christian belief and ceremony. It is for reasons like these that James Sanders, after summarizing Simon's role as one of the main founders of historical-critical biblical studies and after having explained how Simon talked about the composition and editing of the Old Testament, says, "If some of this sounds like postmodern literary criticism, it is, nonetheless, from Simon and from the late seventeenth century."[132]

Richard Popkin, one of the principal historians of the origins of the critical spirit in Europe and of the philosophical roots of the Enlightenment,[133] believed that Simon's influence on the rise of modernity has been too little recognized. Popkin even suggests that Simon's views approach those of the Second Vatican Council. He summarizes Simon's contributions as follows.

---

[130]Le Brun and Woodbridge 39.

[131]André Godin, review of *Richard Simon: Additions aux "Recherches curieuses sur la diversité des langues et religion" d'Edward Brerewood*, eds. Jacques Le Brun and John D. Woodbridge, in *Revue d'histoire ecclésiastique* 80 (1985) 203.

[132]Sanders 52.

[133]See his *The History of Scepticism from Erasmus to Spinoza* (Berkeley: U of California P, 1979).

He is in part responsible for the development of modern methods for studying the past. He revealed the epistemological problems involved, and worked out in great detail the "critical method" of historical research for gaining the best account and evaluation at a given time of past events. Using scholarly tools far beyond La Peyrère's and Spinoza's, he showed how this could illuminate a crucial part of man's behaviour—his religious dimension. He showed how present investigations, in the practices and customs of Jews, the Greek Orthodox, the Nestorians, the Cairites (with whom Simon was fascinated), the Moslems, etc. could throw light on understanding the Bible and its Message. He provided many tools and methods, and an approach that was not only to make religion amenable to social scientific investigation, but was to open the door to a kind of science of man.[134]

This is precisely what I have been arguing here. But what makes Simon particularly interesting is not just that he had a role to play in the rise of modernity, but that he was convinced that this new mentality could be reconciled with Christian faith, with fidelity to the Bible and to Church tradition, a combination that his contemporaries and not a few believers and ecclesiastical leaders even today find hard to accept. As Jacques Le Brun, another expert on the rise of modern Christianity, and on Simon in particular, puts it,

> Richard Simon had two basic convictions: on one hand, his attachment to the ecclesiastical institution and to tradition, to which he himself remained faithful, although representatives of this institution condemned him, and, on the other hand, his attachment to a new legality, of which we have already spoken, that to the *Respublica Literaria.*[135]

It was precisely as a critic, and as such an absolute and universal one, that Simon was one of the creators of modernity. Of course what we call modernity, and the Enlightenment itself, which was about to engulf Western culture, was the product of many forces, some at work long before Simon's day. The Renaissance, the Protestant Reformation, the New Science (Nicolas Copernicus [1473-1543], Galileo Galilei [1564-1642], Isaac Newton [1642-1727]), a revived skepticism (Michel de Montaigne [1533-92], Pierre Charron [1541-1603], François de La Mothe Le Vayer [1588-1672], Pierre Gassendi [1592-1655], Pierre

[134]Popkin, "Bible Criticism and Social Science" 350.
[135]Jacques Le Brun, "Das Entstehen der historischen Kritik im Bereich der religiösen Wissenschaften im 17. Jahrhundert," *Trierer theologische Zeitschrift* 89 (1990) 114.

Bayle [1647-1706]), the rise of modern philosophy (René Descartes [1596-1650], Hobbes, Spinoza, John Locke [1632-1704], Gottfried Wilhelm Leibniz [1646-1616]), and new economic and political realities were all elements in this evolution of consciousness. But the contribution of religious criticism specifically to the growth of modernity, which was to be the greatest challenge to religious belief itself, is often overlooked. It was biblical textual criticism, for example with Erasmus, which gave rise to textual criticism generally. The critique of the lives of the saints pursued by the Dutch Jesuits whom we call the Bollandists, after Jean Bolland (1596-1665) their first leader, and the critique of medieval manuscripts pursued by the monks of Saint-Maur, especially under the leadership of Jean Mabillon (1632-1707), were other important contemporary examples of this critical spirit which came out of and was nourished by religious tradition. But the critical spirit could not be limited to just the text of the Bible or of other ancient works. Criticism extended to religious traditions in the Reformation, to scientific assumptions in the New Science, to philosophical verities in rational philosophies. Simon was part of this larger movement. What made him special was his willingness to apply a very radical critique to the Bible, to its text and its meaning, and to customary interpretations of religious traditions. To some extent Hobbes and Spinoza did this too. But Simon carried out a vast and detailed program of criticism of the Bible and its interpretation, and, on top of that, he maintained that this great project could be pursued while remaining faithful to Christian belief.

Of course, we know that other believers of all persuasions rejected Simon's claim. But they did so at their own peril. Modern critical consciousness could not be contained. Eventually the Churches would have to come to terms with modernity, but for a long time they would have to do so without the benefit of gradual engagement with the antinomies between faith and reason which the Enlightenment presented, an engagement that Simon had boldly proposed in the case of biblical tradition. Simon himself had anticipated the challenge.

I foresee that in the future most disputes in religious matters will have to do with Socianism. The ones we have with Protestants are almost nothing in comparison with the articles of faith contested by those who call themselves Unitarians.[136]

[136]*Lettres choisies* 2:50.

It seems obvious today that if Catholicism had taken Simon seriously in his day, if biblical scholars could have pursued the leads he pointed out, then, doubtless with many false starts and dead ends, but eventually, the Church could have worked out the sort of assimilation of modernity that the Second Vatican Council attempted to achieve without the miserable travesties of the antimodernist crusade which persisted right up to the council itself. But seventeenth century Churchmen found Simon and his science too strange to merit a serious hearing in the community of faith.

Jean Steinmann, who has provided the most detailed study of Simon in modern times and who himself was one of those biblical scholars who suffered under the inquisitorial pressure of modern day Bossuets,[137] perhaps put the case a bit too strongly, but it is hard to discount the basic validity of his lament.

> It wasn't Bossuet who triumphed over this little, sickly and disagreeable man, it was Voltaire. D'Alembert's atheism, not theological integralism, took the place of the despised biblical criticism. Renan was right. Bossuet's victory over Richard Simon was the Church's most crushing defeat in modern times.[138]

It is perhaps an exaggeration to say that Simon was completely ignored or that the encyclopedists would have been dissuaded by Simon's critical faith, but it is certainly true that Christian Churches generally and the Catholic Church in particular paid dearly for their refusal to face the fact that the modern critical mind could not be eliminated by anathemas and excommunications. Only an honest openness to the stranger that stood before the Church in the form of modernity could lead to the construction of a modern critical faith, a task which is far from over even today and a challenge which was put off at the price

---

[137]Steinmann was a prominent Catholic priest and biblical scholar who died tragically on a pilgrimage to the Holy Land in 1963. He was the author of a number of important biblical and literary studies. His own *Vie de Jésus* (1959) was put on the Roman *Index* in 1961, a year after the publication of his study of Simon. Steinmann had reason to see parallels between Simon and his own experience of church resistance to critical biblical studies and its continuing opposition to strange new ideas generally.

[138]Steinmann 7. Note the qualification of this judgment in note 8 above. Scholars in France, Germany, and England did know Simon's work and he eventually did have influence in academic circles, but over all and for a long time Simon's views were unwelcome in orthodox religious milieux.

of great losses for the faith and for human growth and solidarity in general.

I would like to conclude this essay with an attempt at listing some of the principal critical contributions of Simon which have eventually become part of the apparatus of modern or even post-modern religious faith and even part of the critical mind generally. I don't pretend that the following list is exhaustive or that Simon could be said to have articulated each of these insights in quite the explicit way I do here. Nevertheless, I think that all of them are justified on the basis of his work, and, together, they explain why Simon was such an important figure in the evolution of the encounter between faith and modernity in the Christian West.

First, Simon, in his almost endless analyses of the biblical text, shows how complicated a matter the production of literary texts is, especially, though not exclusively, ancient compositions. There is a history of the biblical text that must be taken into account. Perhaps, in some sense or other, there is a history behind the composition of any text, hence his critical work in all sorts of different areas besides the Bible itself.

Second, texts come out of a cultural matrix, they can only be understood in the context of their own time and within the worlds of their authors and listeners or readers. To understand the Bible one must enter the cultural milieu of the ancient Near East. To do that, one ought to pay attention to vestiges of that world preserved in the Jewish, Oriental Christian, even Islamic worlds of later times, even of one's own day.

Third, the language of the text must also be understood within the world of its cognate tongues. To understand Hebrew it is helpful to study the rabbis' Aramaic, to read Syriac and Arabic, and other similar linguistic families. Furthermore, the ancient versions of the Bible in other languages must also be studied, since they too provide a variety of insights into the background of the text we have before us.

Fourth, customs and ceremonies can also be read as texts. They too have a context. These customs and ceremonies illumine the meaning of the written text, and they themselves, in turn, are explained by the written text. There is a symbiotic relationship between written text and life, hence, Simon's extensive studies of the customs and ceremonies of Judaism, Islam, and Oriental Christianity.

Fifth, in the interpretation of a written text, the primary meaning is what was usually called the literal sense, that is, the sense the text had for its authors and their audience, not some later symbolic meaning read into a text. These spiritual and allegorical meanings might be quite valid witnesses to the faith of the community as it existed in later times, but they should not be regarded as the proper meaning of an ancient text as such. This is not to say that the original authors or their audience always understood themselves in a literal sense. Rather, what is meant is the understanding they in fact did have, whatever literary category later readers may assign a text to.

Sixth, since successive readings of a text are themselves subject to the cultural influences of later times, and since later readers only imperfectly grasp the original world of the text at issue, interpretations will always be only approximate and, consequently, there always will be a history of the interpretation of, as well as a history of the composition of, a text. The composition of and the understanding of these interpretations are both also subject to the same complexity of historical forces and cultural horizons which conditioned the original texts. No one, neither author nor critic, can stand outside all cultural and historical conditions.

Seventh, Christian theology will always be radically historical. Its foundational texts are products of a long historical, as well as a providential, process. Furthermore, the unfolding of the centuries of Christian understanding of these texts and of the community's self-consciousness of its faith, are also subject to manifold historical conditioning. There can be no escape from history. Believers must enter into the interplay of these forces in order to understand their faith.

Eighth, criticism is an open field. In arriving at a history of the composition of texts, in checking the evolution of interpretations, in harvesting the contributions of alien cultures, there is room for observations from all sorts of heterogeneous sources. Other kinds of believers, citizens of other ancient or modern cultures, even apparently foreign or hostile creeds and civilizations might have valid insights to contribute, worthwhile corrections (even painful ones) to make, to the received wisdom of the faith community.

Finally, there is a certain serene joy in Simon's conception of religious criticism. He was an incorrigible wit and even, at times, a malicious satirist. In spite of all the attacks he was subject to, from all sides, he never seemed to feel defeated. People like Bossuet couldn't understand his lightheartedness any other way than in terms of a cynical contempt for religious faith. Simon, however, couldn't seem to understand why his ecclesiastical enemies were so worked up about his criticism. He, apparently, remained supremely confident that all his revamping of the biblical text and of customary interpretations of this and that in Judeo-Christian tradition could never touch the essence of faith. This trust, if real, and I am convinced it was real, could only have been based on a childlike faith in the divine guidance of the Church. The Catholic community, as a whole, he believed, could never depart from the essence of faith. Certainly its understanding of its faith must be subject to constant refinement, and, in that sense, critical work would always be necessary to distinguish authentic tradition from transitory assumptions. Though that task would never end, the believer should always trust that the Spirit will preserve the Church from fundamental error. To put this another way, Simon's critical faith lay somewhere between the flippant sneer of Voltaire and the artless smile of the medieval madonna. His remained a critical faith.

8

THE ROLE OF ESTRANGEMENT IN CONVERSION

The Case of John Henry Newman

Kenneth L. Parker

An essay on conversion may seem at first misplaced in a volume devoted to the theme of the stranger in Christian tradition. Yet on closer examination no topic is more apposite; for conversion results in estrangement from the convert's previous religious world view and from the society that nurtured that vision. By reflecting on the role of estrangement in the experience of conversion, we gain a clearer understanding of the nature of conversion itself. While many cases could be selected to explore this topic, few are as complicated or intriguing as that of John Henry Newman (1801-90). This nineteenth century Anglican divine led a dynamic movement in the 1830s which made a deep and lasting mark on the Church of England. Yet in October 1845, Newman quietly left the Church to which he had been deeply committed and was received into the Roman Catholic Church, a Church he had reviled and against which he had worked most of his adult life. Polemicists, biographers, theologians, and historians have struggled to understand his motivations for a century and a half.

The extreme parameters of the debate were established even before Newman's conversion to Roman Catholicism, but were crystallized in the published controversy between Charles Kingsley, sometime Regius Professor of History at Cambridge, and John Henry Newman in 1864. Kingsley charged that Newman had behaved deceptively and had consciously sought to undermine the Church of England before publicly declaring himself to be Roman Catholic. Newman's *Apologia Pro Vita Sua* was written to demonstrate that his Anglican years had been lived with integrity and honesty, and that his conversion was the result of his pursuit of Christian truth.[1]

---

[1] For the complete collection of the published works and correspondence see

This debate has taken on renewed significance in recent years, for the controversy over the ordination of women in the Anglican tradition has caused some to invoke the example of John Henry Newman. They assert that, like Newman, their renunciation of the Church of England and embrace of the Roman Catholic Church is an act of fidelity to a higher Christian truth. With this in mind, it seems crucial that one reexamine the historical context of Newman's life and his personal development during the Anglican years. To borrow a phrase from the *Apologia*, this investigation may clarify, "humanly speaking,"[2] some of the reasons for Newman's estrangement from the Church of England and his conversion to the Church of Rome.

Conscience, according to Newman, was the force that gave him assurance that his conversion was God's will. While the historian cannot discern his interior experience of the divine, it is possible to consider the external forces and life circumstances that shaped and influenced his interpretation of that experience. In considering this issue, three dimensions of Newman's life and times will be examined. First, Newman's development must be placed in the context of early nineteenth century England and the dramatic changes that occurred in that society during his Anglican years. These changes brought major shifts in the economic, social, political, and religious structures of the nation, and sent many—Newman prominent among them—searching for a source of stability and certainty as old verities crumbled. While Newman fixed his hope on religious faith as an adolescent, the other forces at work in English society affected his life and shaped his response to the world. Second, Newman's personal experience of alienation and estrangement from individuals and groups which did not share his world view must be examined. These personal estrangements coincided with major crises in his life and significant shifts in his religious commitments. While he continued to admire and even correspond with former friends and alienated colleagues, he seemed unable to maintain close relationships with those who did not share his most deeply cherished convictions. Finally, his role as a controversialist in defending his religious world view will be explored.

Charles Kingsley and John Henry Newman, *Mr. Kingsley and Dr. Newman: A Correspondence on the Question, Whether Dr. Newman Teaches that Truth is no Virtue?* (London: Longman, Green, Longman, Roberts, and Green, 1864).

[2]*Apologia Pro Vita Sua* (London: Longmans, Green, Reader, and Dyer, 1881) 5.

This section selectively considers Newman's work during the 1830s and examines the circumstances surrounding his alienation from the Church of England. Through this study, one may gain a greater understanding of the complex circumstances surrounding Newman's conversion.

Social Changes

By the time of John Henry Newman's birth in February 1801,[3] England was in the midst of changes that would dramatically alter the character of the nation. During the eighteenth century, England experienced what one historian has described as a "silent revolution."[4] The growth of manufacturing and the related enterprises of transportation and shipping accelerated the expansion of urban centers. During the eighteenth century towns grew at more than twice the rate of the total population. The first decades of the nineteenth century witnessed the consolidation of cotton, iron, and coal as the key industries in England's changing economy, and urban centers grew at a rate two and a half times that of the whole population of England.[5]

Throughout the eighteenth century political power and social influence remained in the hands of the aristocracy and landed gentry, a privileged class with firm roots in an hereditary system that supported a Protestant king and the Church of England. It was the firm conviction of those in power that the stability of the state required religious conformity. Any departure from this imperative would bring disaster. Until the creation of new peers by the younger Pitt, the lay peerage included no more than 170 persons—men whose wealth came from vast estates in the countryside. The landed gentry were also a small portion of the population. At the end of the eighteenth century only 700 to 800 families were included among the higher gentry, with another 3,000 to 4,000 families numbered among the lesser gentry. It was from these privileged classes that the lay peers of the Lords and

[3]Sheridan Gilley, *Newman and His Age* (London: Darton, Longman, and Todd, 1990) 7.

[4]John W. Osborne, *The Silent Revolution: The Industrial Revolution in England as a Source of Cultural Change* (New York: Scribner's, 1970).

[5]F.M.L. Thompson, "Town and City," in *The Cambridge Social History of Britain 1750-1950: Regions and Communities*, ed. F.M.L. Thompson (Cambridge: Cambridge UP, 1990) 1:9-10.

the MPs of the Commons were almost exclusively derived.[6] Each member of this triad of king, aristocracy, and Church reinforced and defended the place and privileges of the others.

The mercantile and financial elite of London and the towns came to share in the social prestige formerly reserved for landed families. The Newman family benefitted from these changes, for John Henry's father was a prosperous banker.[7] However, this new elite was largely denied a share in political power.[8] As a result of the egalitarian thought of John Locke and the events of the French Revolution, an increasing number of Englishmen began to question the constitutional structures that limited political power to a small number of landed families. Of great concern were constitutional provisions which excluded Roman Catholics and Dissenting Protestants from full participation in the national life. While exceptions can be found, those who did not conform to the Church of England were routinely refused degrees at Cambridge, denied admission to Oxford, and barred from standing at municipal, corporation, and parliamentary elections. As the first decades of the nineteenth century unfolded, the pressure for change could not be ignored.[9]

While change came early to the University of Oxford, it was reactionary in nature. Because of the political events of Europe in the 1790s, Oxford mobilized to reform its system of education, which had declined in rigor during the eighteenth century.[10] The university was

---

[6]W.A. Armstrong, "The Countryside," in *The Cambridge Social History of Britain 1750-1950: Regions and Communities*, ed. F.M.L. Thompson (Cambridge: Cambridge UP, 1990) 1:89-90; J.C.D. Clark, *English Society 1688-1832* (Cambridge: Cambridge UP, 1985) 418.

[7]Gilley, *Newman and His Age* 7.

[8]Thompson, "Town and City" 1:17.

[9]Peter Slee, "The Oxford Idea of a Liberal Education 1800-1860: The Invention of Tradition and the Manufacture of Practice," in *History of Universities*, ed. Laurence Brockliss (Oxford: Oxford UP, 1988) 7:62; Sheldon Rothblatt, "The Student Sub-culture and the Examination System in Early 19th Century Oxbridge," in *The University in Society*, ed. Lawrence Stone (Princeton: Princeton UP, 1974) 1:284-85.

[10]Edward Gibbon, *Memoirs of My Life* (Harmondsworth: Penguin, 1984) 76-82; Rothblatt, "The Student Sub-culture" 1:247-303. For further evidence of the problems in Oxford during the eighteenth-century see William J. Baker, *Beyond Port and Prejudice: Charles Lloyd of Oxford, 1784-1829* (Orono: U of Maine at Orono P, 1981) 12-18; Charles E. Mallet, *A History of the University of Oxford* (London: Methuen, 1927) 3:123-26.

a bastion of Tory politics and aristocratic privilege, and the dons introduced measures intended to minimize the impact of revolutionary ideals on the undergraduates of the university. John Eveleigh, the Provost of Oriel College, stated publicly in 1791 that the university should counter the harmful impact of the irreligious philosophies of the Enlightenment by refocusing undergraduate attention on orthodox theology.[11]

But the fears of university officials were not just religious in nature. Their concern was for the political stability of the nation. The heads of Balliol, Christ Church, and Oriel, all men with close ties to the prime minister, William Pitt, were instrumental in enacting the New Examination Statute in 1800. One historian has observed that the new examination's purpose was to instill those ideals which enabled the student to assume his position as a leader in the nation, and prevent him from becoming a critic of society and its institutions.[12]

The new examinations produced the disciplinary results desired by the heads of Balliol, Christ Church, and Oriel. The impact of the reforms was felt throughout the university. However, the examinations had unexpected consequences: the narrowing of the curriculum to a few subjects, the need to supplement college teaching with expensive private coaches, and the division of the undergraduates into two groups—those studying for honors and pass men. It was into this university culture that the young Newman entered in December 1816, and he proved eager and willing to conform to the new expectations.[13]

From 1828 to 1832 England was forced to confront its social, political, and religious challenges. An old order passed and new structures were established. The Church of England initially stood with the Tory party against reform, and bishops voted with the lay peers against parliamentary reform. This solidarity with the traditionally privileged resulted in the abuse of clergy in city streets and the burning

[11]Rothblatt, "The Student Sub-culture" 286.

[12]Ibid. 283-86.

[13]Slee, "The Oxford Idea" 7:68-69; Rothblatt, "The Student Sub-culture" 297-98; Arthur Engel, "The Emerging Concept of the Academic Profession at Oxford 1800-1854," in *The University in Society*, ed. Lawrence Stone (Princeton: Princeton UP, 1974) 1:312-13. For an example of the relationship between a private tutor and his pupil see John H. Newman, *Loss and Gain* (London: Burns and Oates, 1881) passim; *The Letters and Diaries of John Henry Newman*, ed. Ian Ker and Thomas Gornall (Oxford: Clarendon, 1978) 1:28; xiii-xiv.

of a bishop's palace. On Guy Fawkes day 1831, effigies of local bishops took the place of Guy Fawkes and the pope in the bonfires. Many called for the disestablishment of the Church of England. Prelates were intimidated into submission, and the Reform Act of 1832 passed in the Lords with no episcopal opposition.[14]

The changes in the social and political life of England had an inevitable impact on the Church of England. This shift in the social matrix required a reassessment of the Church's place in the power structures of English society and its claims to be the normative expression of Christianity for the nation. This reassessment was complicated by the battle raging within the Church itself, as evangelicals, liberals, and High Churchmen struggled for dominance within the Church of England. Newman understood this struggle intimately, for since his religious conversion as a young man, he had passed through each of these traditions. The rapid alterations of England's public life forced Newman and others within the Church of England to seek a new place for the Church in the life of the nation.

The aftershocks of the Reform Act of 1832 were felt during the winter of 1833. As Parliament debated the suppression of the Irish bishoprics and confiscation of Irish Church property, a former Tory leader reflected on the consequences of the recently acquired Whig domination of parliament. Wellington observed on March 6, 1833, that,

> The revolution is made, that is to say, that power is transferred from one class of society, the gentlemen of England, professing the faith of the Church of England, to another class of society, the shopkeepers, being dissenters from the Church, many of them Socinians, others atheists.[15]

Even as Wellington wrote, far away from the turmoil of English political life, John Henry Newman anguished over the fate of England and her Church as he toured the Forum and Coliseum of Rome.[16] In late May of that year, as Newman prepared to return to England, his Sicilian servant found him sobbing violently on his bed. When asked

---

[14]Owen Chadwick, *The Victorian Church* (London: SCM Press, 1987) 1:25-28, 32.

[15]John Wilson Croker, *The Croker Papers: The Correspondence and Diaries*, ed. Louis J. Jennings (New York: Scribner's, 1884) 2:9.

[16]*Letters and Diaries* 3:237-38, 242.

what afflicted him Newman could only say, "I have a work to do in England."[17]

Newman returned to defend a Church he perceived to be threatened and in crisis. However, he did not defend the traditions and practices received from previous generations. Newman sought to redefine the premises and goals of the Church of England. While self-consciously controversial and initially influential, Newman ultimately found himself isolated because of his theological experimentation. Anglicans of the evangelical and liberal parties rejected his agenda from the outset. Traditional High Churchmen came to realize that his cause was not their own. Bishops eventually denounced his teaching and refused to ordain his disciples. Public opinion labeled him a closet papist. The causes of Newman's estrangement from his friends and Church must now be explored.

Personal Estrangements

Newman's early life was deeply affected by the changing nature of English society. The firstborn of a London banker, his early years reflected the ease and comfort of the rising urban elite. Yet the family's fragile prosperity was shattered in the financial crisis that followed victory over Napoleon. Shortly after Newman's fifteenth birthday in 1816, his father's bank was forced to close and the family moved from a much loved home. Though Newman senior became the manager of a brewery, he was devastated by the bank's failure. The prosperity of the Newman family was never revived. John Henry spent much of his early adult life supporting several family members.[18] These shifting economic circumstances profoundly affected Newman's life at a crucial juncture in his life, leaving him with a distrust of the social honor and privilege that had proven so precarious for his father and family.

The young Newman, who had been tantalized by the controversial ideas of Paine, Pope, Hume, and Voltaire shortly before the family crisis, became worried and introspective.[19] In May of 1816 he wrote

---

[17]*Apologia* 35.

[18]Gilley, *Newman and His Age* 13-14, 56, 68, 77.

[19]*Apologia* 3; John Henry Newman, *Autobiographical Writings*, ed. Henry

on the vanity and futility of fame and was disdainful of those who pursued it.[20] Because of the family's dislocation, Newman remained at Ealing School that summer and passed through a serious illness which also marked a turning point in his life—his religious conversion.[21] From August 1 to December 21, 1816, under the influence of Walter Mayers, his evangelical classics master, and the books he lent, Newman was converted to "a definite Creed" and absorbed dogmatic principles which were to have a lasting influence.[22]

Having lost the childhood security of home, Newman arrived at university with a resolve to cultivate his newly found faith and to apply himself to studies. He adopted personal disciplines that facilitated these goals. However, this resolve set him in opposition to the dominate student culture of his college. On entering the university at Trinity College in 1817, Newman was perplexed by the neglect of the tutors in his largely unreformed college and repulsed by the lax and irreligious behavior of Oxford undergraduates.[23] Newman quickly took his stand against the pass men—a position that only strengthened with time. Reflecting on the blasphemous combination of religious observance and excessive drinking on Trinity Monday 1819, Newman observed,

> As it is, I keep quiet, for all have pledged themselves to go; yes, all but one, a poor despised, awkward man, of unprepossessing appearance and untidy person, who, I really think, has more proper sense of religion than them all together.[24]

This self-image of one separated and despised for his firm religious convictions and academic diligence is illustrated in other parts of his early autobiographical writings.[25]

Newman's severe evangelical discipline, combined with excessive intellectual labors and academic ambitions, was an unrelenting

and Correspondence of John Henry Newman, ed. Anne Mozley (London: Longmans, Green, 1891) 1:22.

[20]*Letters and Diaries* 1:19-21.

[21]*Autobiographical Writings* 268.

[22]*Apologia* 4; *Autobiographical Writings* 181.

[23]*Autobiographical Writings* 31-35.

[24]Ibid. 38.

[25]Ibid. 37-38, 156-57.

pressure. He responded to the challenges of the new examination system with the earnestness of youthful zealot. These physical, mental, and emotional strains proved too much for Newman as he sought honors in the Schools. He failed to achieve his ambitions and experienced the humiliation of a pass degree in late 1820.[26] This experience, like his father's humiliation in banking, profoundly affected his religious world view.

Newman's spiritual interpretation of this event is crucial to note. In January 1821, he wrote to Walter Mayers,

> There is a great difference between believing a thing to be good, and feeling it; now I am thankful to say, I am not only enabled to believe failure to be best for me, but God has given me to see and know it. I never could before get my mind to say heartily "Give me neither poverty nor riches." I think I can now say it from my soul. I think I see clearly that honour and fame are not desirable. God is leading me through life in the way best adapted for His glory and my own salvation. I trust I may have always the same content and indifference to the world, which is at present the *prevailing* principle in my heart—yet I have great fears of backsliding.[27]

These reflections reveal two important dimensions of Newman's religious world view. First, he served a God who dashed human goals and ambitions to save his followers and illustrate his power in the world. Second, he struggled with the conviction that indifference to "the world" and earthly acclaim, in pursuit of salvation, should be the guiding principle of his life. The rejection of worldly honors, first recorded shortly after his father's financial troubles in 1816,[28] was thoroughly integrated into Newman's personal spirituality after his humiliation in the Schools. While one might regard this as a negative assessment of divine action in the world, for Newman it had the effect of freeing him from pressures to conform. His independence of thought and action in the 1820s and 1830s confirm this conclusion. Yet this period also illustrates that Newman's fears of "backsliding" were well founded.

In 1822 Newman's academic career was revived by his election to

---

[26]*Letters and Diaries* 1:31n, 36, 43, 44-47, 50-51, 66, 79-99; *Autobiographical Writings* 30-50, 156-57.

[27]*Letters and Diaries* 1:99.

[28]Ibid. 1:19-21.

the fellowship of Oriel College, one of the most intellectually vigorous and academically reformed colleges of Oxford. The master, Edward Copleston, championed Newman's election; for while he promoted the revised exams as a means of improving discipline in university life, he rejected them as a measure of intellectual ability. As he noted later to his successor, Edward Hawkins,

> Every election to a fellowship which tends to discourage the narrow and almost the technical routine of public examinations, I consider as an important triumph. You remember Newman himself was an example. He was not even a good classical scholar, yet in mind and powers of composition, and in taste and knowledge, he was decidedly superior to some competitors, who were a class above him in the Schools.[29]

What Newman had perceived as a humiliation was understood by the Oriel fellows to be the result of a flawed examination system. He was welcomed into a fellowship that cultivated and guided his intellectual curiosity and scholarly enterprise. In this setting Newman flourished.

In the *Apologia* Newman described the powerful influence of Edward Hawkins, Blanco White, Richard Whately, and other fellows of Oriel. He attributed to Hawkins his rejection of Calvinist doctrines and a greater regard for tradition. From White, Newman received "freer views" on the inspiration of scripture. Whately was credited with teaching Newman how to think and to use his reason.[30] In the common room of Oriel College, Newman willingly submitted to the formative influence of men regarded by many as controversial. By 1827 he "was beginning to prefer intellectual excellence to moral [excellence]...[and] was drifting in the direction of the Liberalism of the day."[31]

Yet Newman was not passive in this setting. Against the strong opposition of Hawkins, he received holy orders in 1824.[32] Despite Whately's influence on his intellectual skills, Newman resisted his "special theological tenets."[33] While Newman could be deeply influenced by others, he also retained an independence of thought and action that resisted conformity at the cost of personal convictions.

---

[29]*Autobiographical Writings* 64.
[30]*Apologia* 8-9, 11.
[31]Ibid. 14.
[32]*Autobiographical Writings* 87-88; *Letters and Diaries* 1:177.
[33]*Apologia* 13.

Newman's strong sense of detachment from temporal honors, first noted in 1816 and again in 1820, was reenforced by the events of late 1827 and early 1828. Pressed by the academic demands of a new term, an aunt's financial distress, political shifts in the college, and the strain of overzealous preparations for his debut as an examiner in the Schools, Newman collapsed after only two days as an examiner in late November 1827. This event, occurring on the seventh anniversary of his own failure in the Schools, left him with "an inability to think or recollect." On the advice of his physician, Newman left the university for a period of rest and recuperation.[34] This was not the end of Newman's pain.

In early January 1828, he experienced what he described shortly after to be "the heaviest affliction with which the good hand of God has ever visited me." In a sudden and unexpected illness, Newman's favorite sister Mary died. Deeply affected by her death, he seemed to assume responsibility for her passing, finding in it God's judgment on him for his excessive attachment to her. Thirteen weeks after her death he observed,

> For some time I had a presentiment more or less strong that we should lose dear Mary. I was led to this by her extreme loveliness of character, and by the circumstance of my great affection for her.... It must have been in October 1826 that, as I looked at her, beautiful as she was, I seemed to say to myself, not so much "will you live?" as "how strange that you are still alive!"[35]

Newman understood himself to be disciplined and chastened by God once more. He received his public humiliation in the Schools and the death of his beloved sister as divine warnings. They changed the course of his life.

Ecclesiastical Estrangement

England passed through the final stages of its social and political transformation from 1828 to 1832. During this period the previously marginalized Dissenters and Catholics pressed for civil rights denied

[34]*Autobiographical Writings* 212.
[35]Ibid. 213.

them, and parliament was forced by public pressure to reform itself. This atmosphere threatened much that had seemed established and essential to social stability, among these was the place of the Church of England. It was in this climate of rapid change that Newman rejected his former evangelical and liberal world views and assimilated a High Church vision of his reality. In this turbulent process Newman distanced himself from former friends and mentors with whom he was no longer in accord, and cultivated close relationships among the High Churchmen. In this period he was either barred from or relinquished former pursuits, and took up new tasks. While 1828 and 1829 represented a period of transition, by 1830 Newman was among Oxford's most ardent High Church Tories. The events of the nation and Newman's personal life conspired to transform his personal, religious, and public outlook.

In the two years that followed Newman's "chastening," men who formerly had been mentors and important friends were perplexed and repelled by Newman's changing views and causes. Hawkins and Newman fell out over changes Newman sought to establish in Oriel's tutorial system.[36] Whately and White were offended by the illiberal nature of his shifting views on Catholic emancipation.[37] Also during this period he preached at the funeral of Walter Mayers—laying to rest the guiding influence of his evangelical experience.[38] Each of these estrangements had the effect of severing Newman from previous religious attachments and freeing him to assimilate a new religious vision. Men to whom he had looked for friendship and guidance prior to this period were viewed with detachment, caution, and at times with harsh criticism. Like the irreligious pass men of Newman's undergraduate years, in the late 1820s Newman distanced himself from those who did not share his new vision of reality.

That change was facilitated by two friends that powerfully reshaped Newman's Christian world view. Although he had known John Keble and Hurrell Froude long before this period, he became open to their influence during 1828. Keble had been an object of admiration since Newman's undergraduate years—a legend even as a youthful don at Oriel. Yet Keble's departure from the university to assume parochial

---

[36]Ibid. 86-107.
[37]Gilley, *Newman and His Age* 73.
[38]*Letters and Diaries* 2:64.

responsibilities and Newman's earlier religious and political views had prevented the two from developing a personal rapport. It took Hurrell Froude, a mutual friend, to bring them together. Through Keble and his writings, Newman was opened to what might be termed a High Church aesthetic and a greater appreciation for aspects of Christian belief that are not confirmed by rational argument. Newman named Keble as the primary influence on him and what came to be called the Oxford Movement.[39]

Hurrell Froude, a former student of Keble and fellow of Oriel, left clear and identifiable marks on Newman's newly found High Church character. These marks were more extreme than the High Churchmanship typical of the late eighteenth and early nineteenth century. Through this friendship, Newman was reenforced in his dedication to virginity. Froude drew him into a devotion to the Blessed Virgin, and slowly brought him to believe in the real presence of Christ in the Eucharist. Most significantly, under Froude's influence Newman came to admire the Church of Rome and hate the sixteenth century reformers.[40]

Through Keble, Froude, and other High Churchmen, Newman was strengthened in his distrust of nineteenth century rationalism and suspicion of evangelical enthusiasm. While the old alliance of king, aristocracy, and Church crumbled, and the foundations of society shifted, Newman and his new friends sought solutions to the current crisis by looking to the history and traditions of primitive and medieval Christianity, and the example of the Caroline divines of the seventeenth century.

Newman and those with whom he came to associate were keenly aware of the challenges they faced. Writing to his mother in March 1829, Newman observed,

> We live in a novel era—one in which there is an advance towards universal education. Men have hitherto depended on others, and especially on the Clergy, for religious truth; now each man attempts to judge for himself.... Christianity is of faith, modesty, lowliness, subordination; but the spirit at work against it is one of latitudinarianism, indifferentism, republicanism, and schism, a spirit which tends to overthrow doctrine, as if the fruit of bigotry, and discipline as if the instrument of priestcraft. All parties seem

[39]*Apologia* 17-23.
[40]Ibid. 23-25.

to acknowledge that the stream of opinion is setting against the Church.[41]

Although recent scholarship has argued to the contrary,[42] Newman and his associates perceived great weakness in the intellectual powers of their party. In the same letter he observed that "the Church party...is poor in mental endowments. It has not activity, shrewdness, dexterity, eloquence, practical powers." Newman implicitly revealed his, perhaps subconscious, agenda when he observed that within the High Church party "there may be latent talent, and great times give birth to great men." He added later in the letter that, "moral truth is gained by patient study, by calm reflection, silently as the dew falls, unless miraculously given."[43] Circumstances soon gave Newman a period to prepare for the work he was to launch in the 1830s.

Shortly after becoming a public tutor of Oriel College in 1826, Newman was distressed by the detached relationship between tutors and pupils at Oriel. He decided to introduce a more pastoral model for college tutors. With the help of Hurrell Froude and the other tutors, Newman developed, and in 1828 implemented, a tutorial reform in the college. Because they were uncertain that Hawkins, then master of Oriel, would approve, Newman convinced the other tutors to enact the changes without his knowledge or consent. When the changes were discovered, Newman and the others resisted a return to the former system. His personal certitude in this matter ended Newman's career as an Oxford tutor, for in 1830 Hawkins dealt with the matter by assigning students to the care of other tutors. While Newman continued to care for the students in his charge, by 1832 his role as public tutor came to an end.[44] Thus freed from the labors of undergraduate teaching, Newman was able to devote more of his attention to scholarship and political controversy.

Not long after Mary Newman's tragic death, Newman took up a new role that was of great importance to his personal and public life. In March 1828, he succeeded Hawkins as vicar of the parish of Saint Mary the Virgin. While the parish was primarily the place of worship for college servants, local tradesmen, and their families, in the years

---

[41]*Letters and Diaries* 2:129-30.

[42]Peter Nockles, "Continuity and Change in Anglican High Churchmanship in Britain 1792-1850," 2 vols., diss., U of Oxford, 1982.

[43]*Letters and Diaries* 2:130.

[44]*Autobiographical Writings* 86-107.

that followed Newman used the liturgy and the pulpit of Saint Mary's to cultivate and nurture his new found High Church vision. As he later observed in his *Apologia*, "It was to me like the feeling of spring weather after winter; and, if I may so speak, I came out of my shell; I remained out of it till 1841."[45] During the first years much of his labors focused on normal parochial responsibilities.[46] Yet it was also here that Newman reintroduced the observance of saints' days,[47] a daily service of Morning Prayer in the chancel,[48] and other practices largely discontinued in the Church of England. However, the most important change was not in the liturgical life of the parish, but in the congregation that was attracted to Newman's preaching. Through the pulpit and in public lectures Newman drew increasing numbers of students under his influence. In the course of the 1830s his assaults on liberalism and promotion of High Church ideals shaped the religious imagination of a generation of Oxford undergraduates.

One last change in Newman's life following the traumatic experiences of late 1827 and early 1828 must be noted. In late June 1828 Newman began a chronological reading of the *"Patres Apostolici,"* starting with Barnabas.[49] He later described his deepening interest in the early Fathers as corresponding to his disaffection with liberalism.[50] Through this study Newman nourished his developing High Church vision, turning to the sources that had inspired the Caroline divines of the seventeenth century.[51]

These apparently conflicting priorities, active engagement in public controversies, parochial duties, and scholarly reflection, nourished one

---

[45]*Apologia* 16.

[46]Gilley, *Newman and His Age* 70.

[47]*Letters and Diaries* 2:200.

[48]Ibid. 4:289.

[49]Ibid. 2:76. Many sources cite Newman's inaccurate account in the *Apologia*, which marks the beginning of his reading with Ignatius. See *Apologia* 25.

[50]*Apologia* 25.

[51]It is unclear how intensively he read the patristic sources. While Newman studied these sources regularly through the summer of 1828, public controversies and his college and parochial duties appear to have kept him from returning to a systematic study of the Fathers until the summer of 1831. An examination of his journal entries suggest that Newman did not return to serious scholarly research on the early Fathers until he was invited to write a history of the councils in the spring of 1831. See letters and journal entries in *Letters and Diaries* 2:76-81, 88-96, 100, 245, 245n, 319-24, 338.

another as Newman's High Church world view crystallized and his role in the crisis of the times became clearer to him. Yet Newman's synthesis was idiosyncratic. It did not conform to the High Churchmanship of previous generations or that of his contemporaries.

During the late 1820s and early 1830s, Newman became deeply convinced that the Church of England was facing a crisis that required unusual measures. Anxious and agitated by the "republican" spirit he found growing among the students, Newman commented to his sister, Jemima,

> I am more than ever imprest too with the importance of staying in Oxford many years—"I am rooted etc"—nay feel more strongly than ever the necessity of there being men in the Church, like the R Catholic friars, free from all obstacles to their devoting themselves to its defence.[52]

Noting numerous examples of clergy who had been intimidated into silence over Catholic emancipation, he saw his celibate state and relative freedom from the pressures of preferment a great advantage in fighting against the liberalism of his time.[53] Newman's action took three forms: first, preaching sermons that denounced the liberal threat; second, publishing his first book, *Arians of the Fourth Century*, which drew a parallel between the threat of Arianism in the fourth century and the contemporary crisis in the Church of England; and finally, forming a movement to promote a "return" to the Anglican orthodoxy he perceived to be found in the neglected writings of the early Fathers and the Caroline divines.

Using his pulpit at Saint Mary the Virgin, Newman preached and published sermons that were intended to defend the Church of England against the liberal threat. As the political pressure for Catholic emancipation and parliamentary reform increased in the late 1820s and early 1830s, Newman's assaults on liberalism took two forms. First, he asserted that the Church of England had inherited a definite body of doctrines from the early Church. This was a tradition the Church was called to obey, preserve, and defend. Second, he claimed that liberals were tainted by an ethos or character that rejected authority and therefore orthodoxy.[54]

[52]*Letters and Diaries* 2:133.
[53]Ibid. 2:133-34.
[54]Stephen Thomas, *Newman and Heresy: The Anglican Years* (Cambridge:

In the second of Newman's university sermons, preached in 1830, he compared the revealed system of the Church with the natural system of the liberalism of that period. He remarked,

Such, then, is the Revealed system compared with the Natural—teaching religious truths historically, not by investigation; revealing the Divine Nature, not in works but in action; not in His moral laws, but in His spoken commands; training us to be subjects of a kingdom, not citizens of a Stoic republic; and enforcing obedience, not on Reason so much as on Faith.[55]

In this passage Newman stressed the historical and revelatory nature of Christian truth, rejecting the contemporary emphasis on rational investigation. He also subtly tied this understanding of Christian truth to a condemnation of republican politics. As Englishmen had believed since the Reformation, he was convinced that any alteration in the religious, political, or social order would threaten the nation. Newman's concern with obedience to the Church, reverence for the Christian past, and disapproval of contemporary religious and political developments can be found in other sermons preached during this period.[56] What he failed to recognize was that his own response to the liberal threat was an aberration, for it differed significantly in basic points from that which maintained consensus within the Church of England.

In 1831 Newman was given an opportunity to bring his scholarly, religious, and political interests together in a book for the *Theological Library*, a series of theological texts edited by two High Church scholars. Originally conceived as an introductory history of the ecumenical councils, Newman finished in the autumn of 1832 a volume entitled *Arians of the Fourth Century*. The volume was rejected for the series, not only because its subject had shifted, but also

Cambridge UP, 1991) 27.

[55]John Henry Newman, *Fifteen Sermons Preached before the University of Oxford* (London: Rivingtons, 1880) 30.

[56]John Henry Newman, *Parochial and Plain Sermons* (London: Rivingtons, 1870) 3:190; see also John Henry Newman, *Parochial and Plain Sermons* (London: Longmans, Green, 1901) Sermons VI, XV. For a collection of sermons that reflect Newman's polemics against the liberals of his time, see John Henry Newman, *Newman Against the Liberals*, ed. Michael Davies (New Rochelle, NY: Arlington House, 1978) passim.

because the editors were concerned that it did not reflect an Anglican understanding of tradition. As expressed in a letter between the editors,

> Mr Newman's notions about tradition appear to me directly adverse to that which Protestant writers of our own Church have contended for...and seem to me more favorable to the Romanist writers, than I should like to put forward in the *Theological Library*.[57]

Newman's idiosyncratic High Churchmanship was to become more pronounced with time.

This study of a fourth century heresy combined Newman's concern over contemporary political and religious developments with his interest in the early Church. The result was a historical monograph that was a thinly veiled commentary on his own times. He drew comparisons between figures in the two periods, and found analogies in events of the fourth and nineteenth centuries. Most interestingly, he asserted that rationalism was a link between the Arianism of the fourth century and the liberalism of the nineteenth century. In the concluding paragraph Newman noted,

> We may take comfort in reflecting, that, though the present tyranny has more of insult, it has hitherto had less of scandal, than attended the ascendancy of Arianism; we may rejoice in the piety, prudence, and varied graces of our Spiritual Rulers; and may rest in the confidence, that, should the hand of Satan press us sore, our Athanasius and Basil will be given us in their destined season, to break the bonds of the Oppressor, and let the captives go free.[58]

This passage not only reflected the challenge of the times, as Newman perceived it, but reasserted themes that reflected his own sense of purpose and detachment from worldly acclaim. As Newman finished writing his book, political life in England was passing through the final stages of reforms that would seriously affect the Church of England.

Newman may not have been conscious of his desire to play the "Athanasian" role as he prepared for his Mediterranean holiday in late 1832. However, his sense of mission was clear to him in Sicily in the spring of 1833 when he tearfully confessed to his servant, "I have a

[57]*Letters and Diaries* 3:104-05.

[58]John Henry Newman, *The Arians of the Fourth Century* (London: J.G. and F. Rivington, 1833) 422.

work to do in England."[59] In this frame of mind he wrote on the journey back to England his famous poem, "The Pillar of the Cloud":

Lead, Kindly Light, amid the encircling gloom,
Lead Thou me on!
The night is dark, and I am far from home—
Lead Thou me on!
Keep Thou my feet; I do not ask to see
The distant scene,—one step enough for me.

I was not ever thus, nor pray'd that Thou
Shouldst lead me on.
I loved to choose and see my path, but now
Lead Thou me on!
I loved the garish day, and, spite of fears,
Pride ruled my will: remember not past years.

So long Thy power hath blest me, sure it still
Will lead me on,
O'er moor and fen, o'er crag and torrent, till
The night is gone;
And with the morn those angel faces smile
Which I have loved long since, and lost awhile.[60]

This poem restated the theme that has already been found in Newman's life following the closure of his father's bank, his failure to gain honors in the Schools, and his collapse at the Schools as an examiner. After each of these events, Newman deepened his commitment to a God who chastens and demands detachment from worldly acclaim. In the autumn of 1833, Newman and his friends embarked on a campaign to reform the Church of England—calling it back to its ancient traditions, as Newman and his colleagues perceived them. Their activities became known as the Oxford Movement.

Controversy and Estrangement

While the details of Newman's involvement in the Oxford Movement lie outside the scope of this essay, it is crucial that we

---

[59]*Apologia* 35.
[60]John Henry Newman, *Verses on Various Occasions* (London: Burns, Oates, 1880) 152-53.

consider his role as a controversialist in defending his religious world view. This will be accomplished by first considering two key issues espoused by Newman and others who led the Movement. Second, the strategies used to promote their work will be explored, with special attention to Newman's concerns in this regard. Finally, Newman's increasing marginalization within the Church of England from 1833 to 1841 will be analyzed.

At the heart of the movement launched by Newman and his colleagues in 1833 was a firm belief that the Church was in danger. They perceived the breakdown of the old alliance of king, aristocracy, and Church as leaving the Church of England defenseless against those who would attack her. Because of parliamentary reform, the Church's practice and property had become subject to a parliament no longer exclusively Anglican in composition. Shortly after returning to England in July 1833, Newman wrote to a friend, decrying the recently passed parliamentary bill authorizing the dissolution of many Irish bishoprics and the confiscation of Irish Church property.[61] Having described his serious illness in Sicily and his recovery "*by nature* without medicine," Newman said, "I trust my life thus restored will be given up to Him who restored it—I am not conscious to myself of wishing for any thing but to be spent in His service, if I knew how."[62] Newman's work as England's Athanasius had already begun.

The movement launched in late summer 1833 rested on the premise that the Church of England was the one true Church in England. Newman and his colleagues asserted that their Church was bound to preserve and transmit the catholic (universal) tradition which had been received from primitive Christianity and defended by the Caroline divines of the seventeenth century. All of their efforts flowed from a defense of this position.

While many other issues became part of the Oxford Movement's agenda, two causes proved of central importance from the beginning—defense of apostolic succession and the Book of Common Prayer. By defending apostolic succession, Newman and his colleagues stressed the ancient roots of their ecclesiastical authority. The Church of England was not a "parliamentary Church," dependent on the government for its existence, but a Church established and maintained

[61]Chadwick, *The Victorian Church* 1:54-60.
[62]*Letters and Diaries* 4:14.

on the authority of the apostles. As the movement began Newman published a tract addressed to the clergy, observing that the Church had too long depended on station and social position to establish its authority. He asserted, "I fear we have neglected the real ground on which our authority is built,—OUR APOSTOLICAL DESCENT."[63] While Keble and others were reluctant to press this issue to its logical conclusion, Newman was willing to risk disestablishment in defense of this principle. It was this firm conviction that was to be the final cause of Newman's estrangement from the Church of England eight years later.

Also central to the movement was a defense of the Liturgy of the Church, found in the Book of Common Prayer. In preceding years liberal and evangelical Churchmen had urged revisions of the Prayer Book. Newman wrote a tract against such alterations, noting that those who sought changes in the liturgy were not simply seeking changes in words and phrases, "they dislike the *doctrine* of the Liturgy." Observing that "the rage of the day is for concession," he asked, "have we not already granted (political) points, without stopping the course of innovation?"[64] He urged the clergy to stand firm against any alterations, in defense of the ancient traditions of the Church of England.

During the autumn of 1833, two strategies were implemented in defense of what Newman regarded as the ancient catholic tradition of the Church of England. First, a network of local associations was created among the clergy, in the hopes of mobilizing popular support behind the cause. Second, a series of tracts on issues of the day were published, as well as articles in magazines and journals sympathetic to their views. Yet a crucial point should be made about the strategies employed—Newman rejected the creation of structures that limited his personal ability to act.[65]

At the end of August 1833, Newman confessed to a friend that, "Tory as I still am, theoretically and historically, I begin to be a Radical practically."[66] To another friend he explained, "We have

---

[63]*Tracts for the Times* (London: J.G. and F. Rivington, 1838), vol. 1, Tract no. 1, 2.

[64]*Tracts for the Times*, vol. 1, Tract no. 3, 3-4.

[65]*Letters and Diaries* 4:67-70.

[66]Ibid. 4:35.

everything against us but our cause.... The early Church threw itself on the *people*—now that the Crown and aristocracy have deserted us, must not we do so too?"[67] He was convinced that popular support was essential. In an article sent to the *British Magazine*, Newman made this point clear:

> Hitherto the English Church has depended on the State, i.e. on the ruling powers in the country—the king and the aristocracy.... What is intended by Providence to take the place of the time-honoured instrument, which he has broken (if it be yet broken)[?]... I shall offend many men when I say, we must *look to the people*.[68]

Acknowledging concern that reliance on the people might lower the standards and practices of the clergy, Newman stressed the importance of the apostolic source of clerical authority:

> We have that with us, which none but ourselves possess, the mantle of the Apostles; and this, properly understood and cherished, will ever keep us from being the creatures of a populace.[69]

With this conclusion firmly in his mind, Newman and his colleagues created a local society at Oxford, intended to "rouse the Clergy." The hope was that by using their influence with Oxford men scattered through the country, a grassroots movement would be created.[70] By late August 1833, clergy in various parts of England were persuaded to organize societies that sought to defend the liturgy of the Book of Common Prayer and the doctrine of apostolic succession.[71]

Newman and his colleagues also began a series of tracts that promoted their concerns. In September 1833, the first of the *Tracts for the Times* appeared in print. These tracts were variously addressed to the clergy and general public. Although they began as short pieces of no more than four to seven pages, they evolved into essays of some length, examining in detail doctrinal issues and matters of practice. For

[67]Ibid. 4:14; for further elaboration of this point in an essay on Ambrose written in August 1833 see John Henry Newman, *Historical Sketches* (London: Longmans, Green, 1914) 1:340-42.

[68]Ibid. 1:340.

[69]Ibid. 1:341.

[70]*Letters and Diaries* 4:21; 28-29.

[71]Ibid. 4:9,33,35.

over seven years the *Tracts for the Times* proved an effective organ of controversy, promoting the views and goals of those who led the Oxford Movement. But it remained highly unstructured, with little editorial control. This was largely due to Newman's resistance to a board or committee that would review and edit tracts. He argued that such formal structures should only be established when bishops in various parts of the country chose to take a public stand and lead the movement in their dioceses.[72] However, his primary concern was the inhibiting effect of a committee on the content and rhetoric of the tracts—turning them into "tame dull compositions," in the name of moderation.[73] Newman clearly desired to run ahead of the pack, and did not wish to be held back by the timidity of others.

Newman took great delight in stirring the controversy and sought various means of bringing the movement to the attention of the public. In a letter to Froude, he suggested as an "innocent Economy," an anonymous letter from Oxford to the *Times* which would begin, "'Our bigots are on foot again etc' then give an account of the Association, noticing the inconsistencies of men who were Tories turning Radicals, and who profess Episcopal obedience acting without a Bishop."[74] While Newman may have suggested this in jest, it reveals his clear awareness of the paradox of their professed goals and the strategies used to accomplish them. This conflict was never resolved.

As the 1830s progressed, many other means were found to promote the movement. Newman published articles in a variety of magazines and journals, printed sermons that promoted the causes dear to him, and gained a large following in Oxford among the undergraduates of the university through his sermons and lectures. The network created around the country had some political successes within the university and on the national scene. By the late 1830s, Newman had become a nationally known figure and had achieved his goal of giving orthodoxy, as he understood it, the tantalizing scent of scandal.

However, effective as these strategies were, Newman's labors flowed from an idiosyncratic vision of Anglicanism—a vision that proved disastrous for the movement and Newman's commitment to the Church of England in the early 1840s. From the beginning of the Oxford

[72]Ibid. 4:68-69.
[73]Ibid. 4:55.
[74]Ibid. 4:48.

Movement, Newman's alienation and estrangement from the various Christian traditions outside the established Church and "parties" within the Church of England was clear. He actively opposed the enfranchisement and granting of civil liberties to Dissenters and Roman Catholics. Within the Church of England, he vigorously resisted the influence of liberal and evangelical Churchmen. Yet one must also keep in mind his low regard for the High Churchmen of his day. He sought to create a new High Church synthesis that would not only renew the influence of the High Church "party," but also revitalize doctrines and practices that were moribund. Newman approached this project with little formation in the High Church tradition, and was regarded with suspicion by leading High Churchmen from the beginning. This concern focused on Newman's understanding of tradition, which was considered to be contrary to the position taken by Anglican divines.[75]

While his scholarship reflected a passion for patristics, especially the study of ancient heresies, Newman did not exhibit a corresponding effort to master Caroline divinity. This did not inhibit his rhetorical appeal to these divines.[76] Using the names of great seventeenth century theologians, Newman pushed forward arguments that caused even his High Church supporters great unease.[77]

Perhaps the most grievous flaw in Newman's refashioned High Church theology was the perception that he rejected two principles common to all of the parties within the Church of England—he was thought to have rejected the Protestant character of the Church and abandoned anti-Romanism.[78] This was not simply a problem of public misperception. Newman, deeply influenced by Froude, lamented the ways in which the Protestant tradition had departed from ancient practice and openly admired much that he found in the Roman Catholic tradition. In May 1836, Newman confessed to a High Churchman that he loved the Church of Andrewes, Laud, and Hammond, but "I do not like the Church of the Reformation." He went

---

[75]Ibid. 3:105; 4:169n.

[76]Kenneth L. Parker, "Newman's Individualistic Use of the Caroline Divines in the *Via Media*," in *Discourse and Context: An Interdisciplinary Study of John Henry Newman*, ed. Gerard Magill (Carbondale, IL: Southern Illinois UP, 1993) 33-42.

[77]Gilley, *Newman and His Age* 119-20; *Letters and Diaries* 4:314-15.

[78]*Letters and Correspondence* 2:10; Chadwick, *The Victorian Church* 1:119.

on to observe, "I cannot endure, except by patience and resignation, the insults of the world which she [the Church of England] has worn now three hundred years." Later in the letter he made a declaration that would have sounded treasonous to most English ears: "My heart *is* with Rome, *but not* as Rome, but as, and so far as, she is the faithful retainer of what we have practically thrown aside."[79]

Newman hoped the movement would initiate a second Reformation. Drawing on his love of the early Church, his disdain for the Protestant Reformation, and affection for the seventeenth century divines, Newman created a vision of Anglicanism on which he hoped to build a new consensus within the Church of England. Newman claimed in 1837, "Protestantism and Popery are real religions; no one can doubt about them; they have furnished the mould in which nations have been cast: but the *Via Media* has never existed except on paper, it has never been reduced to practice."[80] Newman hoped his *via media* would steer a course between the corruptions of Roman Catholicism and the heretical innovations of the Protestant Reformation.

By the summer of 1839, Newman's hopes of bringing his "paper religion" to life were weakening. As he studied the Monophysite controversy that summer, he reported in 1864 that he experienced a crisis of conscience. During this period of reading, "for the first time a doubt came upon me of the tenableness of Anglicanism." He explained that, "my stronghold was Antiquity; now here, in the middle of the fifth century, I found, as it seemed to me, Christendom of the sixteenth and the nineteenth centuries reflected. I saw my face in that mirror, and I was a Monophysite."[81] These reflections, written twenty-five years later, cannot be verified by documents from the period.[82] However, his impatience with the leadership of the Anglican Church and frustration with the rejection of his vision of the Church can be documented. On September 1, 1839, Newman stated in a letter to Henry Manning,

I am conscious that we are raising longings and tastes which we are not allowed to supply—and till our Bishops and others give scope to the

[79]*Letters and Diaries* 5:301-03.

[80]John Henry Newman, *Lectures on the Prophetical Office of the Church* (London: J.G. and F. Rivington, 1837) 20.

[81]*Apologia* 114.

[82]Thomas 205-19.

development of Catholicism externally and visibly, we *do* tend to make impatient minds seek it where it has ever been, in Rome...whenever the time comes that secessions to Rome take place...we must boldly say to that Protestant section of our Church—"*You* are the cause of this. You must *concede*...You must make the Church more efficient—more suitable to the needs of the heart, more equal to the external pressures. Give us more services—more vestments and decorations in worship—give us monasteries—give us the "signs of an Apostle"—the pledges that the Spouse of Christ is among us. Till then, you will have continual defections to Rome." This is, I confess, my view."[83]

These observations illustrate the chasm that separated Newman and his disciples from the other parties within the Church. It was only a matter of time before this unconventional vision of the Church of England would lead to his estrangement from the Church. Two events in the early 1840s served as catalysts: the response to Tract XC and the Jerusalem bishopric controversy.

A major obstacle to Newman's synthesis was a doctrinal statement called the Thirty-nine Articles, which had shaped the Protestant identity of the Church of England since the Elizabethan Settlement. This was a problem that Newman could not escape. In the spring of 1840, during a parliamentary debate, Bishop Stanley of Norwich described the English Church as Calvinist in creed and Arminian in liturgy.[84] This statement, with its oblique reference to the Thirty-nine Articles, required a response from the leaders of the Oxford Movement. Newman's *via media* rested on his assertion that the Church of England was faithful to the doctrines and liturgy of the ancient catholic tradition. If the *via media* was to survive, the Articles had to be interpreted in a way that conformed to the catholic tradition as Newman understood it.

The fruit of this reinterpretation was Tract XC, published in February 1841. Newman began the tract with a clear description of the crisis faced by the Church. He observed, "We can do nothing well till we act 'with one accord'; we can have no accord in action till we agree together in heart.... Our Church's strength would be irresistible,

[83]J.H. Newman to Henry Manning, 1 September 1839, Newman Archives, Oratory, Birmingham, England.

[84]Chadwick, *The Victorian Church* 1:181-82. This misquotation of Lord Chatham's observation that the church had a popish liturgy, Calvinist Articles, and Arminian clergy was a source of distress for Newman as early as 1836. See *Letters and Diaries* 5:302.

humanly speaking, were it but at unity with itself."[85] With this plea for unity, Newman proceeded to violate two cherished and enduring sources of Anglican identity: the Protestant character of the Church of England and hostility toward the Church of Rome—both symbolically maintained in the Thirty-nine Articles. In a resolute rejection of Reformation doctrine, Newman violated the Protestant sense of the articles and interpreted them in a way that conformed to his vision of ancient catholicity. In his concluding remarks Newman observed, "It is a *duty* which we owe both to the Catholic Church and to our own, to take our reformed confessions in the most Catholic sense they will admit; we have no duties toward their framers."[86]

In an age when the term "Catholic" was synonymous with "Roman Catholic," the reaction was swift and forceful.[87] Less than three weeks after the tract's publication the hebdomadal board of Oxford condemned Newman's attempt to evade the Protestant sense of the articles. The popular press agreed. An example was the *Morning Chronicle* which derisively observed, "According to the authors of the *Tracts* we are all good papists without knowing it."[88] A series of episcopal condemnations soon followed. Bishop Sumner of Chester summarized the conclusions of many of his episcopal colleagues when he insisted,

> I understand the Articles subscribed officially before me, as Articles, not of the Universal Church of Christ, but of the United Church of England and Ireland, of which the subscriber is a member. They do not therefore admit of interpretation borrowed from any remote or undefined authority, professing to be that of a Church calling itself, or imagined to be, the Church Catholic.[89]

Bishop Monk of Gloucester and Bristol observed that,

> The real object at which the writer seems to be labouring is to prove that the differences in Doctrine which separate the Churches of England and

---

[85]John Henry Newman, *Tracts for the Times: Remarks on Certain Passages in the Thirty-nine Articles* (London: Gilbert and Rivington, 1841) 3.

[86]Ibid. 83.

[87]Chadwick, *The Victorian Church* 1:183.

[88]Ibid. 1:185.

[89]W. Simcox Bricknell, *The Judgment of the Bishops upon Tractarian Theology* (Oxford: J. Vincent, 1845) 536.

Rome will, upon examination, vanish. Upon this point much ingenuity, and, I am forced to add, much sophistry is exerted; and I think exerted in vain.[90]

Newman had taken a doctrinal statement that symbolically had united the Church, and given it a meaning that evangelicals, liberals, and traditional High Churchmen recognized as a distortion of their Church's identity. Employing a tactic used by evangelicals and liberals against the Book of Common Prayer, he had rejected the reformed sense of the Thirty-nine Articles, in favor of interpretations that others perceived as savoring of Romanism. Despite the deep divisions within the Church of England, all parties could—and did—unite in rejecting Newman's vision of Anglicanism. He had violated two essential components of Anglican identity that had remained sources of unity—the Protestant character of the Church of England and hostility toward the Church of Rome—and it was on these grounds that Newman found himself isolated and estranged from the Church he had sought to defend.

Newman's initial response to the criticism suggests a feeling of relief that his views were at last clearly and publicly stated. In a letter to Arthur Perceval on March 12, 1841, he explained that Tract XC had been written to reassure those who contemplated defection to Rome. He also added, "it was necessary for my own peace so much as this, that I felt people *did not know* me, and were trusting me when otherwise they would not."[91] By September 1841, Newman was feeling keenly the contradiction of his loyalty to the Church of England and his doctrinal conflicts with those who spoke for the Church. In a letter to Keble he stated,

What *is* heresy?—is the Protestant doctrine of justification? is the denial of the real presence? or the denial of Episcopal grace, or of the Catholic Church?—I really fear that the majority of our Bishops at this moment would be on the Protestant side on all these points.[92]

His fears concerning the Protestant character of the Church of England

[90]Ibid. 537.

[91]J.H. Newman to Arthur Perceval, 12 March 1841, Newman Archives, Oratory, Birmingham, England.

[92]J.H. Newman to John Keble, 4 September 1841, Newman Archives, Oratory, Birmingham, England.

were soon confirmed.

Newman's rejection of the Church of England required more than official and popular condemnation of Tract XC. He needed clear evidence that fundamental principles of primitive Christianity had been rejected by the Church. For Newman, proof of the Anglican tradition's break with catholic tradition came in the Jerusalem bishopric controversy of 1841.[93] It not only illustrated the negative affects of Erastianism on the Church, but also confirmed the Protestant character of the Church of England. For Newman, this was shocking proof of the heretical condition of the Church of England.

The cause of Newman's crisis was a decision by the government to use the Anglican Church to further British interests in the Middle East. As the Ottoman Empire decomposed, the European powers sought ways of establishing their interest in the region. Russia and France had already used the protection of Orthodox and Roman Catholic Christians as a pretext for expanding their influence in the region. In June 1841, Friedrich Wilhelm of Prussia proposed to the British government that their two nations establish a joint Lutheran-Anglican bishopric in Jerusalem, which would provide protection and pastoral care for the few Protestants in that region.[94] The Prussian ruler not only hoped to gain influence in Palestine, but also to use this joint venture as a means of reestablishing episcopal polity in his state Church.[95] The proposal was accepted by the government and Church of England, and a treaty was signed in July 1841.[96]

Few events could have more clearly confirmed Newman's growing doubts about the Church of England. Newman was appalled by the flagrant use of the Church as an instrument of foreign policy.[97] But even more repugnant was the underlying assumption that the Lutherans

---

[93]*Apologia* 140-46.

[94]Chadwick, *The Victorian Church* 1:189; Kurt Schmidt-Clausen, *Vorweggenommene Einheit: Die Gründung des Bistums Jerusalem im Jahre 1841*, Arbeiten zur Geschichte und Theologie des Luthertums, vol. 15, ed. Max Keller-Hueschenmenger, et al. (Berlin: Lutherisches Verlagshaus, 1965) 19; P.J. Welch, "Anglican Churchmen and the Establishment of the Jerusalem Bishopric," *Journal of Ecclesiastical History* 8 (1957) 193-204; Ernst Benz, *Bischofsamt und apostolische Sukzession im deutschen Protestantismus* (Stuttgart: Evangelisches Verlagswerk, 1953) 149. I am grateful to Austin McCaskill for these references.

[95]Gilley, *Newman and His Age* 207.

[96]Chadwick, *The Victorian Church* 1:190.

[97]*Letters and Correspondence* 2:353-4.

of Prussia and the Anglicans of England shared a Protestant heritage. Newman expressed his outrage to Keble in early October 1841, stating, "It really does seem to me as if the Bishops were doing their best to uncatholicize us."[98] In November 1841, Newman sent a statement of protest to the archbishop of Canterbury and the bishop of Oxford. This protest, filled with premises not shared by other Anglicans, set out the principles which were to force him to renounce the Church of his birth. He asserted,

> Whereas the Church of England has a claim on the allegiance of Catholic believers only on the grounds of her own claim to be considered a branch of the Catholic Church:
>
> And whereas the recognition of heresy, indirect as well as direct, goes far to destroy such claim in the case of any religious body:
>
> And, whereas to admit maintainers of heresy to communion, without formal renunciation of their errors, goes far towards recognizing the same:
>
> And whereas Lutheranism and Calvinism are heresies, repugnant to Scripture, springing up three centuries since, and anathematised by East as well as West:
>
> And, whereas it is reported that the Most Reverend Primate and other Right Reverend Rulers of our Church have consecrated a Bishop, with a view to exercising spiritual jurisdiction over Protestant, that is, Lutheran and Calvinistic congregations in the East...thereby giving in some sort a formal recognition to the doctrines which such congregations maintain:
>
> And, whereas the dioceses in England are connected together by so close an intercommunion, that what is done by authority in one immediately affects the rest:
>
> On these grounds, I, in my place, being a Priest of the English Church, and Vicar of St. Mary's, Oxford, by way of relieving my conscience, do hereby solemnly protest against the measure aforesaid, and disown it, as removing our Church from her present ground, and tending to her disorganization.[99]

Newman's protest, based on a concept of the Catholic Church which had been publicly rejected by members of the Anglican episcopate, denounced as heretical Protestant movements that other Anglicans

---

[98]J.H. Newman to John Keble, 5 October 1841, Newman Archives, Oratory, Birmingham, England.

[99]*Letters and Correspondence* 2:362-63.

acknowledged as kindred traditions. Even among his closest friends and allies, Newman's views were not shared. Although supportive, Pusey did not consider Lutheranism heretical. Keble opposed its publication.[100] Though Newman focused on the doubts of his followers during this period, fearing that the Jerusalem bishopric controversy "may be the last straw that breaks the horse's back," Newman later acknowledged in the *Apologia* that "it brought me on to the beginning of the end."[101] Although Newman was not received into the Church of Rome until October 1845, he later confessed that "from the end of 1841, I was on my death-bed, as regards my membership with the Anglican Church."[102]

Conversion and Estrangement

John Henry Newman illustrates that the theme of the stranger in Christian tradition takes a poignant turn when applied to the issue of conversion. His estrangement from a cherished and deeply loved Church raises questions that are not satisfied by simplistic answers or partisan judgments. One must examine the complexities of his society and culture. The impact of personal experiences and the influence of mentors and friends must not be neglected. The power of the written word to persuade and direct requires serious examination.

A key factor in Newman's religious quest was the transitional nature of English life in the first half of the nineteenth century. Dramatic swings in the British economy that had brought prosperity and material comforts as a child, also brought hardship to John Henry and his family, and instilled in Newman a distrust in the material world and the honors society bestows. His youthful flirtation with religious skepticism ended during this crisis, and he experienced a religious conversion that marked him for a lifetime. Perhaps most significant for his future was the impact of his earliest religious beliefs, which had the effect of "isolating me from the objects which surrounded me, in confirming me in my mistrust of the reality of material phenomena, and making me rest in the thought of two and two only absolute and

[100]Ibid. 2:365-66.
[101]Ibid. 2:354; *Apologia* 146.
[102]*Apologia* 234, 147.

luminously self-evident beings, myself and my Creator."[103] Newman's first estrangement was from the world and any security and affirmation society might offer. This conviction became a highly developed part of his spirituality, as Newman confronted the challenges of university life at Oxford in the 1820s and the crises in England's political and religious life in the 1830s.

Unlike others who stopped short of decisions that might bring personal pain and public humiliation, Newman's spirituality sustained him through a series of disruptive and dramatic turns in his personal and public life. Though deeply influenced by others, he did not hesitate to reject those who did not hold his convictions or break with friends and mentors he left behind in his quest for truth and certainty. This trait has been viewed as callous and arrogant by some and courageous by others. At the least, it was an expression of his ability to resist the pressures to conform.

Another factor which must not be minimized was the impact of the written word on Newman's life and actions. From the Calvinist books and tracts lent to him in 1816 to his study of the early Church Fathers and ancient heresies in the 1820s and 1830s, Newman's vision of reality was profoundly influenced by the ideas and reflections of previous generations of Christian thinkers. However, he brought to his reading a keen and creative mind. While abhorring the notion of innovation in theology, he was not passive in his reception of their vision of Christianity.

All of these factors made Newman a dynamic force during the 1830s—a man capable of creating a new synthesis for a Church that needed fresh answers to new challenges. Yet these great strengths were also the source of his estrangement from the Church of England. Because he was distrustful of the material world, Newman frequently stood in opposition to the established norm, finding it impossible to compromise principles that he perceived to be divine and eternal. Human attachments and personal loyalties had to be sacrificed in the name of religious truth, as Newman understood it. As a controversialist, he did not scruple at using the tactics and methods of those he opposed, in order to achieve goals that he considered worthy and just. His creative synthesis of ancient, medieval, and early modern theology resolved, in Newman's mind, the dilemma facing the English

---

[103]Ibid. 4.

Church. However, his rejection of the Protestant character of the Church of England and the nation's deeply ingrained hostility to the Church of Rome, marginalized and alienated Newman from his Church and countrymen. His detachment from the "world" ultimately estranged him from the Church and society that had been his frame of reference for a lifetime.

Given these factors, it is not surprising that Newman spent four years reassessing and reshaping his religious world view. His idiosyncratic vision of Anglicanism had been shattered by the rejection of his coreligionists. Newman was forced to look for truth and certainty elsewhere. He set his sights on the Church of Rome—a communion he had castigated all of his adult life as a corrupt and distorted image of primitive Christianity. The factors that led to Newman's alienation from the Church of England, also proved decisive in his conversion to Roman Catholicism. While the historian may not be able to judge the role of the divine in Newman's decision to become Roman Catholic, "humanly speaking," the factors that led to Newman's alienation from Anglicanism played a critical role in his conversion to the Church of Rome.

9

HOW OUTSIDERS BECAME

SUBVERTERS OF CHRISTENDOM

The Jew as Quintessential Stranger

Ronald E. Modras

In what was virtually an aside in a 1938 article on Zionism, the editors of *La civiltà cattolica* characterized Judaism as a religion that was "*profondamente corrotta*," profoundly corrupt.[1] Although jarring by contemporary Catholic standards, the accusation in the 1930s was hardly unique but on the contrary quite commonplace. For the Italian Jesuits who published the Roman journal, the charge was justified by what they regarded as Judaism's "corrupt," materialistic messianism, which made it not only the "antithesis of Christianity" but a source of disorder and a "permanent danger" for the world. Jews, believers and unbelievers alike, were gripped by the "fatal desire" to achieve a financial domination of the world. Despite this "danger" (a word the Jesuit journal used regularly regarding Jews), Christian charity precluded persecution. But prudence required segregation. With an appeal to the precedent of the ghetto imposed on Jews in the former papal states, the editors of *La civiltà cattolica* suggested that Jews might enjoy continued Christian hospitality but should be kept at a distance. In short, the "civil co-existence" (*convivenza*) of Christians and Jews should be "*in maniera simile a quella che si usa con gli stranieri*," similar to that which is customary between strangers.[2]

La civiltà cattolica was and is not just another Catholic periodical. Founded in 1850 by the Italian Jesuits, it proposed "always and in all matters to reflect the thinking of the Holy See."[3] Formally approved

---

[1]"Intorno alla questione del sionismo," *La civiltà cattolica* 89.2 (1938) 76-77.
[2]Ibid.
[3]*New Catholic Encyclopedia* (1967) 13:305. See also *Encyclopedia Italiana*

with a papal letter by Pope Pius IX (1866), later reconfirmed by Pope Leo XIII, it has long been justifiably regarded as a "semi-official organ of the Holy See."[4]

From its very beginnings the Roman journal enjoyed a unique relationship with the Vatican. Not only was it scrupulous in its fidelity to Vatican directives, its editorial positions were openly known to have been given prior approval by the curia. Its merited reputation for enjoying the confidence of the popes gave it a unique authority for Catholics. Within its pages one could receive clarification for the sometimes encoded or merely suggestive language of official Vatican documents. Certainly this was true of what *La civiltà cattolica* regarded as the "Jewish danger," or what most others in interwar Europe called simply the "Jewish question."

Treating Jews as strangers was, for the editors of *La civiltà cattolica*, the proper way for Catholics to relate to Jews, a prudent and Christian middle stance between the "extremes" of anti-Semitism and what the Roman journal called "semitism."[5] In 1928 the Vatican's Holy Office suppressed an organization of bishops and priests called the Friends of Israel (*Amici Israël*), pledged not only to pray for the conversion of Jews but also to defend them as peculiarly loved by God. The reason for the suppression, according to the Vatican decree, was that the Friends of Israel acted and thought in a manner "contrary to the opinion and spirit of the Church, to the thinking of the Holy Fathers, and to the liturgy itself."[6] But the Holy Office took the occasion of its action against the Friends of Israel to express condemnation as well of "that hate that today is called by the name of anti-Semitism."

Writing the following year on "The Jewish Danger and the 'Friends of Israel,'"[7] the editors of *La civiltà cattolica* defended Vatican policy as an exercise of both justice and charity. Charity excluded the

---

(1949) 10:515. The 1949 anniversary issue of the journal boasted of its "very special links to the Holy See and the favor which it enjoyed from the Popes" (*La civiltà cattolica* 100.2 [1949] 3).

[4]Roger Aubert, *Le pontificat de Pie IX (1846-1878)* (Tournai: Bloud et Gay, 1952) 40.

[5]"Il pericolo giudaico e gli 'Amici d'Israele,'" *La civiltà cattolica* 79.2 (1928) 335.

[6]*Acta Apostolicae Sedis* 20 (1928) 103-04.

[7]"Il pericolo giudaico" 335-40.

"excesses" of anti-Semitism, which the Roman journal described in terms of hatred, violence, and unjust harassment. In condemning anti-Semitism, the Church was protecting, as it has always done, "even its enemies and fiercest persecutors such as the Jews." But justice required that the Church not close its eyes to the "semitism" represented by the Friends of Israel, an "extreme no less dangerous" than anti-Semitism and in fact "even more seductive" (*anche più seducente*), because it posed under the aspect of good.[8]

The most succinct description of what the Jesuit journal meant by "semitism" was the "social predominance (*prepotere*) in all areas of modern life, especially the economic," afforded to Jews by liberalism. Granting Jews equal rights before the law had allowed them to become bold, powerful, and constantly more dominant (*preponderante*) in modern society. Jews had now attained the highest positions in industry, banking, diplomacy, and "even more in secret sects, plotting world domination" (*più ancora delle sètte occulte, macchinanti la loro egemonia mondiale*). For the editors of *La civiltà cattolica*, all the world, but especially Christian nations, were endangered by the "undeniable alliance" (*innegabile alleanza*) between liberal Freemasons and Jews, both of whom were responsible for the persecution being suffered by Catholics and the clergy.[9]

The Second Vatican Council's declaration on non-Christian religions (*Nostra aetate*) marked a watershed in the way Catholics and subsequently other Christians view Jews and Judaism. It repudiated the traditional "teaching of contempt" (Jules Isaac) that declared Jews as rejected by God for their supposedly collective responsibility for the death of Jesus. But as one can see from the highly illustrative *La civiltà cattolica*, these were not the issues that troubled Catholic Churchmen in the interwar period. Jewish guilt for Jesus' crucifixion may have been assumed and the idea of rejection below the surface, but the principal reasons for Catholic antagonism against Jews were much more contemporary, this worldly, and, if I may suggest, political.

The conviction that Jews were a "question" was a commonplace in interwar Europe, even for Jews, especially Zionists. How and why they were a "question" was more often than not vague and ill-defined for most who wrote on the subject. But not so for traditionalist Catholics

[8]Ibid. 339-40.
[9]Ibid. 340-44.

for whom the Jewish "question" was seen as largely originating in 1717. Catholic theologians found it striking that Providence seemed to unleash Satan at two-hundred year intervals: first in 1517, then 1717, and most recently in 1917. Virtually anyone with a sense of history will recognize 1517 as the onset of the Protestant Reformation and 1917 as the year of the Bolshevik Revolution. But these days even professional Church historians and those given to serious reflection on Jewish and Christian relations ignore or give short shrift to the founding of the Grand Lodge in London and the organization of modern Freemasonry in 1717. I can think of no more telling measure of the Catholic Church's aversion to liberalism and Freemasonry than to have the founding of the Grand Lodge likened to the Protestant Reformation and Bolshevik Revolution.

The notion of a sinister alliance between Freemasons and Jews to subvert traditional European society originated in Germany but first flourished in France, where it played a conspicuous role in the turn-of-the-century Dreyfus Affair. Although a staple in the anti-Semitic arsenal of the 1930s and closely connected with the notorious *Protocols of the Elders of Zion*, the idea of a Masonic-Jewish alliance has been largely forgotten today, neglected even by writers on Christian-Jewish relations.[10]

Jews and Christians had been estranged since the first century, a condition both rabbinical and ecclesiastical leaders found satisfactory to their respective interests. Following the thinking of Saint Augustine (354-430), the medieval Church saw Jews as marked with the sign of Cain, cursed to wander the earth as fugitives, but not to be killed (Gen 4:11-15). In effect, they could be tolerated as resident aliens in Christian society so long as they were in a condition of subservience,

---

[10]The enormously important book by Jacob Katz, *Jews and Freemasons in Europe, 1723-1939*, trans. Leonard Oschry (Cambridge, MA: Harvard UP, 1970), has not had the impact on scholarship that it deserves, in my opinion. Hans Küng in his encyclopedic *Judaism: Between Yesterday and Tomorrow* (New York: Crossroad, 1992) appears unaware of Katz's work. And even in its revised, updated edition, Edward Flannery's excellent history of anti-Semitism, *The Anguish of the Jews: Twenty-three Centuries of Anti-Semitism* (New York: Macmillan, 1965), gives the supposed alliance only brief notice. For the interconnection between anti-Semitism, anti-Masonry, and anti-Modernism, see C.J.T. Talar, "Anti-Masonry as Anti-Modernism, in *Modernism as a Social Construct*, eds. George Gilmore, Hans Rollman, and Gary Lease (Spring Hill College, AL: Working Group on RC Modernism, 1991) 52-66.

giving "witness" to the victory and superiority of Christianity by their condition of inferiority.[11] But the process of social leveling, represented by Freemasonry and exponentially advanced by the French Revolution, radically changed the condition of European Jews and, with that change, the attitude of Catholic Church leadership toward them as well. Jews were no longer mere strangers. They were agents of modern secular liberalism, joined with Freemasons in undermining Christian culture. Jews were no longer subservient outsiders but dangerous subversives in the heart of what once was Christendom.

Freemasonry and Liberalism

The origins of Freemasonry date back to early eighteenth century England, where lodges of working masons began admitting non-working members into their numbers, sharing secret symbols and passwords. When these "honorary" masons outnumbered the operatives, the lodges became schools of morality which used the older symbols to inculcate ethical lessons.[12] Four such lodges banded together in London (June 24, 1717), to form the Grand Lodge of England. In an era torn by religious dissention, it was decided not to make religious affiliation a test for membership. Not only members of the established Church of England but dissenters and even Roman Catholics were allowed to join their ranks.

Under the quite obvious influence of deism, the 1723 constitution, written by Presbyterian minister, James Anderson, required Masons to believe in God and in the immortality of the soul and to adhere to a sacred law, such as was found in the Bible. Points of dissention were

---

[11]"Iudei tamen manent cum signo.... Non sine causa Cain ille est, qui cum fratrem occidisset, posuit in eo Deus signum, ne quis eum occideret. Hoc est signum quod habent Iudei.... Iam factum est: per omnes gentes dispersi sunt Iudei, testes iniquitatis suae et ueritatis nostrae." (St. Augustine, *Enarratio in Ps.* 58.1.21-22 [*Corpus Christianorum,* Series Latina 39.744]). See also *Enarratio in Ps.* 40.14.15-35 (*CCL* 38:459); *Enarratio in Ps.* 77.9.42-50 (*CCL* 39.1074); *Sermo* 201 (Migne *PL* 38.1032.52); Bernhard Blumenkranz, "Augustin et les juifs, Augustin et le Judaïsme," *Recherches Augustiniennes* 1 (1958) 225-41.

[12]By its own definition, Freemasonry is a "peculiar system of morality, veiled in allegory and illustrated by symbols" (Alec Mellor, *Nos frères séparés, les francs-maçons* [Paris: Mame, 1961] 246).

bracketed off for the sake of "conciliating true friendship."[13] In the original Masonic conception, religion, like politics, was not to be discussed within lodge meetings. Other Masonic principles were the equality of all members within the lodge, no matter what their religious affiliation or social class, and the right of all Freemasons to visit other lodges. As a result of its socially leveling principles, Freemasonry provided an access into elite circles that otherwise would have remained closed to outsiders like Roman Catholics and Jews.

Within less than a decade, Freemasonry spread to Ireland and the continent. By 1738 lodges were established in France, Germany, Poland, the English colonies, Spain, Portugal and Italy. It was with the establishment of lodges in Tuscany that Pope Clement XII in 1738 issued the first in a series of papal condemnations (*In eminenti*), excommunicating any Catholics who joined the Freemasons. The reason offered for the papal condemnation was the masonic oath of secrecy which gave rise to the "strong suspicion" that the Masons were "acting ill." Pope Clement claimed that there were "other just and reasonable causes known to ourselves," but left them unnamed.[14] Pope Benedict XIV repeated the condemnation in 1751 (*Providas Romanorum Pontificum*), but once again the reasons given were not heresy or philosophical errors but secrecy and the Masonic oath.

Despite the papal prohibitions, Catholics continued to enter the ranks of Freemasons. Some lodges in Ireland consisted entirely of priests and Catholic laymen like the patriot, Daniel O'Connell. A convent of nuns in Nantes in northwestern France sent George Washington a gift of a masonic apron. John Carroll, the first Roman Catholic bishop of the United States, had a brother, Daniel, who was both a Catholic and an active Freemason. When asked his opinion on the matter, Bishop Carroll wrote (1794) concerning the papal bans: "I do not pretend that these decrees are received generally by the Church, or have full authority in this diocese."[15] According to ancient but now all too neglected Church practice, a doctrine or law had to be "received" by the Church in order to have "full authority." In the view of Bishop John Carroll, Catholics "generally" were still refusing to acknowledge

---

[13]Ibid. 78-79.
[14]William J. Whalen, *Christianity and American Freemasonry* (Milwaukee: Bruce, 1958) 101-02.
[15]Ibid. 103.

the papal ban against Freemasonry in 1794.

Three years later, in 1797, all that changed, thanks greatly, I would argue, to the publication of a four volume work by Abbé Augustin Barruel, *Memoires pour servir d'histoire au Jacobinisme*. In it Barruel ascribed the French Revolution, especially its excesses, to a Masonic plot to overthrow Christian civilization. Barruel had already written sixteen volumes on the French Revolution and the disestablishment of the Church in France without making any anti-Masonic allusion. A Eudist priest named Lafranc had first raised the thesis of a Masonic plot in 1791, but it was Barruel who popularized it. A best-seller in French with translations into English, Italian, Spanish, and Russian, his *Memoires* not only made Barruel a fortune but afforded the popes fresh reasons for their condemnations of the Masonic order.

Modern scholarship recognizes that eighteenth century Freemasonry in France was aristocratic rather than republican. Contrary to the myth popularized by Barruel, Masons were rather to be found among those who fled or were victims of the French Revolution than among its adherents. Freemasons neither provoked nor facilitated the chain of events that commenced in 1789.[16] But by the latter part of the nineteenth century, the myth of masonic responsibility for the Revolution had become so much a part of conventional wisdom that French Freemasons themselves embraced it. By that time they were anti-clerical republicans happy to take credit for the Revolution ascribed to them by their monarchist Catholic adversaries.[17]

When the Napoleonic empire replaced the First Republic, the revolutionary ideas of 1789 spread to Italy. In opposition first to Napoleon and then to the monarchist restoration, the Carbonari were a secret society founded to create a united Italy. At first even Catholic clergy joined its ranks. Though neither generated by nor affiliated with Freemasonry, the Carbonari were influenced by Masonic symbolism, and the two organizations, theoretically distinct, eventually so interpenetrated each other's memberships, that they became indistinguishable one from the other. In 1821 Pope Pius VII condemned the Carbonari as an imitation of the Masons. When

---

[16]For a detailed refutation of the legend, see Alec Mellor, *Histoire de l'anticlericalisme français* (Paris: Mame, 1978) 224-34.

[17]Robert F. Byrnes, *Anti-Semitism in Modern France* (New Brunswick, NJ: Rutgers UP, 1950) 1:126, n.61.

Giuseppe Mazzini formed Young Italy in 1831, once again those who joined him in his efforts at Risorgimento were Italian Freemasons.

The pontifical condemnations did not distinguish between English and North American Masons who avoided political involvement and those of the Grand Orient lodges on the continent who did not. Neither were distinctions made between Masonic and other secret societies, nor between anti-clericals and those Christian liberals who claimed a Christian basis for democratic principles. All were identified as intent on revolution, on overturning the existing social order and, in the case of Italy, posing a very real threat to the Pope's temporal sovereignty over the Papal States and thus his political independence.

The Roman Catholic hierarchy's hostility to liberalism hardly needs a detailed review here. The reaction of the popes to the revolutionary ferment of the nineteenth century can be encapsulated in a short litany of phrases sure to appear in any history of the era. For Pope Gregory XVI (*Mirari vos*), the idea that "liberty of conscience must be maintained for everyone" was "shameful" and "absurd" (*insanis*).[18] Of the eighty propositions Pope Pius IX condemned in his celebrated *Syllabus of Errors*, the most quoted is certainly the last, that the "Roman Pontiff can and should reconcile himself to progress, liberalism, and modern civilization." As for what Pius IX and subsequent popes meant by liberalism, the most succinct description seems to me to be that found in the encyclical accompanying the Syllabus (*Quanta cura*). There the Pope declared it to be an "impious and absurd principle" that society should be governed "without distinction being made between the true religion and false ones."[19]

Pope Leo XIII was no liberal, but he is generally regarded as less extremist than his immediate predecessors when he pronounced in a 1888 encyclical (*Libertas*) that freedom of speech and worship might be "tolerated" when there was "just cause" and "moderation."[20] But it was also Leo XIII who in 1884 published the longest and most detailed papal denunciation of Freemasonry before or since (*Humanum genus*), precisely for its efforts on behalf of what he called the "great error of this age," namely, treating the Catholic Church as equal to other

---

[18]Claudia Carlen, *The Papal Encyclicals: 1740-1981* (1981; Ann Arbor, MI: Pierien, 1990) 1:238.

[19]Ibid. 1:382.

[20]Ibid. 2:169-81.

religions.[21] Pope Leo charged Freemasons with responsibility for depriving the papacy of its temporal sovereignty and for introducing secular education, civil marriage and divorce into Italy. He accused Freemasons of misunderstanding the true meaning of liberty, equality, and fraternity.

One can see clearly from Pope Leo's writings that Barruel's association of Masonry with the French Revolution had made its impression upon the highest echelons in the Catholic Church. In one of his addresses, Pope Leo described Freemasonry as "the permanent personification of revolution."[22] In 1892 (*Custodi de quella fede*) he called on Italian Catholics to wage war against it with a Catholic press, schools, and organizations. Catholics were to avoid familiarity or friendship not only with known or suspected Masons, but even with "those who hide under the mask of universal tolerance, respect for all religions, and the craving to reconcile the maxims of the Gospel with those of the revolution."[23]

In France and Italy alike, the Vatican saw its war against Freemasonry as identical with its struggle against liberalism. With the establishment of the Third Republic in France (1875), a series of laws secularizing the French school system, requiring civil marriage, and permitting divorce culminated in the 1905 separation law that rescinded the concordat between France and the Vatican. Despite the fact that the Church was now freed from considerable control by the French government, Pope Pius X condemned the separation law as the work of the Church's Masonic enemies (*Vehementer nos* and *Une fois encore*).[24] As a matter of fact, there is no denying that Freemasons played leading roles in the Third Republic, and that at one point the Grand Lodge of Paris served as a virtual think-tank for anti-clerical legislation. For France's secularizing republicans, "*Le clericalisme, voilà l'ennemi*" was no empty slogan. And for their French Catholic adversaries as well, there was no doubt as to their nemesis—*la judéo-maçonnerie*.

[21]Ibid. 2:91-101.
[22]*Acta Apostolicae Sedis* 34 (1901-02) 526.
[23]Carlen 2:302, 304.
[24]Ibid. 3:45-48, 67-69.

Freemasonry and Jews

The first known instance of a Jew being admitted to a Masonic lodge was in London in 1732. There is no indication that the authors of the English Masonic constitutions intended their toleration of Christian diversity to allow for Jewish membership. But when Jewish candidates applied, the principle was extended to them as well. Inasmuch as membership in a Masonic lodge offered access to social elites coupled with significant business advantages, in England and Holland alike significant numbers of Jews applied and were admitted. In France the original constitution made baptism a requirement for Masonic membership, but this was dropped after the French Revolution. In Germany Jewish efforts to join Masonic lodges met staunch resistance. Barriers against Jewish membership were let down somewhat in some areas of Germany, but generally anti-Semitic forces bent on preserving the old social order and its values prevailed well into the late nineteenth century.[25]

So it was that Eduard Emil Eckert's book, *Der Freimauer-Orden in seiner wahren Bedeutung*, made little impact in Germany. He argued that Masonry was under the influence of Jews and that both groups were in an alliance to undermine traditional society. In Germany Eckert's book was dismissed even by those who were in principle antagonistic to Freemasonry. His thesis was too palpably contrary to the facts. But when in 1854 it appeared in French translation, the situation was altogether different, and Eckert's ideas found much more fertile ground. Jews were well represented in French Freemasonry, particularly when Adolphe Cremieux, the president of the Alliance Israélite Universelle, served at the same time as the grand master of the Scottish Rite in France.[26]

Gougenot des Mousseaux, a Catholic theologian, took up Eckert's thesis in his (1869) book, *Le Juif, le judaisme, et la juidaization des peuples chrétiens*, treating it, however, incidentally, alongside the deicide charge and the blood libel. An otherwise obscure village priest, E.N. Chabauty, not only gave central focus to the thesis but sharpened it. According to his (1880) book, *Franc-Maçons et Juifs*, Jews were

---

[25]Katz, *Jews and Freemasons in Europe* 15-19, 208-18.

[26]See Jacob Katz, *From Prejudice to Destruction: Anti-Semitism, 1700-1933* (Cambridge, MA: Harvard UP, 1980) 144.

not only in league with the Masons but in control of them. "The Jew with his gold and his genius had seized supreme power within Masonry and secret societies."[27] Again, the allegation was hardly credible in counties like Germany where anti-Semitism was present within Masonic lodges, or in Great Britain, where lodges were resolutely apolitical. But in France, where lines were drawn between Catholic royalists and secularizing Masonic republicans, Jews and Freemasonry were easily associated in the popular mind. With more than a little justification, French Catholics saw their Church as the most important institutional victim of the French Revolution. And they blamed France's Freemasons, the self-appointed champions of the Revolution, and Jews, arguably its foremost beneficiaries.

Chabauty's book was too cumbersome and prolix to be a best-seller, but it became a primary source for one of the most popular works of anti-Semitica in history. *La france juive* by Eduard Drumont, appearing in 1886, went through two hundred editions within twenty-five years. The longest part of Drumont's two-volume work was taken up with what he called the "persecution" of Catholic France by Masons and Protestants, both under the influence of Jews.[28] Drumont's attitude toward Christianity is not altogether clear, but he presented himself as a Catholic writing for Catholics, and his book was received warmly by the Catholic press. Encouraged, he claimed, by the clergy, he went on to found the *Ligue nationale antisémitique de France* and its anti-Semitic daily newspaper, *La libre parole* (1892).

During the Dreyfus Affair (1894-1906), Drumont associated Dreyfus' "treachery" with a Jewish plot to rule France, and by 1900 there were three periodicals taken up with Masons and Jews, each sponsored by an anti-Masonic organization. The most important of these periodicals was *La revue internationale des sociétés sécrètes*, founded in 1912 by a Catholic priest, the Abbé Ernest Jouin. Published right up to 1913 and the Second World War, Abbé Jouin's review combined anti-Semitism, anti-Masonry, and the anti-modernist integralism of Pope Pius X.

The point at issue between Catholic conservatives and liberal republicans was no less than the definition of what it meant to be

---

[27]Katz, *Jews and Freemasons* 270, n.55.
[28]Pierre Pierrard, *Juifs et catholiques français: De Drumont à Jules Isaac, 1886-1945* (Paris: Fayard: 1970) 38-44.

French. As such, the "Jewish problem" figured intrinsically. Active in the debate were the Assumptionist priests who published the most influential Catholic daily newspaper in France, *La croix*. With a circulation of almost two-hundred thousand and fraternal ties to the French bishops, *La croix* described itself unabashedly as "the most anti-Jewish newspaper in France."[29] *La croix* saw Jews and Masons as the natural enemies of Catholic France. Jews were the revolutionaries par excellence, whose long history of insurrection began at Calvary. According to the Assumptionist Catholic daily, Jews were driven by two dominant desires: "to fight the religion of Jesus Christ and to dominate the world by the power of money."[30]

With the onset of the First World War, all parties, left and right, even the most extreme, were compelled to unite in France's common defense. Catholic valor on the battlefield demonstrated Catholic loyalty to the Republic, and after the war more moderate forces came to determine policy, both in the French government and in the Roman Catholic Church. In the persons of Pope Benedict XV and Pope Pius XI, the Vatican was willing to make its peace with both the French Republic and modern pluralist society. At least, it would seem, when the Church's leadership could do nothing else.

Pope Pius XI

Pope Pius XI is favorably remembered for his encyclicals criticizing the totalitarian regimes in Nazi Germany (*Mit brennender Sorge*) and the Soviet Union (*Divini Redemptoris*). Those pronouncements, however, did not make him in any way an advocate of democratic principles. In his first (1922) encyclical (*Ubi arcano Dei*), he made it quite clear that he intended to uphold the teachings of his predecessors on Church-state relations and what he called the socio-political "prerogatives" of the Church and the Holy See. He promised a "holy battle" to vindicate the rights of the Church over education. There was, he declared, a species of legal and social modernism to be condemned

[29]Oscar L. Arnal, *Ambivalent Alliance: The Catholic Church and the Action Française, 1899-1939* (Pittsburgh, PA: University of Pittsburgh P, 1985) 33.
[30]Ibid. 38.

no less than theological modernism.[31]

That inaugural of Pius XI proved to be programmatic for his pontificate. He continued to protest the separation of Church and state in France and, in instituting the Feast of Christ the King in 1929, reasserted the rights of the Church within civil affairs. Government leaders, he wrote, were bound to give public honor to Christ and to his empire over nations. It was the fault of impious anti-clericals that parliaments avoided mentioning Christ's name and "ignominiously" placed the Catholic Church on the same level as "false religions."[32] In his 1929 encyclical on education, he forbade mixing Catholic and non-Catholic children in schools where they would receive lessons from non-Catholic teachers. Justice, he insisted, required that the state provide Catholic pupils not only with religious instruction but with teachers and textbooks supervised by Catholic Church authorities.[33]

Popes since Pius IX and Leo XIII had been linking communism with socialism and socialism with liberalism. Pope Leo had censured socialism not only for its ideas on property but its theory of equality, insisting that in the state as well as in the Church there was a hierarchy of dignity and power.[34] So Pius XI was not being original when, in his 1937 encyclical on communism (*Divini Redemptoris*), he described it as following logically from economic and political liberalism. At the same time he indicted the international press for not adequately reporting the anti-Christian violence in Russia, Mexico, and Spain. There was a "conspiracy of silence on the part of a large section of the non-Catholic press of the world," he wrote, favored by "various occult forces which, for a long time have been working for the overthrow of the Christian Social Order."[35]

The Pope did not make explicit whom he meant by the "various occult forces" bent on overturning the Christian social order. He did not make any mention of Jews in connection with communism or with the "conspiracy of silence" on the part of the non-Catholic press. If any group was ever to be singled out for subverting the Christian social order, they were the Freemasons. In addressing a group of Polish

---

[31]Carlen 3:225-39.
[32]Ibid. 3:265-69, 271-79.
[33]Ibid. 3:353-69.
[34]Ibid. 2:13.
[35]Ibid. 3:537-54.

pilgrims to the Vatican in 1929, the Pope warned them against traps being set by the "enemy of all good." He went on to explain: "I have in mind here above all the Masonic sect, which is spreading its perverse and destructive principles even in Poland."[36]

Pope Pius XI did not mention Jews when he referred to "occult forces" or a "conspiracy of silence" in the international press. But as I indicated at the outset, *La civiltà cattolica*, displayed no such reticence. The Roman journal denied any intention of ascribing all the ills of modern society to Jews, but it was clear that there was a "prevalence" of Jews in the Russian and Hungarian revolutions, just as Jews had been involved in the French Revolution.[37] The theses of Barruel, Eckert, Chabauty, and Drumont had plainly made an impact on the Roman Jesuits whose task it was to interpret and defend the pronouncements of the Holy See. In his (1928) book, *Sur les ruines du temple*, French Jesuit Joseph Bonsirven had attributed the frequency of Jewish participation in modern social revolutions to their materialistic concept of messianism.[38] For the editors of *La civiltà cattolica*, this "authentic Jewish mentality" was responsible for the bloodshed in Bela Kuhn's Hungary, Bolshevik Russia, and the anti-clerical atrocities in civil war torn Spain.[39]

Bishops and the Catholic Press

If the Roman Jesuits at *La civiltà cattolica* were only quasi or semi-official interpreters of the Holy See, the same cannot be said of bishops, who not only interpret the teaching of popes but apply them to their local Churches. The local Church with the greatest number of Jews in Europe was by far that in Poland, restored or "resurrected" as Catholic Poles preferred to put it, after well over a century of being partitioned. There, in the name of a Catholic Poland and Christian culture, the Church fought the self-same struggle against liberalism between the two world wars that it had fought earlier in France and

[36]*Mały Dziennik*, July 25, 1938.

[37]*La civiltà cattolica* 79.2 (1928) 342.

[38]Joseph Bonsirven, *Sur les ruines du temple* (Paris: Grasset, 1928); English translation: *On the Ruins of the Temple* (London: Burns, Oates, & Washbourne, 1931).

[39]*La civiltà cattolica* 87.4 (1936) 43.

Italy. In a joint pastoral letter in 1934, the Polish bishops accused liberals of the "deep things of Satan" in trying to introduce the spirit of the French Revolution into Poland. Separation of Church and state could only mean war between Church and state.[40]

Leading the Church's war against liberalism in Poland during the interwar period was its Primate, Cardinal August Hlond. In a 1932 pastoral letter he attacked the idea of a secular, non-confessional state as "perverted," at least in Catholic countries like Poland. It was inconceivable to him that a "circle of liberals and free-thinkers" would influence public policy contrary to the convictions of a Catholic majority.[41] In an oft-quoted 1936 pastoral letter, Cardinal Hlond made it clear that this "circle of liberals and free-thinkers" included not only Freemasons but Jews. "It is a fact," he wrote, "that Jews are waging war against the Catholic Church, that they are steeped in free-thinking, and constitute the vanguard of atheism, the bolshevik movement, and revolutionary activity."[42]

Cardinal Hlond made it clear that he was not speaking of all Jews. So too Cardinal Aleksander Kakowski of Warsaw, in complaining to a group of rabbis about Jews ridiculing Catholic dogmás in the press, noted that the rabbis could not be held responsible for the acts of Jewish free-thinkers. But the Cardinal was sure that the Jewish community, which united in solidarity to defend its own interests, should be able to guarantee respect for the faith and traditions of Christians.[43] Other bishops did not always make the distinction between religious and apostate Jews. Archbishop Józef Teodorowicz of Lwów called the Church to imitate Jesus, whose life, he wrote, was "one prolonged war with the Pharisees and synagogue." At the center of that war was a fundamental conflict between a supernatural Christian messianism and a this-worldly Jewish messianism.[44] For Bishop Teodor Kubina, capitalists and communists both had embraced the "Jewish" battle-cry, "We do not want Christ to rule over us."[45]

The Catholic press in Poland followed the lead of the bishops in

---

[40] *Wiadomości Archidiecezalne Warszawskie* (1934) 49-60.

[41] August Cardinal Hlond, *Na Straży Sumienia Narodu* (Ramsey, NJ: Don Bosco, 1951) 53-75.

[42] Hlond 164-65.

[43] *Wiadomości Archidiecezalne Warszawskie* (1934) 248-49.

[44] *Ruch Katolicki* (1933) 387-90.

[45] *Mały Dziennik*, October 29, 1936.

their struggle for a Catholic Poland. That meant opposing civil marriage and divorce and combatting liberal efforts on behalf of religiously neutral public schools. Pope Pius XI had insisted that Catholics had a right to schools in which all the teachers were Catholic and the entire organization was under the supervision of the Church.[46] In Poland that meant that Catholic pupils were not to share schoolrooms with Jewish children or be taught by Jewish teachers. *Prąd*, a moderate Catholic periodical, acknowledged that Jewish teachers were behaving in a most proper manner, more proper than some nominal Christians. But Jews could not help but represent a culture in conflict with what the children were learning at home and in Church.[47] A much less moderate Catholic periodical simply stated that Jews could not be trusted to teach Catholic children in a Catholic manner because "by background, religion, and history, a Jew was an enemy of Christianity."[48]

The largest publishing center in all of Poland was that founded by Father (now Saint) Maximilian Kolbe and the Conventual Franciscans at Niepokolanów. As a student in Rome, Kolbe received papal approval to found the Knights of the Immaculata, an association to combat Freemasonry. The periodicals emanating from Niepokolanów, regularly linked "Masonic liberalism" with communism and Jews. Their popular monthly *Rycerz Niepokolanej* (The Knight of the Immaculata) explained that "communism and Masonry not only agreed with each other but worked hand in hand toward the same goal, bringing about the savage Jewish dictatorship over the whole world."[49]

Poland had a negligible number of Masons but well over three million Jews. At the opposite extreme, Spain had been virtually *Judenrein* since 1492. But that did not mean that Jews were exonerated from responsibility for Spain's bloody civil war and its anti-clerical atrocities. Entirely without justification, the bishops of Spain in a joint letter blamed the civil war and its atrocities on Spanish communists and liberals. Individual bishops, however, were more explicit. Cardinal Isidor Goma of Toledo designated the war as a punishment for secularism: "The Jews and Masons had poisoned the national soul with

---

[46]Carlen 3:365.
[47]*Prąd* 28 (1935) 3-6.
[48]*Przewodnik Katolicki*, 40 (1934) 642.
[49]*Rycerz Niepokolanej* (1938) 228-30.

absurd doctrines."[50] Bishop Feliciano Rocha Pizarro of Plasencia denounced "communism, Judaism, and Masonry in an infernal amalgamation" to destroy Spanish civilization. Bishop Albino Menendez Reigada of Tenerife attacked "international Marxists and the great Jewish press lords" for publishing calumnies against Spain.[51] For Bishop Antonio Garcia Garcia of Tuy, the war between Spain's liberal Republicans and Francisco Franco's right-wing nationalists was simply a war "waged by Anti-Christ, that is by Judaism, against the Catholic Church and against Christ."[52]

Between Poland and Spain there was Germany, where Bishop Gröber of Freiburg im Breisgau defined Marxism as founded by "the Jew Karl Marx" and "led mostly by Jewish agitators and revolutionaries."[53] Austria's Bishop Alois Hudal, living and working in Rome, defended the 1935 Nuremberg race laws that disenfranchised Germany's Jews; he pointed out that in the nineteenth century it was the liberal state and not the Church that had first torn down the walls of the ghetto.[54] Earlier Bishop Johannes Gfoellner of Linz, Austria, called on Catholics to combat the pernicious influence that Jews were having over all domains of modern civilization. Bishop Maurice Landrieux of Dijon, France, criticized the Talmud for promoting the idea of Jewish world domination. And Bishop Ottocar Prohaszka of Hungary denounced "this so-called Liberalism that expels us from our own house to hand it over 'liberally' to Jewry."[55]

In the United States, such statements were cited in self-defense by Father Charles Coughlin for his own anti-Semitic diatribes.[56] Coughlin's major inspiration, however, was a priest-professor in Ireland, Father Denis Fahey. Fahey, who studied in Rome during the

---

[50]Hugh Thomas, *The Spanish Civil War* (New York: Harper, 1977) 512.

[51]Victor Manuel Arbeloa, "Anticlericalismo y guerra civil," *Lumen* 24 (1975) 171, 260, 264.

[52]*Social Justice*, August 21, 1939.

[53]Guenter Lewy, *The Catholic Church and Nazi Germany* (New York: McGraw, 1964) 277.

[54]Gerhart Binder, *Irrtum und Widerstand: Die deutschen Katholiken in der Auseinandersetzung mit dem Nationalsozialismus* (Munich: Pfeiffer, 1968) 267-69.

[55]*Social Justice*, December 12, 1938; August 21, 1939.

[56]Ronald Modras, "Father Coughlin and Anti-Semitism: Fifty Years Later," *Journal of Church and State* 31 (1989) 231-47.

integralist, anti-Modernist pontificate of Pius X, argued on the basis of papal encyclicals that those who advocated separation of Church and state were enemies of Christ's kingdom. Putting the Catholic Church on the same level as "heretical sects" and the "Jewish perfidy" was the work of diabolical forces. Freemasonry was one of those diabolical forces, but the "most active and most energetic Masons" and the "leaders of the other Masons" were Jews.[57]

Conclusion

From the age of Augustine to the eighteenth century, a Jew was the "only one possible outsider in a Christian world."[58] Pagans, Manichees, and heretics were outlawed; Jews alone were tolerated, allowed to live as resident aliens, as strangers, in the midst of Roman Catholic Christendom. It could have been otherwise. Jews too could have been put under the ban that other outsiders suffered. They too could have been suppressed. That they were not disallowed can be attributed to the forcefulness and success of Saint Augustine's analogy. Augustine had used any number of biblical metaphors for describing Jews (broken-off olive branches; the carpenters who built the ark but did not enter in; the older brother who serves the younger). But when he argued that Jews should not be killed, it was the analogy of Cain, forced to wander but protected by God with a sign. Jews were "witnesses of their iniquity and our truth."[59]

The influence of Augustine's argument was such that it became the common coin of Western Christendom, disconnected from his name.[60] But it made sense only so long as Jews were socially degraded, legally maintained in a position of inferiority. When Enlightenment thinking

[57]Denis Fahey, *The Kingship of Christ According to the Principles of St. Thomas Aquinas* (Dublin: Browne and Nolan, 1931) 144-45. See also his *The Mystical Body of Christ in the Modern World*, 2nd ed. (Dublin: Browne and Nolan, 1938). For an excellent treatment of Coughlin's dependence on Fahey, see Mary C. Athans, *The Coughlin-Fahey Connection: Father Denis Fahey, C.S.Sp., and Religious Anti-Semitism in the United States, 1938-1954* (New York: Lang, 1992).

[58]Peter Brown, *Religion and Society in the Age of Saint Augustine* (New York: Harper, 1972) 141.

[59]See note 11 above.

[60]Blumenkranz 240.

endorsed the equal rights of individuals, when the French Revolution reduced the Catholic Church to equality with other religious bodies, the analogy of Cain no longer held. More sinister analogies were devised, as Jews, among the foremost beneficiaries of the French Revolution, were identified with the Revolution's reputed architects, the Freemasons. As such, Jews were no longer merely alien but subversive, advancing if not engineering the disestablishment of the Catholic Church and the secularization of formerly Catholic cultures.

Just as much as the statement on Jews (*Nostra aetate*), the Second Vatican Council's declaration on religious liberty (*Dignitatis humanae*), constituted a revolution in Catholic thinking. Prior to the council, the prevailing Catholic teaching was that only one faith could be true, and error had no rights. Thanks to the theological arguments of American Jesuit, John Courtney Murray, the council broke with that essentially anti-liberal stance and taught that neither truth nor error, only people have rights, in virtue of their human dignity, whether they are in error or not.

Obviously this teaching has implications which the Catholic Church's pastoral leaders have yet to develop, implications not only for the nature of just governments but for defining the appropriate role of the Church in modern pluralist society. Not all governments with established Churches or religions necessarily discriminate against religious minorities or dissenters. But experience argues that separation of religion and state make both for better government and better religion. The new possibilities for dialogue, cooperation, and respect among Christians and between Christians and Jews would have been unthinkable without the kind of democratic thinking traditionalist Catholics once called Masonic.

If co-existence as strangers no longer describes the appropriate relationship between Christians and Jews, it is not thanks to any extrapolations from traditional Catholic (let alone Augustinian) thinking. The concept of a "spiritual bond" between Christians and Jews has replaced estrangement, but not only because of appeals to biblical sources. Catholic theologians and pastoral leaders have yet to acknowledge the Church's indebtedness to its Enlightenment critics and the secular state.

10

FUNDAMENTALISM

How Catholics Approach It

William M. Shea

Interpretations of texts have suppositions that are more or less known by the author and the interpreter. A text has not only an author who means something and an community to which the text is addressed (in fact or in imagination), but also a "communal authorship," a tradition, a stance which promotes as well as limits the author's intention and composition. The same is true of an interpreter. Here we deal with "Catholic" materials, that is, the texts have Catholic authors and communities of reception; furthermore, behind its authors are a Catholic tradition and a communal authorship. This means little more than the old Catholic claim that the scriptures are the "book of the Church," the Church creating as well as listening to them. The community is "behind" the text and "in front" of it. *Mutatis mutandis*, the same is true of the novels of John Updike whose audience in front includes Catholics and whose community behind is secularized Protestantism.

As David Tracy has pointed out, all communities and traditions are morally ambiguous.[1] No one yet stands in the City on the Hill. We need a term that will highlight the pre-reflective character of the community's cohesion in meaning and value, as well as the inescapable ambiguity of its moral character. The community is a product of first order intentionality and practice (that is, it is built), and its intensity and necessity bring to birth both a life-giving inclusivity and a death-dealing exclusivity. In the sixth and seventh chapters of Bernard Lonergan's *Insight: A Study of Human Understanding* we find a fascinating discussion of scotosis and group bias, and in that discussion he regards not only what may be the case but also what is in fact the

[1]David Tracy, *Plurality and Ambiguity* (San Francisco: Harper, 1987).

case: the Fall envelops all.[2] We must take it for granted that we are bent by our interests and the accumulated interests of our communities. To put the matter in the terms suggested by the theme of these essays, when the stranger appears he or she becomes not only an object of curiosity but also one of awe and fear, and, in the presence of the stranger, the moral ambiguity of the community is exposed.[3] It is faced once again by a *krisis*, by a call for judgment and decision.

At the outset, then, I should like to say something about tribes and tribalism. By the term I mean an important element of religion and culture, but also an important element in the horizon of the interpreter of religion. The term in this context is not a metaphor of opprobrium. We can ill afford to look down on tribes, for we belong to them; without them we are nothing. By tribe I mean the community established by bonds of common experience, understanding, and inter-subjectivity that set a people apart in the sea of humanity: the tribe has its common past and its hopes for the future.[4] The family, the extended family, the clan, the ethnic group, the people, the nation, even the political party would more or less fall under my usage, but so, too, do the Catholic Church and such Enlightenment movements as Marxism and secular humanism.

Even the modern academic class, a child of the Enlightenment, is a tribe, although not an especially cohesive or attractive one. Few academics, for example, have ever been heard to say "I regret I have but one life to give for my university." But the tribe excludes as well as includes, it not only distinguishes but it draws lines beyond the pale of which are those about whom the tribe cares not. The term "tribe" brings out that moral ambiguity more sharply for our purposes than the more morally neutral "community."

We may belong to several tribes and find our loyalties divided among them. I for example, am a Roman Catholic, an American citizen, an academic theologian, a student of religions, a Democrat, and confess that I do not find my multiple tribal membership at all easy. In addition, we may be at odds with other members of our

---

[2]Bernard Lonergan, *Insight: A Study of Human Understanding* (New York: Philosophical Library, 1957) 191-206, 214-41.

[3]Darrell Fasching, *Narrative Theology after Auschwitz: From Alienation to Ethics* (Minneapolis: Fortress, 1992).

[4]I.M. Lewis, "Tribal Society," in *International Encyclopedia of the Social Sciences*, 1968 ed.

tribes—witness the liberal-conservative split which runs across the Christian Churches in the United States.[5] The ample number of tribal memberships possible for us characterizes the modern world—it is called pluralism by academics. There were always many tribes, but I doubt that there ever was an equal possibility of multiple memberships—perhaps with the exception of Hellenistic culture with regard to religion.

Moreover, the tribe today often recognizes itself as such, not as the norm of the human as was reportedly the rule in tribal, archaic, and classical cultures, but now as one tribe among many, in relation to others, a situation which counters claims to normativity. Nazism and the Communist movements are counter-examples to this claim, but they remain the aberration rather than the rule in the twentieth century.

There is a certain irony to this pluralism: the Enlightenment, which is at least in part responsible for it, is responsible by indirection, for the Enlightenment set out to liberate us from the old tribes in favor of a new tribe, a universal tribe of the Enlightened which would embrace all, if only the Enlightened could get the rest of us into public schools and keep us there until we are civilized.[6] This is typical, for tribes suspect one another. One of their characteristics is suspicion of the stranger and unease in the presence of the strange. The tribe lives by its inherited common sense wisdom and aesthetics, and by its unquestioned and unquestioning group loyalty, and the stranger threatens these. When the tribe meets the stranger or a tribe of strangers, there is swift recognition "They are not us," and the conclusion that "They are perverse insofar as they are not like us," and the imperative, "Draw the wagons round." The modern world, the modern mind, the left wing of modern culture has been suspicious of the old religious tribes, their traditions and their authorities, and deeply hostile to them, as well they might be.

The irony is twofold: the Enlightenment meant to transcend tribalism and became another tribe in its very efforts to destroy

---

[5]See Robert Wuthnow, *The Struggle for America's Soul* (Grand Rapids, MI: Eerdmans, 1989); see also William Shea, "Divided Loyalties," *Commonweal* 119 (9 January 1992) 9-14.

[6]Dewey's theory of education is perhaps the best example of this. See John Dewey, *Democracy and Education* (New York: Macmillan, 1966), and John Dewey, *A Common Faith* (New Haven: Yale UP, 1934). On classicism, see Bernard Lonergan, *Method in Theology* (New York: Herder, 1972).

tribalism; and, second, the Enlightenment thereby set conditions in place which assured the resurgence of tribalism, for, in its destruction of the "old ways," myths, and traditions, it left a vacuum which its own spare myths of progress and equality could not possibly fill, a vacuum soon to be filled at times with new and raw versions of the ancient myths.[7] Some of the worst of that resurgence we see in the ethnic war in Bosnia and acts of racism in Germany; some of the best we see in the persistence and renewal of ethnic communities in other parts of central Europe and in the United States, and, above all, in the survival and health of the Western Jewish and Christian tribes and the renewed vigor of Islam.

But these are high and great matters. I have in mind a much narrower and more lowly focus: tribalism and the study of fundamentalism. The bonds of affection and loyalty over time and the sharing of meaning which constitute religious communities are ambiguous. The religious tribe not only gives life and spirit and provides the beginning of any understanding we possess, it also breeds bias, it blocks understanding, it demands a loyalty that cuts into the very freedom that brought it into existence.

Religious tribes, like others, outlaw the very questions of meaning and value that constituted them in the first place. Christianity whose foundation involves a Man who is regarded as a Stranger and even, by his murderers at very least, an enemy and a Christianity, which itself has claims to universality, can only contradict itself when it outlaws the stranger and oppresses the strange in its midst. It would appear that this tribe's very existence and meaning is bound up with welcoming the stranger as the bearer of God. A tribe which presents itself as the "one true tribe" and separates itself from its many less true neighboring tribes has only a surface logic in its favor, for it acts on the logic of survival, the ordinary logic of the tribe; it has lost the logic of its Master who, according to its own traditions, did not choose survival over other values. What may be expected in view of historical tribal warfare may become an irony indeed if the tribe claiming eternal affinity with the Stranger-in-our-midst should become, in the attitudes

---

[7]Ernst Cassirer, *The Myth of the State* (New York: Doubleday, 1955); John Herman Randall, *The Meaning of Religion for Man* (New York: Harper, 1968); and Carl Raschke, *The Interruption of Eternity: Modern Gnosticism and the Origins of the New Religious Consciousness* (Chicago: Nelson-Hall, 1980).

and action of his earthly body the Church, the systematic enemy of all that is strange.

Enlightenment liberalism, as was remarked above, does not escape ambiguity. It set out to teach us all tolerance, yet has not gotten beyond patronizing and scornful tolerance toward the old religious and ethnic tribes. The "mere tolerance" of the Enlightenment carries in its bosom a secret wish for my death and the death of my tribe. At bottom, the Enlightenment tribe doesn't think the others should exist. No wonder then, that the others, the religious tribes of Christians such as the Catholics and the fundamentalists, retain their antagonistic attitudes toward Western tribes descendent from the Enlightenment—political tribes like liberals and socialists, cultural elites like the academic tribe, and task-based tribes like the bureaucrats.

The instinct of the modern tribe for survival and for dominance of the environment (whether literal or metaphorical), and so on, has little changed, though its specific forms differ markedly in many instances from older examples. The modern and post-modern tribes, too, confront the stranger in ways continuous with the ancient forms. In the first essay to this volume Bernhard Asen lays out for us the biblical understandings of the stranger and of the stranger's basically ambiguous self-presentation, an ambiguity which puts the tribe in moral crisis. Thus, not only the sojourner in Israel is the stranger, but Yahweh and Jesus may be the Stranger; and the hated stranger (the Samaritan) may turn out to be the neighbor to one in need. Thus, the response of the Christian and Jew to the stranger is complicated well beyond politics, economics, inter-tribal rules of hospitality, and even the memory of a former state of oppression. The stranger can be a bearer of God.

As Catholics have been found strangers to Protestant Americans throughout our history, and to secularist Americans in the twentieth century, the secularist period of hegemony, so fundamentalists now present themselves to Catholics as strangers and even enemies, and fundamentalists so regard Catholics. I intend in the rest of this essay to analyze the literature on American fundamentalism produced by American Catholic academic and ministerial leaders over the past two decades. It reveals the moral ambiguity of the tribe confronted by the stranger very well.

Approaching the Literature

Catholic reactions to American Protestant fundamentalism began in the wake of the political and cultural resurgence of evangelicalism marked publicly by the election of Jimmy Carter in 1976. The Catholic anti-Protestantism of the centuries prior to the Second Vatican Council made no significant distinction between mainline and evangelical Protestantism, and so in twentieth century America no particular distinction set off fundamentalism from Protestantism in general. A change occurred when the Second Vatican Council fueled Catholic theological interest in the achievements of Protestant theologians; consequently, in both popular and scholarly publication, study and dialogue replaced the wariness of pre-Second Vatican Council days. But in 1976 it became clear that there is another Protestantism, in addition to our new found ecumenical friends, and that this Protestantism has its effect in politics and, above all, it poses threats to Catholic belief and practice. As the ecumenical dialogue with mainline Protestantism matured, it more and more sharply set off evangelicals and fundamentalists from other Protestants.[8]

Between 1976 and 1992 over eighty essays were published in Catholic periodicals, ranging from scholarly analyses in journals aimed at pastors and intellectuals to articles and columns in the national Catholic weekly press (diocesan newspapers, with one exception, are not included in this study); over thirty of those essays appeared in journal issues dedicated entirely to fundamentalism; in addition, five general readership monographs and one collection of scholarly essays on fundamentalism were published by Catholic theologians; and there were at least five public statements by American bishops on fundamentalism and one document issued by the Vatican which touches directly upon Catholic attitudes toward "sects and new religions." While not massive (it would be outweighed considerably by the Catholic literature on abortion and on peace and justice questions), the literature is significant. In terms of popular publications for Catholics, this stream replaces the earlier flood of literature on mainline Protestantism.[9]

---

[8]See Wuthnow.

[9]There are hermeneutical problems in approaching this body of literature, beginning with wide variety of types. The literature may be classified (1) by

Sorting out the literature on the basis of its reactions to fundamentalism poses a problem. A good deal of the literature is common sense history and description, with predictable doctrinal contrasts which are accurate as far as they go, but which are of very little theological interest and value. The literature gets interesting when particular theological insights flash, when the common is put in a particularly clear fashion, when strategies of response are developed and promoted, when particularly abysmal ignorance is displayed, and when the canons of a methodical theology and even Christian virtue are violated. The literature, while it is as complex as the Church which spawns it, is not especially profound. How should one approach it?

Three questions arise, questions from the point of view of which we may read the literature, as a whole and as individual pieces. The questions are these: (1) *Is the literature intellectually serious and responsible?* Does it exhibit clarity on what it wishes to understand and does it approach the subject from a theoretic standpoint or not? What unquestioned suppositions are at work? Are there major problems of method in theology?

(2) *Insofar as the literature is pastoral* (most, if not all, of this literature is such), *is it pastorally responsible?* What are its goals and are they worthy? What are the strategies of response adopted and urged, and are they worthy—or are the strategies in conflict with the religious message which they can be presumed to rest on? Are there problems of justice and charity? Does the literature propose new pastoral strategies in the face of a new challenge—or are we being

literary form: reflective essay, scholarly (historical or theological) assessment, apologetic, polemic, exposé, dialogue, homily; (2) by strategy of response: denigration, caricature, methodological reduction, dialectical argument, irenic approach, irony, alarms, pastoral self-reflection aimed at reform, reactive doctrinal instruction; (3) by audience: the American church as a whole or, in the case of the Vatican statement, the universal church, theologians, ministers/clergy, lay and clerical intellectuals, church-going Catholics, other Christians, fundamentalists (rarely), college constituencies such as campus ministers, right or left wing Catholics depending on the bias of the medium; (4) by media: official ecclesiastical statements, popular monographs, articles in academic journals, articles in pastoral-professional journals, edited collections of essays, general religious intellectual periodicals, popular periodicals and newspapers; (5) by author: academic theologians or other professors, bishops, campus ministers, concerned lay persons or ministers, journalists; (6) by theology: location on the spectrum of Catholic theological options, and theological quality or level. These distinctions and classifications are at work throughout this essay.

handed a (modified) version of an old strategy indicating that the enemy is not new at all? Specifically, in this case, is it more of the same old "Catholic versus Protestant" stuff or is there something else going on?

(3) *Finally, and most difficult of all to ascertain, what does the literature reveal about the authors and their concerns about the present condition of the Catholic Church?* Does the literature reveal currents of unsettlement or conflict? Anxiety? Fear? Resentment? Bad conscience? Attitudes of superiority? Lack of genuine interest in the subject matter? Double consciousness: the manipulation of the overt (ecclesially external) subject matter for other covert (ecclesially internal) objectives?

I shall use these three questions to address three different sorts of literature: first, the periodical literature ranging from academic/pastoral journals to newspapers; second, five books which more amply display Catholic attitudes (discretely omitting the collection of essays I have edited); and, finally, six pieces of literature which serve as a sample of the response of the Roman Catholic hierarchy. Finally, at the end, I shall attempt a characterization of the literature as a whole.

Periodical Literature

Of the some eighty essays which have been written by Catholics on fundamentalism since 1976, none is to be found in a Catholic scholarly journal.[10] Not one of the essays has fundamentalists among its intended readers. Fewer than a handful seem to envisage scholars among their readers, and most are written for those engaged in ministry, the theologically literate lay audience, and for the readers of the weekly Catholic press.

---

[10]For example, the indexes of *Theological Studies, The Thomist, Horizons: The Journal of the College Theology Society* list none. Only one of the essays to be discussed appeared in *Theological Studies*, and that is a general piece on sects and cults and not chiefly on fundamentalism. See John A. Saliba, "The Christian Church and the New Religious Movements," *Theological Studies* 43 (1982) 468-85. The closest one comes to scholarly journals in our list are those which publish materials by scholars for the non-specialist but theologically interested audience of intellectuals, such as the *Biblical Theology Review, Communio,* and *The Bible Today.*

Although many are well-informed, they are so almost entirely by virtue of their familiarity with scholarly and critical literature on fundamentalism and few reveal any direct acquaintance with the primary literature of fundamentalist history and doctrine.[11] As a whole the literature makes plain the fact that Catholics are not in the slightest interested in fundamentalism as a phenomenon in its own right, but only insofar as it poses a "pastoral problem." All of the literature, in other words, has a pastoral as distinct from an academic interest, and so a close reading of secondary sources will do: evangelical histories such as those of Marsden, Noll, and Hatch, mainline Protestant anti-fundamentalist polemic (Barr's books), and works of serious "American Studies" scholarship (Sandeen).[12]

The most evident distinction in the literature is between those essays which seek to inform Catholics *about* fundamentalist belief and practice and to contrast it with Catholic belief and practice, leaving the critique of fundamentalism muted and indirect, on one hand, and those essays in which a direct argument *against* fundamentalism is mounted, on the other. Those in the latter class typically attempt to explain fundamentalism, its attractiveness and its growth, as an aberration of the age, while the former typically attempt to set up comparisons which will lead to a clarified commitment to Catholicism. Much of the literature explicitly or implicitly regards fundamentalism as a radically incomplete, not to say "false" Christianity (there are some exceptions), as inadequate or distorted. In terms of explanations," many of the essays link American fundamentalism to a perceived rise of religious

---

[11]The two essays which display interest in fundamentalist literature itself are: John McCarthy, "Inspiration and Trust: Toward Narrowing the Gap between Fundamentalist and Higher Biblical Scholarship," in *The Struggle Over the Past: Fundamentalism in the Modern World*, ed. William M. Shea (Lanham, MD: U Press of Am, 1993) 121-36, and Zachary Hayes, "Fundamentalist Eschatology: Piety and Politics," *New Theology Review* 1 (May 1988) 21-35.

[12]George Marsden, *Fundamentalism and American Culture: The Shaping of Twentieth Century Evangelicalism, 1870-1925* (New York: Oxford UP, 1980); Mark A. Noll, *A History of Christianity in the United States and Canada* (Grand Rapids, MI: Eerdmans, 1992); Nathan Hatch and Mark Noll, eds., *The Bible in America: Essays in Cultural History* (New York: Oxford UP, 1982); James Barr, *Beyond Fundamentalism* (Philadelphia: Westminster, 1984); *Fundamentalism* (Philadelphia: Westminster, 1978); and Ernest Robert Sandeen, *The Roots of Fundamentalism: British and American Millenarianism, 1800-1930* (Chicago: U of Chicago P, 1970).

fundamentalism world-wide, and some link it with what is called by some "Roman Catholic fundamentalism."

While many of the essay are pastorally serious, very few of them are academically serious. That is, they do not get beyond the commonplace in areas such as biblical hermeneutics and ecclesiology. They mean to report and give advice, but not to open up questions or establish new questions and research possibilities. While some raise serious questions about current Catholic practice, none raise questions about fundamentalism which lead to more inquiry. A few are irenic (and fewer yet ironic!), a good number appeal to Catholics to ponder the lessons for the Catholic Church arising from the conversions of millions of Catholics to fundamentalist Churches, and these sometimes offer critical reflections on the current state of the Catholic Church as a basic condition permitting the defection of Catholics.

Since a report on the contents of over eighty essays is out of the question, I shall discuss a relatively few representative pieces and relegate comparable ones to footnotes. The mass is divided under the following six categories: essays by scholars for a theologically literate audience; essays in popular journals and weekly newspapers; essays which display a marked tendency to reduce fundamentalism to individual and social psychological aberration; essays which are deeply if not primarily concerned with the phenomenon of a "Catholic fundamentalism"; a review of four journals which devote an issue entirely or in greater part to essays on fundamentalism; discussion of five books; and, finally, episcopal and Vatican statements.

Scholars for a Theological Audience

To Brigid Frein's "Fundamentalism and Narrative Approaches to the Gospels,"[13] an essay on hermeneutical possibilities, there is appended

---

[13]Brigid Curtin Frein, "Fundamentalism and Narrative Approaches to the Gospels," *Biblical Theology Bulletin* 22 (1992) 12-18. Not discussed in this essay is the volume on fundamentalism edited by Hans Kung. Though it does contain essays by Catholics and on Catholic fundamentalism, it is chiefly concerned with international and world religions fundamentalism rather than with either American or Protestant fundamentalism, and the only one among its authors who is considered a Catholic theologian is Hans Kung himself and his contribution is concerned with fundamentalism in Catholicism. See Hans Kung and Jurgen

a bibliography which is long on works of critical hermeneutical theory and short on works by fundamentalists and evangelicals. She refers to two collections of essays by evangelical and fundamentalist hermeneuts,[14] and her "main source" for the fundamentalist approach is the "Chicago Statement on Biblical Hermeneutics," printed in the collection of essays by Radmacher and Preus. The essay is a careful and respectful contrast of the two "approaches," including the presuppositions, methods, and goals of the two. The two share certain characteristics. Both take the gospels as unified compositions rather than compilations of previously independent units; both are primarily concerned with the general reader's understanding of the text rather than with an audience of technicians of historical-critical method; and both have a lack of confidence in historical method's ability to shed light on the meaning of the text.

But the approaches collide irreparably on several counts: inerrancy, the unity of the Bible as a whole, and the goals of interpretation (the intention of the individual author versus the openness of the text to multiple interpretations which go beyond the intention of the author): narrative approaches are at odds with the fundamentalist doctrines of exact historicity and of the mono-significance of the text and...cannot be used as a way of avoiding the difficulties of historical critical approaches."[15] The essay is aimed at an audience not only of theological interest but of some theoretic sophistication. She treats fundamentalism as a hermeneutical option and in no way as a competing religious movement. Her criticism of it moves with the same deliberation as if she were addressing the limits and glories of Marxist literary criticism.[16]

Moltmann, eds., *Fundamentalism as an Ecumenical Challenge*, Concilium (London: SCM Press, 1992).

[14]E. D. Radmacher and Robert D. Preus, eds., *Hermeneutics, Inerrancy and the Bible* (Grand Rapids: Zondervan, 1984), and Donald McKim, ed., *A Guide to Contemporary Hermeneutics: Major Trends in Biblical Interpretation* (Grand Rapids: Eerdmans, 1986).

[15]Frein 16.

[16]Below, in a discussion of the contents of an issue of *New Theology Review*, I will refer to the essay of Zachary Hayes whose discussion of fundamentalist hermeneutics rivals Frein's essay for detachment. For another essay by a Catholic biblicist, but in a journal aimed at a less sophisticated audience, see Leslie Hoppe, "The Bible Tells Me So," *The Bible Today* 29 (1991) 279-84. His point is that dispensationalist interpretation contradicts itself in that it does not interpret

Clifford G. Kossel writes in the conservative journal, *Communio*.[17] Aimed at Roman Catholic intellectuals, the essay promotes a mutually critical and constructive engagement of the Moral Majority by Catholic conservatives. While the approaches to politics by the two groups may differ, significant features in common remain. There are fundamentals, after all, of the Christian faith which are non-negotiable and are expressed in the creeds of the Church and which can serve as the basis for cooperation. But there are differences as well which need attention, namely "ecclesial unity and the relationship of Christianity to culture."[18]

Catholic ecclesial unity is built on the eucharist which constitutes the body of Christ; the eucharist along with the magisterium allows Catholics a gradualist and open attitude toward cultural change. The Catholic struggles over the direction of culture and its implications for faith

> are not carried out without a great deal of controversy about the boundaries of orthodoxy and about the strategies employed. Nor is it without some confusion, shock, pain, and losses. But the Eucharist goes on and the Magisterium stands, the two centers of the whirlwind.... [But] it is difficult to understand how a group which apparently has no inherent principles to prevent religious fragmentation can supply a public philosophy to put brakes on the individualist-pluralist tendencies in our society.[19]

Thus, the argument of Isaac Hecker and, more recently, of Richard Neuhaus, is revived[20]—Catholicism has the ability to provide a public philosophy, while the Moral Majority (fundamentalists) cannot appeal to the broad public (they can argue publicly only on biblical grounds) and tends to divide the world between "good guys" and "bad guys." The Catholic retention of the natural law argument and a universal appeal to reason, along with its ability to stand back critically from

the text literally at all, but through a set of non-biblical beliefs.

[17]Clifford G. Kossel, "The Moral Majority and Christian Politics," *Communio: International Catholic Review* 9 (1982) 339-54.

[18]Ibid. 346.

[19]Ibid. 348.

[20]Isaac Hecker, *The Church and the Age: An Exposition of the Catholic Church in View of the Needs and Aspirations of the Present Age* (New York: Office of the Catholic World, 1887), and Richard J. Neuhaus, *The Catholic Moment: The Paradox of Church in the Postmodern World* (San Francisco: Harper, 1987).

capitalist economic theory and national interest politics, makes its contribution to the public debate firmer and steadier.

But fundamentalism has its gifts to bring. First, there is its emphasis on the importance of education of the young at the very time Catholics schools have been decreasing; second, the fundamentalists are setting the example by their activist role in politics for the sake of Christian values. In sum:

> Catholics, then, have reason to applaud the active participation of the Evangelicals in the political process and to support several of their positions. On the religious plane Evangelicals do not seem very open to ecumenical moves, but they may be ready for some advances in the social and political areas. Certainly we must be honest about our differences, but Catholics might contribute to the broadening of their perspectives and a toning down of their more abrasive (and counter-productive) tactics. And Evangelicals might communicate to us some of their vigor and enthusiasm—as well as their skills in organization and in the use of electronic media.[21]

The author sees practical and convictional avenues of cooperation without confusing the profound differences in ecclesiology and culture. The essay is a model of constructive criticism, entirely without anti-fundamentalist ranting, polemic, and stereotyping. The attitude displayed here in matters of political cooperation might be displayed again on religious and theological issues, with what success or avidity it is hard to say. Kossel's essay, however, does not entirely fit the profile of this investigation, for the subject matter is cooperation with conservative evangelicals and not their wilder and more virulently anti-Catholic cousins, and the author is not concerned with the state of relations between Catholics and these people. Kossel refers in footnotes to the "usual suspects" Marsden and Barr, and to a few essays on evangelicals and politics. The essay itself is a piece of contemporary relevance, more an editorial than a piece of scholarship. It is distinguished by its balanced and constructive approach rather than any expert knowledge of fundamentalism.

Roy Barkley, an "orthodox" and "loyal" Catholic (thus distinguishing himself from liberal and presumably heterodox Catholics) and member of the Fellowship of (orthodox and loyal?) Catholic Scholars, is an author, editor, scholar of Middle English who

[21]Kossel 354.

is a convert to Catholic Church from "hardbitten Fundamentalism."[22]
In the wake of the *America* special issue in 1986 (reviewed below),
Barkley wants to set the record straight on what fundamentalism is,
why Catholics join the movement, and what to do about it:

> The authors [of the essays in *America*] consider themselves an intellectual
> in-group and speak with the condescending evasion that Fundamentalist
> attitudes are too simpleminded to argue against. Furthermore, they fuse
> Catholicism with mainline Protestantism, a juncture which yields bogus
> ecumenism and a bemused revulsion to Fundamentalist proselytizing.
> There, one suspects, is the rub: the centrifugalist Church is flinging droves
> of Catholics to Fundamentalist communions which, though theologically
> confused, are still capable of winning converts, a capacity increasingly
> moribund among mainline groups. The prospect of the "American" Church
> casting out modern Fundamentalism by the use of Modernism...is scarcely
> less hopeful than the attempt to cast out Beelzebub in his own name.[23]

The problem with fundamentalism is not, as liberals claim, its
biblical *literalism*—on selected texts Catholics are as literal as they and
they are as "symbolic" as Catholic exegetes!—but biblical *legalism*, a
fault corresponding to Catholic legalist tendencies. Barkley joins other
Catholics in the claim that the Bible is the book of the Church as the
expression of *its* truth and the locus of its learning. The difference is
ecclesiological, and profound, but that is the difference between
Catholics and all Protestants, and between "loyal" and "dissenting"
Catholics, the latter having joined the Protestant camp on the matter.
Protestants and liberal Catholics do not believe that the Holy Spirit
guides the Church, and do believe that the Holy Spirit speaks finally
in individuals.

But, Barkley maintains, loyal Catholics and fundamentalists have in
common at least a belief in the sinfulness of the world so evidently
displayed in the host of "social issues" confronting us. In addition,
their attitudes toward scripture are "vastly preferable to the
'rationalistic prejudices' that vitiate much modern exegesis."[24] Again,
its problem is not literalism but the legalism arising from a text torn
out of its ecclesial interpretative matrix, its "tradition."

---

[22]Roy Barkley, "The Fundamentalist Threat," *Homiletic and Pastoral Review*
88 (February 1988) 45-53. See page 46 on "hardbitten."
[23]Ibid. 45.
[24]Ibid. 48.

Fundamentalism's problem is that it is Protestant, in its centrifugalism as well as its anti-Catholicism.

Catholics leave the Church because its modernist elements have undercut the Church's ability to provide a reasonable certitude of the truths of faith, and have substituted for it self-worship and subjectivism. What the Church needs in order to stem the tide toward fundamentalism is a reaffirmation of its identity. Finally, his strategy for dealing with the fundamentalist *facies ad faciem* echoes that suggested by Karl Keating, another "orthodox" Catholic, whose book is discussed below: do not duck the important arguments, argue quietly and with conviction, stick with the priority of the Church, express the *whole* teaching of the Church (none of the "dissenters'" selectivism), and "fear no threats; trust God for the harvest."[25]

Barkley's is among the best of the Catholic essays: clear and accurate in its presentation of fundamentalist positions, direct and tough in its criticism of those positions, realistic and charitable in its estimate of the fundamentalist strengths and weakness, and just in its contrasts of fundamentalism with Catholic doctrine and culture. One could hardly ask for more, except perhaps for a more nuanced and charitable judgment of Catholic liberals and mainline Protestants!

For the General Catholic Public

The popular Catholic press (monthly and weekly magazines and national and diocesan weekly newspapers) present us with a decidedly mixed bag of Catholic responses. First, there are essays which respond to fundamentalism with something more than concern and something less than magisterial calm, and of these I shall discuss two very briefly. Then I shall take five examples of essays which, though obviously concerned with the "fundamentalist challenge," take it all quite calmly and judiciously, and offer a strategy of response-by-contrast. Essays of these two sorts are samples of the body of periodical literature, and reflect attitudes which can be found mixed in all of it.

[25]Ibid. 53. For other expressions of orthodox Catholicism see Karl Keating, *Catholicism and Fundamentalism: The Attack on "Romanism" by "Bible Christians"* (San Francisco: Ignatius, 1988), and Steve Clarke, "Those Terrible Fundamentalists," *New Covenant* 18 (January 1989) 9-10. Comments on Keating's book are found below.

Mary Ann Walsh, in "Fundamentalists Give the Bible a Bad Name,"[26] uses a few horror stories of fundamentalist incursion to set up a review of the weaknesses of American Catholicism, and accounts for the defection from the latter to fundamentalism in terms of those weaknesses. She does so for a general Catholic readership. Fundamentalism is scored as "anti-intellectual...closed," unable to handle issues of literary form and historicity of the biblical narrative, pushy and intrusive. Catholics, on the other hand, are vulnerable to conversion for several reasons, among them: poor education in the Bible, a shallow spiritual life, absence of knowledge of their heritage, a weakened sense of identity, a less than engaging experience and sense of community, and poor preaching. ("When was the last time you heard a good homily?") The answer to the problem is clear: "Teach people how to read the Bible!," intensify spiritual life, clarify identity, improve community. The statement of the problem, the analysis of the causes, and the suggested remedies are all typical of the Catholic literature.

Richard Chilson, whose book is discussed below, contributed to the *America* special issue on fundamentalism.[27] Maintaining that "the fundamentalist threat in our country is more real than the Communist threat ever was, yet little is being done in response," Chilson launches into a critical listing of "fundamentalist perversions": its gospel is a version of the American dream rather than a re-presentation of the gospel of Jesus; its understanding of conversion is inadequate to the facts of Christian experience which reveal it to be "a lifelong process of discernment, change and growth nurtured in authentic community"; it abstracts the Bible from the Church; compassion for the sinner is available only at the price of conversion; and its stands against the doctrine of the goodness of creation. He calls on Catholics to "mount a massive response to the fundamentalist threat. It is time to give time, money, talent and energy to face an enemy that openly threatens in the public media to bury us."[28]

---

[26]Mary Ann Walsh, "Fundamentalists Give the Bible a Bad Name," *U.S. Catholic* 45 (April 1980) 26-32.

[27]Richard Chilson, "A Call to Catholic Action," *America* 155 (27 September 1986) 148-50, 154.

[28]Ibid. 154. See also Mary Frances Reis, "Fundamentalism on the College Campus," *Emmanuel* 94 (1988) 490-97. Mary Frances Reis, at the University of Wisconsin in Milwaukee, wants to inform the "unsuspecting" Catholics about the

By way of contrast, there are essays which are meant to inform Catholics about fundamentalist doctrine and practice, and to set up contrasts between Catholic and fundamentalist doctrine and practice. The aim is pastoral education and retention, which aim it shares with nearly all the Catholic literature. Here we have essays which could serve as the opening statements in a theological dialogue and argument.[29]

Thomas Coskren and the two of the previously mentioned authors (Walsh and Chilson) are in the trenches of the proselytizing wars, the college campuses.[30] But Coskren, at Rutgers University, writes a seriously reflective piece on adolescent fundamentalism, catching both the appeal of Bible study to college age Catholics and the shortcomings of such study, and scoring the lack of a sense of Catholic identity among the young which allows them a move toward such groups. He confesses that he himself, after all his training and his experience as a theology teacher in college, was unprepared "for the emotional power generated by small groups concentrating on the Bible in the shared intimacy of dorm rooms."[31] It has led him to the conviction that Catholics have neglected the power of the liturgically unadorned Word. He, too, lists weak preaching and badly understood liturgical practice, as well as ignorance of the history of the Catholic faith, as faults of contemporary Catholicism—but above all else the "power of the Word" experienced raw and the failure of Catholic communal experience account for the loss of young Catholics.

strategies which await them. Primarily a description of campus crusading and the stages of the conversion process (induction, indoctrination, decision), and the tools for recruiting and retaining, the essay is informative and frightening enough to make a parent of a child about to take off for college more than a bit nervous.

[29]In addition to the essays discussed in the text, the same characteristics of clarity in doctrinal contrast, charity in attitude, and self-criticism are to be found in the following: James R. Higgins, "Which Came First, the Bible or the Church?" *Liguorian* 67 (August 1979) 21-25, and "A Catholic Looks at Fundamentalism," *Liguorian* 69 (October 1981) 48-53; Robert J. Hatter, "Fundamentalism and the Parish," *Church* 4 (Winter 1988) 17-25; Leonard Foley, "Catholics and Fundamentalists: We Agree and Disagree," *St. Anthony Messenger* 91 (July 1983) 15-20; and Peter Kreeft, a series on "Fundamentalists," in each issue of *National Catholic Register* during October 1988.

[30]Thomas M. Coskren, "Fundamentalists on Campus," *New Catholic World* 228 (1985) 38-42.

[31]Ibid. 38.

Francis X. Cleary, wrote the earliest essays on fundamentalism included in our bibliography, and may be the first Catholic theologian to take note of the "fundamentalist challenge"—though he does not call it that. Cleary was (and is) a professor of biblical studies at Saint Louis University. He wrote a series of essays for *Universitas*, the alumni/ae journal of the university.[32] Sharply aware of the post-Second Vatican Council turn in Catholic exegesis from a primarily historical and apologetic methodology to more historical and literary critical methods, and at the same time aware of the attraction of fundamentalist Bible study groups for adult Catholics, Cleary in his first piece sketches the development of historical investigation from Pius XII to the current situation. In the second essay he sketches the conservative reaction in Rome which attempted to repudiate the "new criticism" on the eve of the council. However, this criticism was victorious at the council and afterwards. The council canonized the phrase "religious truth" as distinct from historical and scientific information as the proper subject matter of inerrancy.

In the third and last essay, he recounts the story of fundamentalism in early twentieth century America, and adds that the consequential distinction between fundamentalism and Catholicism is not methods of exegesis but ecclesiology: for Catholics the Bible is the book of the Church, and the Church in its concrete historical existence and practice is the sacrament of the Risen Lord. He ends the series with this commonsensical observation, apparently meant to defuse a more negative reaction to fundamentalists on the part of Catholics:

> Fundamentalist Christians are often unfairly judged. All too often it is an insensitive, pushy, self-righteous minority who are encountered by outsiders. Many live a deeply committed religious life, their local community an enviable source of strength, of warm fellowship and practical example, for daily living.[33]

The restraint shown by Cleary is echoed by American Catholicism's premier biblical scholar, Raymond Brown. His comments on fundamentalism are few, but marked by the same expositional concern

---

[32]Francis X. Cleary, "How is the Bible to be Interpreted?" *Universitas* 2.4 (Spring 1977) 13; "Biblical Inerrancy and the New Criticism," *Universitas* 3.1 (Summer 1977) 11; "Literal Interpretation of the Bible," *Universitas* 3.2 (Autumn 1977) 6.

[33]Cleary, "Literal Interpretation of the Bible" 6.

as Cleary's.[34] In his popular book on the Bible, *Responses to 101 Questions on the Bible*, Brown runs a series of four questions dealing directly with fundamentalism. He distinguishes the correct claim of fundamentalists: that Christianity has fundamental doctrines, from what he regards as its fundamental mistake: "I applaud some of the doctrinal stress of fundamentalists but disagree thoroughly with the method they employ. In my judgment, a literalist reading of the Bible is intellectually indefensible and is quite unnecessary for the defence of the basic Christian doctrines."[35]

The two points in Brown's discussion which are relevant to this inquiry are (1) his analysis of just why Catholics now have a problem with fundamentalism, and (2) what to do about it.[36] The advice to some degree is common enough among Catholic authors: Don't argue over individual texts, for the real issues are much larger (for example, the very nature of the Bible). Don't think they are fools or ignorant, for they are often "extremely intelligent," well informed in archeology and languages, with well developed apologetic arguments. Don't try to convert them too suddenly, for they may lose their faith altogether. Like nearly all of our authors, Brown recognizes the serious institutional failures of Catholicism with regard to the Bible and Bible education, of clergy as well as laity. In fact, with others he maintains that only significant improvement in biblical education and in media use by Catholics, joined by mainline Protestants, will be able to slow the advance of fundamentalism. He also makes the usual plea for smaller and more intense Catholic communities: "We may have to break those parishes down, at least functionally, into smaller groups."[37] Finally, he admits as well that our liturgical language is far less vivid than fundamentalist language about the love of Jesus, and calls for more preaching of that love.[38]

---

[34]Raymond Brown, "Catholic Faith and Fundamentalism," *Priests and People* 5 (1991) 134-36. The points made are nearly identical to the appendix to his book, *Responses to 101 Questions on the Bible* (Mahwah, NJ: Paulist, 1990). In addition, however, the book deals with fundamentalism in Questions 29-33, pp. 40-49. I shall discuss both the essay and the sections of the book here.

[35]Brown, *Responses* 44.

[36]Questions thirty-two through thirty-three.

[37]Ibid. 47.

[38]In an appendix to the book, "Expressing Catholic Faith So That Biblical Fundamentalists Will Not Misunderstand It" (137-42), Brown lines up ten

His explanation for the current (1981) problem is not so typical of his fellow commentators. His explanation is cultural and practical rather than in terms of individual and social psychology. There is not a hint that there is anything pathological or even offensive about fundamentalists. He cites three factors to explain the new confrontation. First, in the 1960s Catholics began to move en masse into the Sun/Bible Belt, and so into the culture of fundamentalism; second, the media explosion of the same period made popular Bible preaching available to Catholics in the Snow as well as Sun Belt; and, third, Catholics left their cultural ghetto in the same period and entered the American economic and social mainstream, a mainstream whose religious *lingua franca* is the Bible rather than the Catholic devotional tradition. The innate attraction of the Bible for all Christians, once it has been discovered, plus the lack of serious biblical education of Catholics and attractive preaching, occasioned the peculiar contact of Catholics with these "new" Protestants. What is noteworthy about Brown's discussion is that the grounds for explanation remains socio-cultural and the blame is not pinned on fundamentalist aggressive proselytizing. The thorny issue is discussed with Brown's usual magisterial calm and devotion to objectivity.

Leonard Foley, in "Catholics and Fundamentalists: We Agree and Disagree," attempts to inform a general readership of the history and nature of American fundamentalism.[39] He traces the history, laying stress on the relationship between fundamentalism and evangelicalism, and confesses that fundamentalism is by no means a simple thing. His criticisms of fundamentalism follow closely the one raised by Falwell and others. He then sets up several points of contrast (inerrancy, inspiration, hermeneutics), and ends with some advice about responding to fundamentalists. We agree on much but disagree on premises; so don't argue biblical texts; rather, take fundamentalism (citing in this regard Eugene LaVerdiere) as a personal, social, and pastoral concern. But Foley does not mean that *fundamentalism* is a

---

questions of particular relevance to a Catholic conversation with fundamentalists, all of them doctrinal, and in each he pushes the doctrinal issue back to its scriptural basis or at very least to texts that shed light on the Catholic doctrinal position. There is no defensiveness or polemic involved.

[39]Foley relies heavily on the 1981 edition of Ed Dobson, Ed Hindson, and Jerry Falwell, *The Fundamentalist Phenomenon: The Resurgence of Conservative Christianity*, 2nd ed. (Grand Rapids: Baker, 1986).

problem (as LaVerdiere does).[40] Foley means that we, Catholics and fundamentalists, share problems and concerns: personally we are all bound in common to preach the gospel; we all share the same upsetting social and economic conditions which need transformation; we all need to stop straining gnats (six days of creation) and swallowing camels (frightful social conditions). We do disagree, but

> we must give both the evangelicals and fundamentalists great credit for their zeal, spirit, enthusiasm, dedication (if not their militancy). Perhaps the most telling criticism a fundamentalist can give (some) Catholic communities was tersely put. ... "You Catholics ain't got no *soul*."[41]

Commonweal, a weekly journal of theology and culture for left-leaning Catholics, published two essays by John Garvey, one asserting the claim that secular humanism is a fundamentalism and the other finding something good to say about Jimmy Swaggart. Garvey's problem with modern and contemporary culture is its smugness and intolerance, its assumption of rightness and its privatization of every opposed point of view. This, of course is a standard critique of modernism in the age of post-modernism, and is common among Catholics, right and left. (Garvey is an Orthodox Christian who publishes regularly in this Catholic journal.) The intolerance of the fundamentalist right is balanced by the intolerance of the humanist left:

> Secular humanists and fundamentalists deserve one another. ... They are equally intolerant. Because liberal intolerance pretends to understand, it is not as obvious as fundamentalist intolerance, which thinks it understands the only thing that matters, and to hell (literally) with anyone with any other point of view. But secular humanist intolerance is clear enough. ... What is incredible is the assumption that religious people indoctrinate, and secular humanists guide people toward truth.[42]

In a cultural situation of this sort, where the public voice of religion and of value is silenced by Enlightenment prejudice, and when it is

---

[40]See, for example, Eugene A. LaVerdiere, "The Challenge of Fundamentalism," *Emmanuel* 94 (1988) 488-89; "There is No Such Thing as a Catholic Fundamentalist," *U.S. Catholic* 54 (September 1989) 36-38; and "Fundamentalism: A Pastoral Concern," *The Bible Today* (1983) 5-11.

[41]Foley 20.

[42]John Garvey, "Made for Each Other: The Fundamentalists-Humanist Complex," *Commonweal* 108 (16 January 1981) 6-8. See p. 7.

clear that the offensiveness of fundamentalists pales before the horrors worked upon human beings by the offspring of the Enlightenment, even fundamentalism has its role:

> Fundamentalists are responding—stupidly, all thumbs—to this situation, which really is a threat in many ways. Right wing Christians may be a little like the canaries coal miners used to take into the mines with them, because they were the first to be affected by poison gas.[43]

So even Jimmy Swaggart, whose ignorance is appalling, has his saving grace:

> The man really is pig-ignorant, as stupid about the limitations of his own very recent version of old-time religion as a man could be and still be able to get dressed in the morning and tie his own shoes. I remember hearing him one morning talk about the dying of a famous atheist, and I couldn't remember ever having heard of Voll Terry, and then I realized that he meant Voltaire. ... He is wrong about a lot of things, terribly wrong, but he seems to be a man who thinks that the Bible is true, and that what can be found in it is meant to transform us. This is the claim which embarrasses us, or part of us. ... They come close to the truth, to the fact that there are moments in our lives when we really must make choices that are just as simple and demanding, and finally saving as the ones these preachers rant and rave about.[44]

Of course the vulnerability of the left-leaning Catholic is on the side of Enlightenment privatization and relativism, and Garvey and a journal like *Commonweal* must be on guard about it and about attacks on it from the Catholic right. Thus, Garvey is putting some distance between himself and the failures of the Enlightenment, marked out so sharply in two hundred years of Catholic dissent from it and its excesses. But it is not easy to compliment the right, Catholic and Protestant, for taking a stand where the left wavers, and when the right is so extraordinarily unappealing. Garvey cannot bring himself to that compliment unequivocally.

There is a point in the Catholic literature at which the term fundamentalism shifts denotation, and a new epithet in Catholic politics is born. Catholic liberals began to call Catholic conservatives

---

[43]Ibid. 7.

[44]John Garvey, "Truth Flashes: What's Right about Jimmy Swaggart," *Commonweal* 113 (26 December 1986) 678.

"fundamentalists," and to make stabs at interpreting their post-Second Vatican Council enemies in the Church under that term.[45] Theologian Gabriel Daly, an Irish priest and historian, at the seventy-fifth anniversary of the American Academy of Religion in 1984, in his comments on the Catholic struggle with modernity, wrote:

> Integralism was the form in which Catholic fundamentalism expressed itself. ... Integralism, like other kinds of fundamentalism, is more a state of mind than a corpus of beliefs. It is a *way* of approaching those truths which are perceived to lie at the heart of one's religious faith.[46]

Daly returns to his usage at the end of his wise and generous comments on the struggle of the Catholic Church against the demons of the Enlightenment, a struggle which he regards as necessary and yet badly waged by the leaders of the Church. He offers a piece of advice to liberal Catholics and others, unfortunately unheeded: "The instinct to entertain and where possible to respond positively to the truth in the positions of others should extend also (if unilaterally) to fundamentalism. An attitude of academic contempt achieves nothing."[47] Daly recognizes that fundamentalism (integralism in the Catholic case) preserves a Dionysian element in religious life which a Church often loses in its close encounter with modernity:

> The sensible rationality of Apollonian religion somehow fails to satisfy the deeper receptors of religious symbol in the human psyche. The Kantian ideal of "religion within the limits of reason" is in the end the most unreasonable aim of all, because it neglects an element in human nature [namely mysticism] which is both necessary to spiritual health and impervious to the censorship of reason. ... Dionysus always strikes back—which is only another way of expressing the New Testament conviction that the Spirit breathes where he wills.[48]

What for Daly is a category in the clarification of religious stands

---

[45]Eugene LaVerdiere uses the term of the Catholic right in his article "Fundamentalism: A Pastoral Concern."

[46]Gabriel Daly, "Catholicism and Modernity," *Journal of the American Academy of Religion* 53 (1985) 773-96. See p. 776. See also his book, *Transcendence and Immanence: A Study in Catholic Modernism and Integralism* (Oxford: Clarendon, 1980).

[47]Daly, "Catholicism and Modernity" 795.

[48]Ibid. 796.

and an element in an explanation of the Catholic integralist movement, becomes something else entirely in the hands of American Catholic liberals defending themselves and their recently fragile theological hegemony against the attacks of contemporary Catholic inheritors of the integralist mantle. Along with a frequent use of the epithet "fundamentalist," which for a Catholic is rarely if ever only descriptive, one finds a remarkably harsh attack on the Protestant and Catholic right in terms of psychological analysis and, in some cases, the language of disease.

Amateur psychological analysis occurs frequently in the academic and liberal essays of Catholics (and others) on fundamentalism.[49] The American Catholic bishops, as we shall see, find explanations for the fundamentalist appeal to Catholics in individual and social psychology. But there are several essays which are dominated by their appeal to psychological and even medical categories. For Patrick Arnold, Catholic fundamentalism, just like any fundamentalism, isn't a religious movement at all, but a political, social, and cultural reaction to change that can only be explained in psychological terms:

> Psychological studies describe its strongest adherents as "authoritarian personalities": individuals who feel threatened in a world of conspiring evil forces, who think in simplistic and stereotypical terms and who are attracted to authoritarian and moralistic answers to their problems. ... The Catholic community was not to prove entirely immune from this disease. In the past few years, indications have grown that the fundamentalist virus is mutating and beginning to produce Catholic symptoms. That this neo-orthodox movement is an illness, and not a genuine reform, is first of all suggested by its affinities with the contemporary problems afflicting Islam, Judaism, and Protestantism. At least five unhealthy characteristics are visible within the movements threatening all these religions.[50]

---

[49]For example, in the otherwise careful attempt at understanding and explanation of R. Scott Appleby, "Unflinching Faith: What Fires Up the World's Fundamentalists?" *U.S. Catholic* 54 (December 1989) 6-13, especially page 11; in the essays of Catholic biblicist Eugene LaVerdiere, especially "Fundamentalism: A Pastoral Concern" 7-9; and, in a particularly confused essay by Damien Kraus, "Catholic Fundamentalism: A Look at the Problem," *The Living Light* 19 (1982) 8-16, especially page 15. There is, in addition, examples of reductionism which seem to be professional rather than amateur. See essays by G. Muller-Fahrenholz and G. Hole in *Fundamentalism as an Ecumenical Challenge* 3-35.

[50]Patrick Arnold, "The Rise of Catholic Fundamentalism," *America* 156 (11 April 1987) 297-302, especially pp. 298 and 302.

Fundamentalism, Catholic and otherwise, is an emotional movement whose root is fear and anger at cultural change, always religiously divisive, taking flight into myths of the Golden Age, obsessed with issues of authority and obedience, and usually linked with rightist political movements. Finally, this "religious disease" is unconcerned with Jesus and what concerned him, and is "bereft of any spirituality, preferring instead either partisan political topics or subjects of a largely intramural, ecclesiastical nature."[51]

Jacques Weber, directly addresses the problem of Catholic fundamentalism,[52] and includes some remarkably condescending descriptions, taken in part from Damien Kraus:

> As Catholic, the fundamentalist is more often concerned with doctrinal and moral simplicism [sic] than with biblical fundamentalism, though this also can be part of the mind-set. The Catholic fundamentalist craves the simple and the absolutely certain; he is intolerant of doubt, of doctrinal development, of developmental stages of faith, and of an ongoing search for the truth. He is reductionistic in his theology and antagonistic toward Catholic pluralism.[53]

The stereotyping here reaches depths of absurdity matched only by the crudity of Arnold's medical metaphors. Weber wants to make use of Gordon Allport's work on childhood and adult faith, and Bernard Lonergan's theory of conversions (intellectual, moral, and religious) to "place" what James Hitchcock prefers to call "activist conservative Catholicism."[54] He concludes:

[51]Ibid. 302.

[52]See Jacques Weber, "The Problem of Catholic Fundamentalism," in *Christian Adulthood, 1984-85: A Catechetical Resource*, ed. Neil Parent (Washington DC: USCC, 1984). The use of the term of other than evangelical Protestants is now canonical, given its acceptance in The Fundamentalist Project of almost all militant religious protest against modernity. The habit seems firmly entrenched among Catholic theologians since John Coleman's essay, "Who are the Catholic Fundamentalists? A Look at Their Past, Their Politics, and Their Power," *Commonweal* 116 (27 January 1989) 42-47. Coleman does an admirable job of connecting the concerns of current Catholic conservatives to those of the integralists in the first half of the century. With the connection I agree. The term fundamentalist applied to Catholics like James Hitchcock, however, is potentially misleading. See LaVerdiere, "There is No Such Thing as a Catholic Fundamentalist."

[53]Weber 81.

[54]James Hitchcock and William Dinges, "Roman Catholic Traditionalism and

It is my observation and experience that Catholic fundamentalism as
described above seriously truncates and blocks ecclesial conversion,
intellectual conversion, and wholistic moral conversion. It also creates
"serious deformations" in the area of religious conversion (to the holy) and
Christian conversion (to Christ), causing a distorted view of the holy and
of the humanity of Jesus and his teaching.

I suggest that one caught in the mind-set of Catholic fundamentalism
will have a distorted view of the holy and of one's own human nature and,
therefore, of Christ incarnate. The Catholic fundamentalist would, I
suggest, rate low in all aspects of the conversion process.

I further suggest that the fundamentalist mind-set seriously inhibits the
passage from infantile or childhood faith to adult faith.[55]

It is hard to imagine the loss to the dignity and decency of Catholic
theology displayed in such paragraphs, to its methodological good
sense, and to a proper interpretation of the important work of Bernard
Lonergan who made his suggestions on the various conversions *not for
the analysis of enemies but for self-understanding*![56] Weber uses
Lonergan's "conversions" as a check list for psychological and spiritual
health, a club for battle with his fundamentalist enemy. He ends his
essay with an adventitious homily on our complimentarity in a single
Church, informing us that "we are the body of Christ"! Who would
want to belong to a Church with a man who denigrates others in this
fashion and then calls us to prayer?

Another low point is reached by John O'Donohue, in two articles in
the *African Ecclesial Review*.[57] The first is interesting as an example
of the kind of interchange which takes place these days between
Catholic liberals and conservatives, for it is a response to a paper on
authority and freedom published by Opus Dei, whose position
O'Donohue considers a perversion and which he criticizes with classic
modernist and liberal appeals to religious experience. (With the appeal
I would agree, though I find the particular argumentation vacuous.)

The second essay better fits our purposes. This one is directed to a
more general analysis of fundamentalism which at the very outset is

Activist Conservatism in the U.S.," in *Fundamentalism Observed*, eds. Martin E.
Marty and R. Scott Appleby (U of Chicago P, 1991) 101-41.

[55]Weber 82.

[56]See Lonergan, *Method in Theology* 235-37.

[57]John O'Donohue, "The Dogmatic Perversion of Religion," *African Ecclesial
Review* 28 (1986) 312-22, and "Fundamentalism: A Psychological Problem,"
African Ecclesial Review 29 (1987) 344-50.

characterized as a "demand for absolute certitude in religion" which is traced to "a failure to outgrow the infant's craving for security."[58] The body of the essay is devoted to explication of this claim. The immediate enemy remains Opus Dei and the Catholic right ("ecclesiastical fundamentalism"), though "biblical fundamentalism" takes its lumps as well (the latter is "an obsessive demand for an inhuman certainty...most easily explained as a desire to return to infantile security which, however, the adult must shed if he or she is to grow"). The disease is adequately met only by the invitation to "grow up, painful and even agonizing though this process must always be." He appeals to Marx and Freud in support of his position that fundamentalism "offers illusory psychological security...[in] false and illusory religion" for the poor as well as the "psychologically handicapped."[59]

Finally, Jesus is called in to witness that in the current argument between "'Fundamentalists' and 'Liberals,'" we would find that the legalistic Pharisees (for whom the Mosaic Law and the 'immemorial traditions' were the ultimate tests of truth and ethical righteousness), were fundamentalists, while Jesus, who proclaimed that the Sabbath was made for man, was a liberal." We are brought to the conclusion, then, that fundamentalism is a "radical human failure...an intellectual failure...[and] a moral failure," as well as "an enemy of human progress...the source of insoluble human conflicts...[and] the destruction of all authentic religion."[60]

These essays amount to an astonishingly apt example of psychological reductionism and of the effects of liberal blinders on empirical observation and theological judgment. The only question which fundamentalism raises for these authors is how to get rid of it, and the most that one can say about its effect on them as scholars is that it clearly creates no serious intellectual problem, not to say curiosity, and calls forth the most distasteful of metaphors and similes, vicious stereotyping, and expressions of self-righteous wrath. Dare we suggest, then, that liberal religion is "emotional," at least on occasions

---

[58]O'Donohue, "Fundamentalism: A Psychological Problem" 344.

[59]Ibid. 348. Father O'Donohue does not notice that Marx and Freud were thinking of his religion also.

[60]Ibid. 350. These are the terms in which Pius X used for Catholic Modernists. See *Pascendi* (1907).

when its presuppositions are challenged?

Thomas E. Clarke's essay "Fundamentalism and Prejudice" could have been better titled "Fundamentalism, Liberalism and Prejudice" and might well have been read by Arnold, O'Meara, and O'Donohue, and others.[61] Recognizing the psychological mechanism of projection of the shadow, and aware of the theological shortcomings of fundamentalism, Clarke will not settle for the easy slide into liberal attacks on the stranger:

> A certain forensic violence then begins to characterize the field of ecumenical relationships. Healthy conflict yields to sterile polemic, or to what is worse, the contemptuous ignoring of the adversary as unworthy of serious attention. As one who is more prone to liberalism than to fundamentalism, I have to acknowledge that this dynamic seems to obtain in both parties to the quarrel. ... Liberals are no less prone to "inordinate attachments" and to the resulting prejudices than are fundamentalists. In a way, the spiritual snares of liberalism are the more insidious for being less blatant. The liberal does not differ from the fundamentalist in being free from anxiety or from the absolutizing tendency.... The peculiarly liberal form of idolatry is to canonize the endless quest for truth, to absolutize the value of doubt and to find safe shelter in keeping an open mind.[62]

Hence, Clarke delivers a moral message to the learned and holy despisers of fundamentalism: people in glass houses shouldn't throw stones. The shortcoming of Clarke's essay is that it covers only one of the oppositions to fundamentalist Protestantism, namely Catholic liberalism. But the crucial opposition is between fundamentalism and Catholicism itself, and it is to this pair that Clarke's essay needs to attend.

Special Issues of Periodicals

Four American Catholic journals thought fundamentalists bothersome enough to print issues entirely or chiefly devoted to them, *Catholic Charismatic* (1979), *The New Catholic World* (1985), *America* (1987), and *New Theology Review* (1988). None of these is a theological or scholarly journal; each has in mind broader Catholic

---

[61]Thomas E. Clarke, "Fundamentalism and Prejudice" *Way* 27 (1987) 34-41.
[62]Ibid. 38-39.

audiences. I shall make some comments on the issues as wholes rather than review each piece in each (some have been mentioned above), singling out a few of the best and the worst, and taking them in chronological order.

The *Catholic Charismatic* (1979) is the organ of the more moderate wing of the charismatic movement in the Church, its counterpart *New Covenant* being the voice of the Ann Arbor National Service Committee of the Catholic Charismatic Renewal. The moderate wing tends to publish materials by Catholics who do not belong to the movement, among them scripture scholars and theologians who could not find ready access to the right wing cousins. The early date on the *Catholic Charismatic* issue suggests that the charismatics were among the first to register the attractiveness of fundamentalism for Catholics.

The issue carries short essays by George MacRae and John Haughey, both of which are theological critiques of fundamentalism.[63] The first faults fundamentalism's refusal to accept the humanity of the Bible and so its implicit rejection of the Incarnation, and the second finds it rejecting the analogical character of our knowledge of God and the limitations of all human knowledge, including our knowledge of God.

Richard Rohr, contributes an excellent meditation on the Marian mystery as a key to incarnational and sacramental Christianity,[64] offering an example of the explication of the *res catholica* in the face of Protestant and Catholic legalism. Bill O'Brien and Barbara O'Reilly, in separate pieces, worry about the growth of fundamentalist attitudes among Catholic charismatic groups, especially in "covenant communities,"[65] while Juan Hinojosa details the history of biblical fundamentalism and suggests a psychological reading of its "attitude."[66]

---

[63]George MacRae, "The Poor You Always Have With You," *Catholic Charismatic* 3 (December-January 1978-79) 15, and John Haughey, "Fundamentalism—An Afterword," *Catholic Charismatic* 3 (December-January 1978-79) 45-46.

[64]Richard Rohr, "Mary and Fundamentalism," *Catholic Charismatic* 3 (December-January 1978-79) 16-19.

[65]Bill O'Brien, "A National Overview: The Question of Fundamentalism," *Catholic Charismatic* 3 (December-January 1978-79) 24-25, and Barbara O'Reilly, "Fundamentalism: Leader's Response," *Catholic Charismatic* 3 (December-January 1978-79) 40-44.

[66]Juan Lorenzo Hinojosa, "What Is Fundamentalism?" *Catholic Charismatic* 3 (December-January 1978-79) 34-36.

The *New Catholic World* (1985), in its editorial introduction, links Protestant and Catholic fundamentalism and proclaims its desire "to show our respect for Fundamentalism as a deeply sincere form of Christian commitment, while frankly facing and even criticizing many aspects that are unacceptable to a true Catholic vision of faith."[67] The hope is partially fulfilled when, in its opening essay, Edward Dobson, one time faculty member at Jerry Falwell's Liberty University and co-author with him of *The Fundamentalist Phenomenon*, fashions a history and apologia of the American fundamentalist movement of the early and mid-twentieth century.[68]

Dobson's portrait is followed by Thomas Stransky's contrast of fundamentalist and Catholic teaching, expressing the dangers of psychological explanations of it, yet accepting a softened version of that explanation as basic: "Struggling to find a firm footing in life; longing to break through the bewildering variety of religious/moral/amoral claims which are offered through the media; searching for a buttress against social instabilities and demographic dislocations, so many look for the clear, absolute, not-to-be-disputed word."[69] Yet in the end Stransky wants Catholics to examine their conscience on their loss of a "passion for truth" which is easy to find in fundamentalists.

Peggy Shriver, an official in the National Council of Churches, gives voice to mainline/liberal Protestant distaste for fundamentalism, describing it as a "mindset of certainty, obedience, authority, and absolute truth"—a "fortress faith" and a refuge.[70] To her the troubles of the 80s are a repeat of the troubles of the 20s.

Eugene LaVerdiere explains what a Catholic might mean by "being born again" (it is a departure, not an arrival).[71] Brian E. Curley, in "Fundamentalism and Its Challenge to Catholic Religious Education,"[72]

---

[67]Lawrence Boadt, "Fundamentalism," *New Catholic World* 228 (1985) 2.

[68]Edward Dobson, "Fundamentalism—Its Roots," *New Catholic World* 228 (1985) 4-9.

[69]Thomas F. Stransky, "A Catholic Looks at American Fundamentalists," *New Catholic World* 228 (1985) 10-14. See especially page 13.

[70]Peggy L. Shriver, "Guardians of Fundamentalism's Fortress," *New Catholic World* 228 (1985) 15-19.

[71]Eugene LaVerdiere, "Must A Christian Be Born Again?" *New Catholic World* 228 (1985) 20-22.

[72]Brien E. Curley, "Fundamentalism and Its Challenge to Catholic Religious

attacks fundamentalism rather than answers its challenge: it is anti-incarnational, confrontational, anti-dialogic, escapist. The piece belongs with O'Meara and Arnold for its psychological reductionism, but its ignorance surpasses theirs by far. The collection ends with the essays by Thomas Coskren and Richard Chilson, the latter a brief version of the introductory chapter to his book.[73]

The editorial that heads the collection of articles in the special issue of *America* (1986) repeats the most frequent of Catholic comments: fundamentalism offers "quick and easy solutions to complicated questions of life and belief."[74] Martin Marty, a leading Church historian who has written extensively on fundamentalism, makes his case again against the common misunderstandings of fundamentalism, arguing that fundamentalism is a "truly modern movement," that it is not conservative despite its devotion to certain classic themes of orthodoxy, that it is historically eclectic, that is possesses "astonishing" cultural adaptability and a "multiplex consciousness" carrying "apparently conflicting signals without necessary disruption of psychic health."[75] On the frequently practiced psychological reduction, Marty comments: "To see Fundamentalists as pathological is in many cases a problem of the observer's spectacles." Attempting to place fundamentalism among the many movements reacting to change in the modern world, Marty pleads care in the judgments we make:

> Fundamentalists do not only organize to gain political power or to demonstrate against aspects of modernity. They believe in Christ crucified and risen, and they gladly testify to the experience of Christ in their born-again lives. But they are also parts of social movements that their neighbors and fellow citizens have to understand if they are to coexist creatively in civil and religious life.[76]

Education," *New Catholic World* 228 (1985) 34-37.

[73]Thomas M. Coskren, "Fundamentalists on Campus," *New Catholic World* 228 (1985) 38-41, and Richard Chilson, "Two Visions," *New Catholic World* 228 (1985) 42-44. See also Richard Chilson, *Full Christianity: A Response to Fundamental Questions* (New Jersey: Paulist, 1985), discussed below.

[74]"The Spirit, the Church and Fundamentalism," *America* 155 (27 September 1986) 129.

[75]Martin E. Marty, "Modern Fundamentalism," *America* 155 (September 27, 1986) 134-35.

[76]Ibid. 135.

Marty is followed by Archbishop John F. Whealon's short comment summarizing the contents of the bishops' letter (see below for analysis), and Thomas Stahel interviews Auxiliary Bishop Cuquejo of Asunción, Paraguay, on the growth of "sects" in Paraguay. John Catoir, director of The Christophers, strings out some anecdotes and statistics meant to warn Catholics, including a charge that "a lot of child abuse [is] taking place among Fundamentalists" and a report that Catholics are contributing about sixty million dollars a year to television preachers. Richard Chilson's essay has been reviewed above, and his book is commented upon below. William Dinges, professor at Catholic University of America, writes a careful analysis of the Vatican statement on sects, cults and new religious movements, among the best pieces in the Catholic literature of the last two decades.[77]

New Theology Review: An American Catholic Journal for Ministry, is edited by Robert J. Schreiter, a faculty member of the Chicago Theological Union, who opens his collection with a warning against reductionist explanations of fundamentalism:

> Most attempts to explain the American fundamentalist phenomenon have been reductionist in nature. Some critics maintain that it is primarily a psychological reaction to the ambiguities of modernity. Others see it as a form of theological ignorance. Still others consider it as related to a socioeconomic class that feels itself left out of the mainstream. But therapies, rational debates, and reform programs do not seem to loosen fundamentalism's grip on the heart and minds of people who are not necessarily frightened, uneducated or socially deprived. Reductionist strategies seem to get religious leaders nowhere in combatting fundamentalism. ... Fundamentalism must be understood in its own right and within its own context, and not simply as an anxious reaction to the mainstream movements in the dominant culture. Fundamentalism is a major pastoral problem in the United States. It is a complex phenomenon that

[77]John F. Whealon, "Challenging Fundamentalism," *America* 155 (27 September 1986) 136-38; Thomas H. Stahel, "The Sects in Paraguay," *America* 155 (27 September 1986) 139-41; John Catoir, "Fundamentalists on the Move," *America* 155 (27 September 1986) 142-44; William Dinges, "The Vatican Report on Sects, Cults and New Religious Movements," *America* 155 (27 September 1986) 145-47, 154. In another issue of *America*, Alan Deck, writes on the worries of American Catholic bishops about the numbers of Hispanic Catholics who have defected to fundamentalist churches and makes suggestions on how to tighten up Catholic communities of Hispanics. See Alan Deck, "Fundamentalism and the Hispanic Catholic," *America* 152 (26 January 1985) 64-66.

cannot be reduced to a psychological diagnosis, a theological error or a single social analysis.[78]

The essays which follow keep carefully to this guideline or perhaps the guideline emerged from the essays. Dominic Monti, of the Washington Theological Union, gives a straightforward and balanced survey of the origins and development of American fundamentalism relying on secondary sources.[79]

In perhaps the best single piece on fundamentalism by a Roman Catholic theologian, Zachary Hayes, presents, analyzes, and criticizes dispensational premillennialism.[80] He read Darby and Scofield, catching their own "canon within the canon." The explanation of the technicalities of dispensationalism is clear and accurate. His criticism is vigorous and well-rounded, and almost entirely theological and not at all psychological. He, like Timothy Weber, explains it as an assertion of the final intelligibility and goodness of an otherwise opaque and mean human history. However, he also raises the further question: Why does this particular affirmation of intelligibility and goodness have strong appeal to some and not to others? "But why do some people seem to be satisfied only with clear knowledge of the future while others seem to be willing to live with a hope that thrives in the face of ignorance concerning the specifics of history? Are we here confronted with two different forms of religious consciousness?"[81]

One might suggest as a beginning of an answer to that question that we are probably facing two quite different understandings of human consciousness and of human knowledge, and perhaps the same sort of dispositional leanings account for general stances of liberalism and conservatism. What to make of the differences between these dispositions, however, is forever a mystery. I still cannot account for the fact that, though there are Republicans I like, I do not like Republicans and would allow very few indeed into my family circle. And Republicans only head the list.

Dianne Bergant relies entirely on the work of James Barr in her

---

[78]Robert J. Schreiter, "Introduction: The Challenge of Fundamentalism," *New Theology Review* 1 (May 1988) 3-4.

[79]Dominic Monti, "World Out of Time: The Origins of the Fundamentalist Movement," *New Theology Review* 1 (May 1988) 5-20.

[80]Hayes 21-35.

[81]Ibid. 34.

essay on fundamentalist hermeneutics, "Fundamentalists and the Bible,"[82] and James Wall, editor of *Christian Century*, briefly explains "The Rise of the Religious Right in American Politics."[83]

Gabriel Fackre, a professor of theology at Andover-Newton Theological School, offers a theological analysis and evaluation of fundamentalist doctrines, with expert distinctions at the outset among varieties of fundamentalists.[84] Spirituality and eschatology are the doctrinal threads he follows to the conclusion that hope is the driving force of fundamentalism:

> Whatever one might think of the hermeneutics of Scripture here employed, or the doctrinal specifics concerning the end-time, political apocalyptic fundamentalism constitutes a "theology of hope" for multitudes. All the elements recommended by the Moltmanns and Schillebeeckxes of ecumenical Christianity reappear here: 1) Human suffering as the contextual question to which the Good News must speak. 2) The focus on the future as the reference point for the gospel. 3) Christ's resurrection as the warrant for hope. 4) A doctrine of "hope in action" that disavows escapism and mobilizes the faithful for social change.[85]

Theodore Ross ends the issue with an essay on Catholic integralism, "Catholicism and Fundamentalism," carrying on the now apparently canonical association of the Catholic right with fundamentalism.[86] He traces the "unfortunate" history of integralism which elevated it to the norm for Catholic theology for a century, and catalogues its theological faults: its opposition to historical study of the Bible; its identification of truth with its own theology, one school among many; its identification of authentic Catholic practice with one historical period of that practice. Though the history of integralism as a movement as well as an apologetic deserves as much sympathy and nuance as does the history of fundamentalism, Ross delivers a fair enough sketch of it in an essay that is decisively negative.

---

[82]Dianne Bergant, "Fundamentalists and the Bible," *New Theology Review* 1 (May 1988) 36-50.

[83]James Wall, "The Rise of the Religious Right in American Politics," *New Theology Review* 1 (May 1988) 51-57.

[84]Gabriel Fackre, "Positive Values and Honorable Intentions: A Critique of Fundamentalism," *New Theology Review* 1 (May 1988) 58-73.

[85]Ibid. 64.

[86]Theodore C. Ross, "Catholicism and Fundamentalism," *New Theology Review* 1 (May 1988) 74-87.

The interpretation and criticism of fundamentalist eschatology and spirituality by Hayes and Fackre are insightful. When Fackre charges fundamentalism with "simplistic absolutisms" and "quick-fix ideologies" one has the sense that the criticism is as fair as the presentation and evaluation. Perhaps in part because Fackre is not a Catholic, and has a firsthand experience with Protestant fundamentalism, he produces the most theologically stimulating essay on Protestant fundamentalism to be found in the Catholic literature. Hayes shows just how good a serious Catholic theological critique of an "alien" theological world can be when it is not driven by the immediate concern with "sheep stealing." The essays by Zachary Hayes and Gabriel Fackre, then, make this special issue (the first) of the *New Theology Review* the most valuable of the four special issues just reviewed. It must be said, however, that each editor strove for balance and set a constructive stage for the contributors, and in this regard all deserve credit.

Books

The five books by Catholics echo concerns, themes, and arguments of the periodical literature. They all regard fundamentalism as a threat to Catholics, and judge it to be intellectually, spiritually, and doctrinally inadequate. All five were written for Catholics, all are defensive (only one is genuinely offensive), all set out to enlighten Catholics on what fundamentalism is, and how it arose and why it prospers (the comment on the history is cursory), what its central affirmations are and how these contrast with Roman Catholic doctrines and current scholarly views. All regard fundamentalist anti-Catholicism as both abhorrent and groundless. They attempt to refute fundamentalist doctrines where these depart from Catholic teaching. They are pastoral rather than scholarly, though two are written by established scholars. None can be counted as a work of scholarship though the authors are educated, intellectually able, and even sophisticated. All are driven by pastoral as distinct from a reasoned response to the intellectual challenge which fundamentalism poses. All are at least minimally restrained, avoiding attacks on people and concentrating on teachings and world-views, and all are directly argumentative. They all agree that "irenicism" and "ecumenism" have little or no place between Catholics and fundamentalists, but pin the blame for that on the fundamentalists. All apparently regard fundamentalists as Christians (at least there is no explicit argument mounted that they are not), mistaken though they may be. None displays any interest whatever in fundamentalism as a valuable subject-matter for study in its own right.

The attractiveness of Anthony Gilles' book, *Fundamentalism: What Every Catholic Should Know*,[87] is its pleasant narrative style. Gilles grew up in the Bible Belt, and is able to take a friendly and bemused look at his neighbors' religion. While his objective is to provide Catholics with a response to common fundamentalist charges and to contrast Catholic doctrines with its teachings, he does so in a folksy style laced with stories of his family's encounters with fundamentalists, all gently humorous.

Gilles is able at the outset to provide a balance to his list of "common fundamentalist tendencies" (not good!) by adding a short list of "fundamentalist good points."[88] The former include most of the standard Catholic criticisms: fundamentalists are legalists, docetists, reifiers of the Divine Mystery, ignorant historically, uncritical individualists, and dualists (for they are pessimists on human nature and pay little attention to the creative as distinct from redemptive divine activity). But there is another side: their devotion to the Bible should make Catholics blush; they are typically on a serious quest for holiness in a world which cares little for that; they take moral choice seriously in a world of moral relativism.

Stanley B. Marrow, a Jesuit scripture scholar, authored *The Words of Jesus in Our Gospels: A Catholic Response to Fundamentalism*[89] to inform Catholics of the present state of New Testament scholarship. The book is hardly a book on fundamentalism at all, and uses a sketchy presentation of fundamentalist doctrine on the Bible to frame and provide contrast for a discussion of the outcome of critical approaches to the gospels, which he traces beginning with the oral tradition through the composition of the gospels to the establishment

---

[87]Anthony E. Gilles, *Fundamentalism: What Every Catholic Should Know* (Cincinnati: St. Anthony Messenger, 1984); it is 62 pages long.

[88]Ibid. 14-25.

[89]Stanley B. Marrow, *The Words of Jesus in Our Gospels: A Catholic Response to Fundamentalism* (New Jersey: Paulist, 1979); it is 152 pages long.

of the canon. Fundamentalism is given short shrift (after the introduction, barely a few paragraphs). His basic criticism of fundamentalism is somewhat sophisticated for this literature: implicit in the claim for the infallibility of the text is a claim for the infallibility of the interpreter. Thus, "in addition to the lack of thoroughness in its arguments and the failure to carry them through to their necessary conclusions, the fundamentalist position invariably runs the risk of the tyranny of its presuppositions."[90] Thus, it leaves no room for interpretation, yet it must interpret. It interprets, but must appear not to.

Richard Chilson is a Paulist campus minister. His *Full Christianity: A Catholic Response to Fundamental Questions*, in its body, answers fifty questions derived from fundamentalist-Catholic differences gathered under five topic headings: (1) Scripture, Authority, and Revelation; (2) Jesus Christ; (3) The Church; (4) Christian Life; (5) Other Questions. In the preface he points out the rising tide of fundamentalism on campuses. The Navigators, the Campus Crusade for Christ, and the Inter-Varsity Christian Fellowship are listed as perpetrators. Fundamentalism is placed in direct line with "classical Protestant themes," while his answers rest on a "Catholic vision" now embraced by mainline Protestants and their scholars as well as Roman Catholics. Once again we can feel the post-Reformation ecclesiastical ground shifting under our feet. Protestant liberalism has manifestly failed to solve the problem created for Christianity by "the modern world," and so we are left with these alternatives, fundamentalism and "the Catholic vision." Only "Catholicism" in this broadened, post-Second Vatican Council sense, has clung to the fullness of Christian faith and only it remains in dialogue with the modern world.

In the introduction the two "visions" are contrasted.[91] Catholicism is inclusive, culturally creative, optimistic, incarnational and sacramental. Fundamentalism, on the other hand, is exclusive, culturally reactive, pessimistic, oriented toward the doctrine of atonement, and fixed on the verbal. These are taken to be world views underlying doctrines, and so the specific doctrines are interpreted against the background of the world view. In general, the book is a moderate to liberal Catholic response, with some stereotyping on the

[90]Ibid. 145.
[91]Ibid. 5-9.

author's part, but it is not an angry response. Fundamentalist positions, however, are presented sketchily and dismissed out of hand.

Karl Keating is a lawyer and a layman in the Church of San Diego where he heads a small organization called Catholic Answers, Inc. The organization publishes and distributes a monthly paper and pamphlets on religious topics and tapes of debates and lectures. Keating talks publicly in a variety of contexts, including parish and diocesan meetings, debates with fundamentalist speakers in their own churches, and is available for consultation to other Catholic organizations. He is well known and apparently respected in conservative evangelical circles, both for the strength of his convictions and his knowledge of the Bible, fundamentalism and Catholicism.

His book, *Catholicism and Fundamentalism*,[92] is the most substantial and, from one point of view, the most interesting of the lot. Keating knows fundamentalism and fundamentalist literature, especially its anti-Catholic variety, thoroughly. Secondly, the book is well organized to serve his very clear purposes, and he proceeds dispassionately and unerringly to accomplish them. Thirdly, it represents an intellectual and public style of Catholicism that is out of tune with the Catholic academic-theological mainstream (represented, say, by the College Theology Society, the Catholic Theological Society of America, or the Catholic Biblical Association) but is quite in tune with more conservative Catholic elements (for example, the Fellowship of Catholic Scholars) and with the tendencies of much of popular conservative evangelical apologetics. The style is that of public debate over the truth of religious claims. To read Keating is to re-enter the world of Catholic apologetics which seemed to have slipped beneath the surface of Catholic discourse with the emergence of the Second Vatican Council's ecumenical style. As fundamentalists slip easily into

[92]Karl Keating, *Catholicism and Fundamentalism: The Attack on "Romanism" by "Bible Christians"*; it is 360 pages. The book is published by a press widely regarded in moderate to liberal Catholic academic circles as an organ of conservative Catholicism, much as Paulist Press would be regarded as middle of the road or liberal. Keating himself is occasionally given to speaking of "orthodox" Catholics, and to occasionally expressing suspicions about contemporary Catholic biblical scholarship. On "orthodox" Catholics, see pages 9, 129, 324, 329; on the biblical scholars, see pages 121 (note 2), and 324-25. Keating's basic approach is fully and directly stated, along with his criticism of other Catholic strategies, in "Answering the Fundamentalist Challenge," *Homiletic and Pastoral Review* 85 (July 1985) 32-57.

the clothes of traditional Protestant anti-Catholicism, so Keating is at home in the world of Hillaire Belloc, G.K. Chesterton, and Frank Sheed. It is the world of British Catholic "in-your-face" response to Protestant nonsense that had a determinative effect on American Catholic education and culture in the first half of this century. The book is intelligent, well-written, and, given the methodological premises of apologetical theology, very effective. While Keating shows little of the wit of the English Catholic authors and controversialists whom he admires, he knows how to take an argument apart. There is no impatience here, no liberal petulance indicating that he would prefer to be doing something else, no dismissal of or disrespect for fundamentalists. He is calmly sure, however, that fundamentalism is doctrinally and theologically flawed, that Catholics make a serious mistake in converting to it, and that the only way to staunch the current wound is to display the good sense that Catholicism and the nonsense that fundamentalism make.

Keating thinks that fundamentalist doctrine must be refuted rather than explained away, and that unless Catholics care about "the truth" as much as fundamentalists profess to, no amount of psychologizing or babbling on about the difficulties of the age or even turning up the affective thermometer of Catholic congregations will stop the bleeding. Catholics must be willing to argue doctrine and history with conviction as well as knowledge.

Eight chapters (125 pages) provide a survey of the anti-Catholic fundamentalist landscape, from the work of the "godfather" of fundamentalist bigotry, Lorraine Boettner, to the conversionary antics and pamphleteering of the "fringe" anti-Catholics, Tony Alamo and Jack Chick.[93] Thirteen chapters (180 pages) present and refute the chief fundamentalist charges against Catholic doctrine and practice, from the inspiration and role of the scriptures to the "facts" about the Inquisition. This section is an handbook of responses to fundamentalist attacks. One chapter describes how one should deal with the fundamentalists one is sure to meet, and a last chapter reviews scholarly, especially historical, literature useful in apologetic learning

---

[93]Loraine Boettner, *Roman Catholicism* (Philadelphia: Presbyterian and Reformed P, 1962). He claims that over 100,000 copies have been sold. It is in print. The Chick cartoons and comics can be obtained from Chick Publications, Box 662, Chino, CA 91710.

and debate.

The Catholic scholarly literature Keating relies on, like the style and technique of apologetic debate, is drawn from the previous era of Roman Catholic thought and language. Even the literature which is dated after that period is, for the most part, reprinted or by authors whose formation and primary work is pre-conciliar. That, of course, is an option rather than a flaw, and will surely work for many Catholics, as it just as surely will not for others. He has no place for any of the mainstream-to-left scholarship and theology that currently dominates the American Catholic scene. This is understandable since it would not serve his purposes and it may account for some of the very weaknesses of the Church which makes fundamentalist inroads possible. Catholic theologians, professors and teachers, no longer commonly mount apologetic arguments. They do not, for example, take the Bible as an historical text which gives evidence that Jesus meant to establish an infallible Church whose witness in turn establishes the inspiration of the scriptures which in turn gives evidence that he is the divine Son. The Catholic theologians no longer argue with Protestants whose subjectivist argument for the verification of the inspiration and inerrancy of scripture was formulated so well by Charles Hodge a century and a half ago.[94] Catholic scholastic apologetics disappeared as did the Protestant version, and we are now unfamiliar and uneasy with both. Except fundamentalists and Karl Keating, that is. However, as long as the Protestant rationalism and anti-Catholic bias lives in fundamentalist apologetics,[95] its counterpart, neo-scholastic rationalism, may be needed in Catholicism.

About many things Keating is correct, among them a view of fundamentalism which supports his efforts at respectful apologetic argument. In the midst of his discussion of the background of the argument, he writes:

> Many Catholics who have written about fundamentalism misunderstand it. They psychologize it into a mass of emotional contradictions. They accept the view of the popular press that fundamentalism is not a matter of theology but of pathology. A man subscribes to the fundamentalist position,

---

[94]Charles Hodge, *Systematic Theology*, ed. Edward N. Gross (Grand Rapids, MI: Baker, 1988).

[95]Nicholas F. Grier, *God, Reason, and the Evangelicals: The Case against Evangelical Rationalism* (Lanham, MD: U Press of Am, 1987).

it is said, because he is ashamed of being poor, or because the priest or minister at his previous Church mistreated him and he is out for revenge or for consoling pats on the back. He does not accept fundamentalism the way an enlightened liberal accepts liberalism, with consideration and forethought. Some critics come perilously close to concluding that any fundamentalist is a loon. Granted, some are—but so are some Catholics and more than a few secularists. ... Whatever forces might have steered a man to fundamentalism in the first place—and it must be granted that emotional factors play a part, as they do in most conversions, no matter the direction—he remains a fundamentalist for doctrinal reasons. He might have left his previous Church out of anger or frustration, [but]...as important as those factors might be they were not the reason he converted. His conversion had to do with doctrines.[96]

It is this conviction that grounds Keating's option for apologetic argument. He knows that if fundamentalism is loony, so are we all, and if it would distinguish itself from the rest of us in an argument over doctrine, then questions about what *really* happened and what *really* is the case in the Christian claim may be essential to relations between religious communities and individuals. While this is on the surface of some of the anti-fundamentalist Catholic literature and supposed by much of it, Keating's book has the decided advantage of not loosing sight for a moment of the historical suppositions and essential doctrinalism of Catholic Christianity and of fundamentalism.

Keating's conviction that fundamentalism is a doctrine rather than a psychological disease is directly contradicted by Thomas F. O'Meara, a professor of historical and systematic theology at the University of Notre Dame. His book, *Fundamentalism: A Catholic Perspective,*[97] broadens the discussion of American Protestant fundamentalism to include manifestations of fundamentalism in the Catholic Church, and makes the most vigorous and direct claim by far that fundamentalism is primarily a psychological problem as well as the "great threat to Roman Catholicism in the United States in the period following the Second Vatican Council."[98]

In the first half of the book, O'Meara discusses what he means by fundamentalism, how it exists in Catholicism as well as Protestantism, and a "new ecumenism" between Protestant and Catholic

[96]Keating 24-26.
[97]Thomas F. O'Meara, *Fundamentalism: A Catholic Perspective* (New Jersey: Paulist, 1990); it is 103 pages long.
[98]O'Meara 96.

fundamentalists. In the second part he interprets fundamentalism as a psychological distortion brought on by anxiety experienced in rapid social change. He then presents four Catholic critics of fundamentalism,[99] and sets up a theological contrast of fundamentalism with Catholicism, making the case that they are "polar opposites" as interpretations of Christianity.

O'Meara's contrast is not between doctrines or specific practices, though he has a great deal to say about both throughout the book. In his view the important differences are in theology, psychology, and culture, in what it means to be human and a citizen of the kingdom. Like Chilson, O'Meara places the Catholic "vision" at the center, between theological liberalism which fades into secularism and fundamentalism which identifies God with an object or objects. Taking over Richard McBrien's phenomenology of Catholicism,[100] he finds Catholicism to be a religion of sacramentalism, mediation, and communion. Fundamentalism denies all three: "Christian Fundamentalism is *an interpretation of Christianity in which a charismatic leader locates with easy certitude in chosen words, doctrines, and practices the miraculous actions of a strict God saving an elite from an evil world.*"[101]

For Catholicism, God is a loving creator and redeemer, human life can be trusted, human beings are usually not sinful and dangerous, and the loving God is present in the "ordinary" ways of human beings and makes himself available in sacramental, communal and historical mediation. Fundamentalism, on the other hand, has a god who is an unpredictable trickster, a magician, a god of anger and fear, and their

---

[99]They are Richard McBrien, another theologian at Notre Dame whose views of fundamentalism seem to have had a decided effect on O'Meara's understanding of it; Raymond Brown, a priest who taught Scripture at Union Theological Seminary in New York; the American bishops' letter on fundamentalism; and Flannery O'Connor, a Catholic short story writer and novelist. The first three surely count as critics of fundamentalism; Flannery O'Connor's "criticism" of fundamentalism is hard to separate from her "criticism" of humanity, for which she had the most extraordinary compassion and with whom she was fascinated. None of the first three critics display any similar sympathies for fundamentalists or fundamentalism.

[100]See Richard P. McBrien, *Catholicism* (Minneapolis: Winston Press, 1981), Study Edition, 1169-83; or Mircea Eliade, ed. *Encyclopedia of Religion*, (New York: Macmillan, 1986), s.v. "Roman Catholicism," by Richard McBrien.

[101]O'Meara 18. Emphasis original.

human beings are tricky, corrupt, untrustworthy, and ugly. Fundamentalists demand the extraordinary (the miraculous), they narrow salvation and are generous in condemnation, they are enthusiastic for a violent end to history, and they are humorless. Fundamentalism is "somewhat world-hating," and "a tribal religion from the past."[102]

O'Meara's argument against fundamentalism is boldly psychological. He is not content merely to stigmatize fundamentalism as a psychological aberration, but he argues that this is the way it ought to be approached. While not "contemptuous of the people who find good things in it," nonetheless, "if we want to understand this movement with its various branches, we cannot stay with the Bible but need to reach the aspects of faith and psychology which lie beneath this attitude to scripture."[103] It is the relentless pursuit of the psychology of fundamentalism that sets his work apart from that of his fellow Catholics, though many, including the bishops, take regular and brief steps into individual and social psychology. Although he tells his readers that "psychology is not the author's field, and the following insights do not claim to be theoretically or scientifically verified," he nonetheless claims a validity for them arising from his twenty years experience in seminaries and universities, his experience with fundamentalists of various sorts, and his own theology of nature and grace. The latter demands that he pay attention to the psychology of a theological or religious position. Thus, he puts himself in the curious position of making an analysis of a sort he is not qualified to offer, yet insisting that it is an accurate portrait.

The basic thesis of the analysis is that change produces anxiety, and that the flight from anxiety can involve a distortion of the human psyche.[104] Such change characterizes contemporary America, and the result is an increase in the incidence and appeal of fundamentalism, the signs of which are elitism, the desire for certitude, anxiety before diversity and change, rigidity, compulsive behavior, and anger. The portrait is painted at some length in the fourth chapter, "The Psychology of Fundamentalism," but is not confined there. It pervades

[102]Ibid. 81-93.
[103]Ibid. 7, 49.
[104]Ibid. 10, 13, 14.

the book.[105]

So pervasive is it, in fact, that it overshadows and perhaps in the end even undercuts his hope to present a convincing contrast of the two religious and theological worlds. For the portrait violates a methodological directive commonly held among scholars of religion and theologians, namely, a rejection of psychological reduction. To put it crassly, you must not do unto others what you would not have done unto you. That precept was hard won in the world of the study of religion with its massive initial psychological prejudice against religion as a reasonable practice; as it has been equally hard won in the relations between religious communities and between their theologians. We are familiar with the caricature of Catholicism easily erected on the same principles of analysis followed by O'Meara. We are left by him with a psychological counterpart to the fundamentalist caricatures of Catholicism.[106]

Finally, perhaps in order to avoid criticizing individuals, O'Meara writes in a code which makes it very difficult to know just what he is responding to. For example, in sketching the "new ecumenism" which unites Protestant and Catholic fundamentalists in a common effort to shape contemporary Catholicism to their liking (a conspiracy which is *prima facie* unlikely), we are left guessing at his specific meaning: "neo-conservative political theorists" may mean Michael Novak and George Weigel; "Protestants...who might become mentors of the Catholic Church today" might be Richard John Neuhaus who at the time of writing had not yet become a Catholic; "antiquarians fascinated by the ritual and organization of the Catholic Church" might be Anglo-Catholics who have entered or profess interest in entering the Church, but then again they might not. There follows a section reprimanding the "outsider" or "tourist" for misunderstanding Catholicism, and a warning to "recent converts" who have "a shallow or skewed understanding of Catholicism," the converts not identified.[107] In addition to finding it impossible to identify the "new ecumenists," it is equally difficult to understand his worry about the "new ecumenism." Does he think that the interdenominational right wing of

[105]Ibid. 7, 13-14, 19, 22, 27, 29, 33, 50ff.

[106]See O'Meara's "Fundamentalism and the Christian Believer," *Priest* 44 (March 1988) 39-41, for more of the same. Comments above.

[107]O'Meara, *Fundamentalism: A Catholic Perspective* 38-42.

American Christianity is combining or conspiring to make life difficult for Catholic moderates and liberals? O'Meara has lapsed into the Vatican habit of avoiding specification of his enemies and leaving it to waves of interpreters to figure it out and apply it. He may have created a piece of literature the adequate interpretation of which calls for a practiced dispensationalist![108]

All of these books remain intensely practical and do not become theoretic or scholarly. Even when they are written by scholars, they display no interest in fundamentalism, fundamentalist thought and practice, or in fundamentalists themselves, except insofar as they impinge upon Catholics and the Catholic Church. We cannot say, then, that there is a Catholic scholarship of fundamentalism evident in monographs.

Episcopal and Vatican Statements

To put the statements of American bishops on fundamentalism in perspective one has only to recall the years of preparation and consultation, and then the waves of subsequent reaction and analysis, to the bishops' statements on war and peace and on the American economy.[109] By way of contrast, in 1987 a small committee of the National Conference of Catholic Bishops including three archbishops and three auxiliary bishops (two of the six trained scripture scholars) composed and approved "A Pastoral Statement for Catholics on Biblical Fundamentalism."[110] It received little public attention.

The letter is addressed to "our Catholic brothers and sisters who may be attracted to Biblical Fundamentalism without realizing its serious

---

[108]For further comments on the book, see William Dinges's review in *Record of the American Catholic Historical Society of Philadelphia* 101 (Fall 1990) 64-65. On the problems of psychologizing, see Dinges, "The Vatican Report" 145-47.

[109]National Conference of Catholic Bishops, *The Challenge of Peace: God"s Promise and Our Response* (Washington, DC: USCC, 1983), and National Conference of Catholic Bishops, *Economic Justice for All: Catholic Social Teaching and the U.S. Economy* (Washington, DC: USCC, 1985).

[110]*Origins* 17 (1987) 376-77. The signatories are: Archbishops John F. Whealon (Hartford), Theodore E. McCarrick (Newark), and J. Francis Stafford (Denver); auxiliary bishops Alvara Corrada del Rio (District of Columbia), Richard J. Sklba (Milwaukee), and Donald W. Trautman (Buffalo).

weaknesses...to remind our faithful of the fullness of Christianity that God has provided in the Catholic Church." The letter offers no attempt to analyze fundamentalism theologically or historically but treats it as a "general approach to life which is typified by unyielding adherence to rigid doctrinal and ideological positions." The letter's criticism of fundamentalism is threefold: fundamentalist biblicism eliminates the Church from Christianity; it ignores the historicity of the Bible itself, distorts the meaning of the Catholic doctrine of inerrancy, and ends in a hermeneutical leap from the Bible to contemporary life; and it offers simple and confident answers to complex questions:

> The appeal is evident for the Catholic young adult or teenager—one whose family background may be troubled; who is struggling with life, morality and religion; whose Catholic education may have been seriously inadequate in the fundamentals of doctrine, the Bible, prayer life and sacramental living; whose catechetical formation may have been inadequate in presenting the full Catholic traditions and teaching authority. For such a person, the appeal of finding *the answer* in a devout, studious, prayerful, warm, Bible-quoting class is easy to understand. But the ultimate problem with such fundamentalism is that it can only give a limited number of answers and cannot present those answers, on balance, because it does not have Christ's teaching Church, nor even an understanding of how the Bible originally came to be written and collected in the sacred canon, or official list of inspired books.[111]

The opening attack on fundamentalism as a psychological attitude of rigidity and as primarily a problem for the immature and uncertain youth vitiates the letter's brief presentation of a contrast between fundamentalist and Catholic doctrines, leaving the reader with the impression (once again) that the bishops' responsibility is exhausted by a warning and a simple contrast. The saving grace of the letter is its admission that "the Catholic Church in the past did not encourage Bible study as much as she could have" and that there is currently need for better homilies, warmer liturgical atmosphere, and greater familiarity with the Bible through parish study and faith-sharing groups.[112]

The bishops of Alabama and Mississippi on June 29, 1989, issued their own letter, "Toward Your Happiness: Catholicism and

---

[111]Ibid. 376.
[112]Ibid. 377.

Fundamentalism, a Contrast."[113] It opens with a review of the economic, political, and cultural grounds for the uncertainty and confusion current in American life, a confusion to which even the Church seems liable. The bishops make out the present as a season of opportunity and promise ("After all, the same age that produced Khomeini produced Mother Teresa of Calcutta.") But the bishops see that fundamentalism offers Catholics "a false security." From an essay by Bill J. Leonard, a Baptist historian, they take a sketch of the origins of the fundamentalist movement, and reach the conclusion that "the fundamentalists were looking for simple solutions to the increasingly complex problems of life."[114]

Positions deemed common among fundamentalists are scored by the bishops. The fundamentalists have an unreasonable certainty about the meaning of scripture texts regardless of context; a simplistic certainty of salvation instantaneously achieved; a sense of personal security which identifies God's way with "the American way," namely, with rugged individualism and self-sufficiency; an intimacy with God which excludes others (namely, the Church). At the end, the bishops add a fifth doctrine, dualism of the world and the kingdom, which they apparently draw from fundamentalist apocalypticism, and contrast it with Catholic cultural incarnationalism.[115]

The correct teaching on these matters is put forth: one cannot understand even the existence of the scriptures much less interpret them apart from the Church which determined the canon to begin with. Again, while many American values are to be cherished by Christians, others must be rejected as "exaggerated and selfish." Finally, the incarnation implies commitment to this world, to its peace and well-being, as well as to the world to come. The function of Christian faith—and of the Bible within the Church—is to provide hope and direction as the Christian community makes its way through history. Catholics do not despair of the world and flee to God, *solus cum solo*. They celebrate the gifts of creation and redemption "with unparalleled joy. That is why the eucharist, the greatest sign of our unity in sharing

[113]Oscar H. Lipscomb of Mobile, Joseph Howze of Biloxi, William Houck of Jackson, and Raymond Boland of Birmingham, "'Toward Your Happiness,' Catholicism and Fundamentalism: A Contrast," in *The Struggle over the Past: Fundamentalism in the Modern World*, 333-41.

[114]Ibid. 335.

[115]The four points are enumerated in section 5 and the fifth in section 8.

God's life, is the sun and center of our lives."[116]

The bishops end with a set of recommendations to the Church meant to help Catholics avoid "the temptations and dangers of fundamentalism and at the same time discover that confidence and hope to which the Lord calls all true disciples": Bible reading and study; improved preaching; transformation of parishes into "communities of God's love" through Cursillo programs, charismatic prayer groups, retreat movements, and social ministry. Beware, they say, for "we will not find peace and joy in a simplistic manipulation of biblical texts or in some instantaneous and emotional religious experience." Rather, find the yoke of discipleship in the world.[117] Once again, as in the case of the National Council of Catholic Bishops' letter, these bishops locate the problem in the age and in false teaching that has a surface attraction, and once again they call for changes in Catholic practice to counter that attraction. Again they offer a contrast of true doctrine to false.

Bishop John Leibrecht of Springfield-Cape Girardeau (Missouri), on November 8, 1988, wrote a letter to his flock entitled "Sharing God's Life Together: Being Catholic in the Bible Belt."[118] It is the longest and most interesting of the episcopal documents. It is animated, I think, by a quite different spirit and adopts a markedly different strategy from those of his brother bishops. He opens by expressing his admiration for the faith of his non-Catholic neighbors and writes to explain Catholic belief to his own people who may sometimes find their neighbors' religious language "confusing...frightening or irritating," and does so by offering a reflection on "the kinds of questions and issues we encounter among our neighbors." He then writes successive sections on the topics of salvation, the Church, worship and prayer, mission and hierarchical authority, the Holy Spirit, the Bible and tradition, and Mary. Let us take the first as an example of the strategy pursued in the others.

When a Catholic is asked "Are you saved?" he or she is often shaken, for Catholics are not used to talking easily about their religious life. The question is aimed at a very specific sort of religious

[116]Ibid. 340.

[117]Ibid.

[118]John Leibrecht, *Sharing God's Life Together: On Being Catholic in the Bible Belt* (Diocese of Springfield-Cape Girardeau, November 11, 1988).

experience, "being born again," in which we are "confronted" by God and "surrendered to him." The bishop hopes that every Catholic has had such experiences of Christ and of the presence of God in life. He himself has had several, and they are blessings. But the Catholic doctrine of salvation is broader. It is not the work of a moment but of a lifetime of gradual entry into God's life, and not only concerned with God's entry into ours. "Catholics have peak religious experiences in life, but 'being saved' is not such a singular peak experience. It is a life-long process of growing in the gifts God gives us."[119]

This section of the letter, and those which follow, amount to a "mystagogical catechesis," an introduction to the fuller meaning of the Christian faith rather than an attack on the weaknesses of others. Unquestionably there are contrasts made and implied, since the topics for reflection are chosen from the chief criticisms of the Church by fundamentalists, but there is no offensive mounted and there is a pedagogically effective strategy of unfolding Roman Catholic self-understanding on issues of mutual concern. Bishop Leibrecht has adopted the standard procedure of dialogue, namely, spelling out one's own position without attacking the position of the dialogue partner. The bishop's doctrine is one a fundamentalist will in all likelihood reject but will, along with the Catholic to whom it is addressed, find himself better instructed. There is no anger or annoyance, no accusation, no attempt to explain fundamentalist belief away, and no invidious comparison. The entire focus of the letter is on an explanation of Catholic faith, rather than on a refutation of the faith of others.

Among the American bishops Archbishop John Whealon of Hartford has shown the most concern with fundamentalism. He chaired the National Council of Catholic Bishops' committee which wrote the 1987 letter and wrote two essays on the subject which appeared in *America* in 1985 and 1986.[120] The titles, "Fighting Fundamentalism" and "Challenging Fundamentalism," express well the seriousness with which he views the situation: biblical fundamentalism poses a "massive challenge" to the clergy and catechists.

In the first essay, little more than a summary of the analysis and

---

[119]Ibid.
[120]John F. Whealon, "Fighting Fundamentalism," *America* 153 (12 October 1985) 211-12, and "Challenging Fundamentalism" 136-38.

characterization of fundamentalism found in the National Council of Catholic Bishops' letter to be released two years later, Whealon urges that the means are at hand to meet the challenge in the form of a new liturgical lectionary, a new Catholic translation of the Bible, a second edition of the *Jerome Biblical Commentary* (soon to be released), other commentaries, books, tapes, and so on. The answer to the fundamentalist challenge is "to get this knowledge into the minds and hearts of all our Catholic teachers and students, and also to get it into our textbooks in a way that shows a knowledge and love of the Bible."[121]

The second essay describes at length an address Archbishop Whealon gave on fundamentalism which was attended by a large crowd equally divided between Catholics and fundamentalists, the latter apparently including a good number of former Catholics. In the address he summed up reasons to admire fundamentalist Churches—"Their love of the Bible.... Their spirit of warmth and friendliness. Their care for other members of the congregation. Their dedication to Jesus Christ. Their moral standards. Their missionary outreach."[122] But he noted their deficiencies as well: no authoritative Church, their ecclesiology, their truncated doctrinal sense, their lack of devotion to Mary and the saints, the absence of a sacramental life, their mistaken notion of inerrancy, and the absence of interest in ecumenism and social justice. He noted in the vigorous discussion period which followed that, while anti-Catholicism is present in some forms of fundamentalism, "most Fundamentalists or Evangelical Churches in the United States...are not anti-Catholic. They are interested only in living according to Jesus Christ and the Bible."[123]

Archbishop Whealon admits that statistics are hard to come by, but has no doubts that "hundreds of thousands of baptized Catholics have for one reason or another abandoned their Catholic faith for a Bible Church." What is the Catholic responsibility in this matter? An evangelical minister of a growing Church in Waterbury told him that eighty percent of his congregation are former Catholics and that the Catholic Church is doing a poor job of holding on to its own people. Whealon lists the reasons: catechetical efforts are failing to produce

---

[121]Whealon, "Fighting Fundamentalism" 211.
[122]Whealon, "Challenging Fundamentalism" 136.
[123]Ibid. 137.

educated Catholics; Catholic sense of identity is weak; evangelization efforts must be increased in parishes; in spite of the resources available, Catholics are not "Bible-reading, Bible-loving, Bible-quoting, Bible-living..." people, a state of religious living of which he apparently approves. In the end he quotes the pope on the need for prayer and immersion in scripture interpreted in the light of tradition so that one can "resist the temptation to place one's personal interpretation above or even in opposition to the authentic interpretation of God's word that belongs exclusively to the bishops of the Church in union with the Pope."[124] It seems that in order to "challenge" and to "fight" fundamentalism it is necessary that Catholics become a biblical people subject to the magisterium. The challenge amounts to little other than retention, however, and so the archbishop is in fact challenging Catholics leaders to resist the challenge posed to Catholicism by fundamentalists.

Several Vatican secretariats cooperated in collecting data from national episcopal conferences and other sources to produce the "Vatican Report on Sects, Cults and New Religious Movements."[125] The document is concerned with a more general and geographically more widespread phenomenon than the impact of Christian fundamentalism on American Catholicism. But the concern surely includes the American problem, and sets it in the broader context of an international Church struggling with its identity and defining its reactions to religious pluralism as well as to the ebb and flow of the religious interests and inclinations of a billion souls in hundreds of cultures. The document has its shortcomings, both in terms of the conceptuality drawn from the human sciences (for example, a derogatory definition of sects and cults) and its theological rationale (there is no *theological* understanding of defection in evidence), but it both reflects current attitudes of Catholic leaders toward these challenges and will help shape future Church reactions and strategies.[126] It is the first serious official attempt to face what appears

[124]Ibid. 138.

[125]"Vatican Report on Sects, Cults and New Religious Movements," *Origins* 16 (1986) 1-11.

[126]For a Catholic theological discussion of the problem before the Vatican document was composed, see Saliba 468-85. For a careful criticism of the document itself by a specialist in American religious movements, see Dinges, "The Vatican Report" 145-47.

to be a huge threat in several parts of the vineyard.[127]

What is the situation that the Vatican tries to explain? The concern with new religions and their growth is directed primarily at the phenomenon of massive loss of Catholics to these "sects and cults," precisely the same motive evident in the Catholic episcopal response to fundamentalism. How does the Vatican explain the situation? In three ways. First, there are unmet needs and aspirations that the new religions meet. These are universal, and Catholicism itself seeks to meet them: the desire for community, for clear and decisive answers to questions of meaning, the desire for wholeness, for cultural identity, for personal recognition and importance, for a conviction of transcendence, for specific spiritual guidance, for hope, for participation and involvement. Not only do they offer to meet these needs and aspirations in word, but "the sects seem to live by what they believe, with powerful (often magnetic) conviction, devotion, and commitment."[128] Momentarily, at least, the document has at hand a basic point of contrast between the new religions and the old, namely, vital religions work and tired religions do not.

Secondly, the new religions use recruitment and conversion techniques that are underhanded and directed toward unworthy goals. They aim at achieving mind control by adopting abusive behavior modification techniques. They may meet legitimate needs, but they do so inhumanely. They rob people of freedom.[129] In agreement with some of the American Catholic critics of fundamentalism, the Vatican psychologizes conversion to other religious bodies. But there are significant problems with this "explanation," not the least of which is the fact that it might explain Catholicism itself:

> Ironically, by framing the problem of religious pluralism partially, but not entirely, in the rhetoric of coercion, the Vatican report lends credibility to a perspective laden with secular and behavioral science assumptions. The

---

[127]In his comments on the document, William Dinges mentions the estimate that Brazil will have nearly 34 million Pentecostals by the end of the century, that perhaps 30 percent of Puerto Ricans have joined Pentecostal communities, and that Latin America's Mormon population has tripled to 1 million.

[128]"Vatican Report" 2.1.9.

[129]Ibid. 1.5, 2.2. Dinges remarks that "Nevertheless, there is little substantive evidence that the vast majority of participants in new religious groups are recruited through brainwashing or coercive tactics, or that they are kept in these movements by Orwellian-like mind-control techniques" (Dinges 147).

brain-washing/mind-control metaphor implicitly medicalizes many realities of religious life and commitment, denies free will and conversion and legitimates a Freudian psychoanalytic bias in which virtually all religious experience is viewed as regressive. It is also a perspective that, when emphasized, obviates the need for critical examination and structural change within the Church itself.[130]

The last point, the avoidance of self-criticism, is a rule of Catholic "corporate culture" to which we will return below. The medical metaphor we have already come across in both the periodical literature and monographs. It is the rhetorical technique used in the Catholic response to fundamentalism most open to methodological and theological objection. Its use also reveals how deeply the sects' gains among the (nominally) Catholic population has disturbed the otherwise urbane ecumenical rhetoric of theologians and Church leaders.[131]

The Vatican's solution to the problem calls for a more holistic pastoral care by Catholic ministers, an increased inculturation of Catholic religious practice, especially prayer and worship "with due respect for the nature of the liturgy and for the demands of universality,"[132] and increased lay leadership and participation. It is clear that the Vatican wants the local Churches to better meet the "needs and aspirations" it listed. It warns against naive irenicism which overlooks the "ideological" and "economic forces" sometimes at work in the sects (perhaps an expression of worry that socially and politically conservative American groups are supporting evangelical missions in Latin America), it calls on Church leaders to exercise special care for the young, and it admits that its standard Second

---

[130]Dinges 147.

[131]The paragraphs on fundamentalism in the recent statement of the Biblical Commission on biblical interpretation repeat most of the charges made against fundamentalism by theologians and by the preceding magisterial documents. Most of the reservations and questions expressed in the present essay with regard to them apply as well to this Vatican statement. The final paragraph is particularly unfortunate: it is stated or suggested that fundamentalism is "dangerous," "deceptive," "illusory," an invitation to "intellectual suicide," and "injects into life a false certitude." The document displays a measured and balanced response to other "methods," including liberation theology and feminism, but explodes with revulsion toward fundamentalism. See "The Interpretation of the Bible in the Church," *Origins* 23 (1994) 499-524. The comments on fundamentalism are in section F, 509-10.

[132]"Vatican Report" 3.5.

Vatican Council response to "other Churches and religions" (dialogue) will fail in the case of the new religions.

Nonetheless, lest its concern be taken as a reversal of its positive and constructive attitude toward other religions, the Vatican does not want any diminishment of "true ecumenism." In fact, and in the end, the document is not satisfied with a negative response to the problem: "The challenge of the new religious movements is to stimulate our own renewal for a greater pastoral efficacy."[133] The document on the whole presents a balance of tensions evident in the other literature, voicing at the same time concern for a threat perceived to be huge and recommendations for "more of the same" solutions, with little or no sense that other possibilities of explanation and response exist. For example, the question is never raised whether Catholicism, under certain circumstances and perhaps even constitutionally, is unable to meet those "legitimate needs and aspirations," nor is the possibility faced that a radical change in Catholic practice may be called for, or that its current understanding of the "demands of universality" may be seriously askew.

Finally, most suspect of all is its explanatory appeal to cultural breakdown:

> A breakdown of traditional social structures, cultural patterns and traditional sets of values caused by industrialization, urbanization, migration, rapid development of communications systems, all-rational technological systems, etc. leave many individuals confused, uprooted, insecure and therefore vulnerable. In these situations there is naturally a search for a solution, and the simpler the better. There is also the temptation to accept the solution as the only and final answer.[134]

But these are the very conditions under which religions, including Catholicism and Protestant Christianity, came into existence and spread, took root and prospered (if the last term is not disagreeable). If this is so, then is it not also true that the ones which succeeded spoke most effectively and truthfully to the human situation? This is not to deny that breakdowns do occur, nor that they present grave difficulties, nor that religion is quite properly strongly linked to social and personal breakdowns. It is only to say that the appeal shows a

[133]Ibid. 4.
[134]Ibid. 3.

startling lack of historical self-understanding, one that can be understood religiously as another example of the "mote and the beam."

The episcopal literature has its aims, the most evident of which is to warn Catholics. The bishops clearly think that the situation is no minor statistical variation, but poses a significant pastoral threat. And it is evidence as well of the episcopal perception of the vulnerability of Catholics to appeals from fundamentalists and other "sectarians." They must offer an explanation, and they do so in terms of the characteristics of the age and culture. They must propose a remedy, and so they do in specific terms of pastoral renewal and reform. But this, too, is not enough for them. They must not only explain the appeal of fundamentalism and the fact of widespread conversion of Catholics, but they must point out the doctrinal inadequacies and mistaken practices of fundamentalists. As fundamentalists turn to the Bible to "prove" that Catholicism is not Christian, so the bishops turn to Catholic doctrine and practice to indicate the inadequacies of the fundamentalist understanding and practice of Christianity, and as fundamentalists might "explain" Catholicism as a diabolical distortion of the Christian faith, so the bishops' reach into widely accepted views of the peculiarities of the age and into popular psychological notions to explain the success and attraction of fundamentalism. One of the stark differences between the approaches of the two, and one which will call for further comments below, is that the aggressive evangelization of Catholics is not in the least matched by the Catholic literature, official and otherwise. The bishops show not the slightest sign of targeting fundamentalists for evangelization; their writings are defensive, not evangelistic. In this they continue the centuries long habit of American Catholics of minding their own religious business. For all their official talk of "evangelization," Catholics are not convert hunters.

Although it may be out of place here, I cannot pass from the episcopal and Roman material without mentioning an essay in criticism of the National Council of Catholic Bishops' statement by a former Catholic and now a conservative Protestant, Mark Christensen, a man who has himself done what has prompted this twenty year flurry of Catholic literature. He thinks "the bishops' statement has addressed only a fraction of the problem"[135] when it traces the problem to a

---

[135]Mark Christensen, "Coming to Grips with Losses: The Migration of

quest for certainty and acceptance of simple answers to complex questions. The problem is that Catholicism is a culture as well as a religion, and this Catholic culture obscures Christ:

> The difficulty we had with Catholicism was that this same powerful force that had done such great things in history also overshadows and obscures Christ! The effect of the obscurity for me was that, while I certainly grew up knowing about Jesus, I never realized who He is or why He came to earth in the first place. I knew Catholicism. Like Theresa and my other ex-Catholic friends, I have been shaped by Catholicism as religious system and culture—but I never heard the gospel. ... For reasons I don't nearly understand, millions of other former Catholics besides myself couldn't hear this Gospel within the Catholic Church. I urge Catholic leaders in this country to ask themselves why their most potentially ardent members must go elsewhere to find their spiritual food.[136]

The Literature: General Comments

Catholic discussion of fundamentalist beliefs, practice, and ethos is a new preoccupation with genre roots in traditional Catholic responses to Protestantism. In the *Catholic Periodical Index* (150 periodicals and journals), the category "fundamentalism" begins to be used in 1977—while its neighboring categories, "fund raising" and "funeral fees," predate and will no doubt outlast it. Little of this growth is due to genuine scholarly and ecumenical interest and amounts to the same sort of thin description one would expect to find of Shakers, except that most of it displays deep and anxious pastoral concerns.

The current Roman Catholic interest in and difficulty with Protestant fundamentalism is occasioned by what a few Catholic leaders, with less than acute ecumenical sensitivity to language, have come to call "sheep stealing," and that means to Catholics the evangelizing of Catholics by fundamentalists and evangelicals, to a significant extent in the United States but more notably in Latin America. Fundamentalists have made huge inroads in Latin America, and some suggest that whole nations of Catholics will be lost to the Catholic Church in the next half

Catholics into Conservative Protestantism," *America* 164 (26 January 1992) 58-59. See especially page 58.

[136]Ibid. 59. Steve Clark, one of the national lay leaders of the Catholic charismatic movement, similarly criticizes the bishops's statement, but broadens the basis of attack. See Clarke 9-10.

century. Here in the United States, statistics indicate that while the number of Roman Catholics who drop their practice of Catholicism remains steady (15 to 25%), the number of drop outs who join other Churches, and especially evangelical and fundamentalist Churches, has increased (one estimate puts it at about 5% of Catholics—two and a half million).[137] This is the largest single occasion for the Catholic literature on fundamentalism. Catholics are used to dealing with dropouts—but transfers are another matter.

By far the majority of the periodical literature responding to the fundamentalist challenge regards it as a threat to be met by simple and direct contrast, aimed at strengthening the commitment of the reader to the Catholic Church by means of some doctrinal and practical invidious comparisons—we interpret the Bible better than they do, we have a living and authoritative organ of interpretation and they don't, we have the full panoply of sacramental life and spiritual practice and they don't, we have the ancient tradition and they don't, we have Mary and the saints and they don't, we are civil and they aren't. Though fundamentalists have a bit of Christianity, "We have more, they have less," which is the old Catholic response to Protestants in general.

Some of the literature is uncomplicatedly defensive, while some is markedly polemical. An example of the latter sort is the essay in the *African Ecclesiastical Review*.[138] It is pure and simple reductionism, the methodical practice of which upon Catholics by intellectual elites for the past two centuries ought to have precluded its use by Catholics of others. That Catholics had been charged with being servile followers of a foreign potentate has not deterred some Catholics from charging that fundamentalists are infantile followers of local potentates.

Another concern appears in the liberal Catholic responses to fundamentalism which makes them particularly interesting in terms of the inner life of the Catholic Church. Some of the literature is concerned with *Catholic* fundamentalism, namely with the conservative Catholic attacks on Catholic liberals which have accelerated in recent years and which have engaged not only the passions of the liberals but the political support of Church leaders. These (generally academic) liberals use culturally acceptable denigration talk about fundamentalism

---

[137]Dean R. Hoge, *Converts, Dropouts, Returnees: A Study of Religious Change Among Catholics* (New York: Pilgrim, 1981).

[138]John O'Donohue, "Fundamentalism: A Psychological Problem" 344-52.

to tar their conservative co-religionists. This is a political as distinct from a pastoral concern, though liberals might not like this distinction.

Catholic comments on fundamentalism, then, are of several sorts. Some respond to the question "What is it?" and present analyses of doctrines such as inerrancy, perspicuity, and fundamentalist ecclesiologies, anthropologies, soteriologies, and spiritualities. Here the analysis is quite weak. Some try to explain the existence of the fundamentalist movement and its attractiveness to Catholics in historical, cultural, psychological and theological terms, responding to the question "Why is it?" The typical answer: it is because the age is messed up and some responses to the age are also.

Most of the argument against fundamentalism is meant for Catholics and not for fundamentalists (while popular fundamentalist literature is aimed at converting Catholics), and answers the question "Why should I remain in the Catholic Church?" The typical answer to the question is: "We have more and better, they have less and worse." This argument, when more than a charge, refutes particular doctrines and heads at showing fundamentalism to be an incomplete and inadequate form of Christianity.

Some of the literature seeks to draw lessons from fundamentalist success, and answers the question "But then what should we do to hold and win people?" In general, the answer to this one is either: "More reform," or "Stand and fight!" or both. Finally, the Catholic popular press publishes articles answering the question "How do I handle them when they plague me at the front door or in the office?" Answer: "Don't argue Bible with them," for they have a method of interpretation impregnable to Catholic reason.

In the literature as a whole the authors, whether popularizers or professional theologians, show little sign of any serious interest in fundamentalist or evangelical theology.[139] That is, they do not convey the impression that there is any respectable intellectual life in fundamentalism. One finds no more than a cursory knowledge of its intellectual history or its important texts. Moreover, very little of the literature presents a program for dialogue, common reflection, or

---

[139]John McCarthy 123-36; also Ann Clifford, "Creation Science: Religion and Science in North American Culture," in *The Struggle over the Past: Fundamentalism in the Modern World*, 103-22. There is nothing in the top Roman Catholic scholarly journals *Theological Studies*, *Thomist*, or *Horizons*.

common action.

One is forced to the conclusion that, were fundamentalists to give up evangelism and stop receiving Catholics into their communities, the Catholic literature on it would cease. Fundamentalism apparently raises no theologically or religiously significant questions for Catholics. The case is quite different with Catholic reactions to Protestant theology in the wake of the Second Vatican Council, for the work of Bultmann, Barth, Pannenberg, and the like, is crucial for many Catholics. Protestantism was taken as both an intellectual and spiritual opportunity for Catholics, but none of this appears in the literature on fundamentalism. More recently there is a promising Catholic literature on Santeria, but still fundamentalism is an object only of defence and alarm.[140]

Moreover, there is an irony in Bishops warning Catholics about biblical fundamentalism.[141] The leaders of that Western religious community which most vociferously and dogmatically opposed the Enlightenment, and which was opposed by it, must now warn their flock about simplistic and dogmatic answers to the complex problems and stresses of the modern world! There is a further irony in the leaders of a Church which, for most of a century, asserted without fear of contradiction both doctrines and theological opinions which their successors now with furrowed brow denounce in fundamentalists. What is absent from episcopal letters is an even rudimentary interest in fundamentalism itself, no fellow feeling for it, and no grasp of the possibility that it represents a serious alternative understanding of Christianity. The bishops are defending souls and tribal turf. They can deal reasonably with the possibility of nuclear war and with a systematically unjust economy, and bring some spiritual and intellectual light to those topics, but they can only deal with a competitor Christianity as a threat.

---

[140]See Raul Canizares, *Walking with the Night: The Afro-Cuban World of Santeria* (Rochester, VT: Destiny Books, 1993), and Joseph M. Murphy, *Santeria: African Spirits in America* (Boston: Beacon P, 1993).

[141]See "A Pastoral Statement for Catholics" 376-77. It is also printed in *The Struggle over the Past: Fundamentalism in the Modern World*, 327-32. The statement was likely drafted by a Catholic theologian (or group of theologians) who had already written a good deal on the topic, and the letter does not depart from the typical theological complaints and worries.

Conclusion

My own view of what ought to be the relations between Catholics and fundamentalists is this: they need in common to drop the polemics even though there are plenty of good reasons for them. As Gabriel Daly noted, ecumenical charity ought to rule even when it remains unilateral. Rather, the two Christianities need to explore the religious life and traditions of the other, and especially to analyze together the promise and perils of modernization and even of post-modernism. There is surely enough religious vigor in each community to insure its survival and health, and enough decency in each community to overcome the legacy of fear and hatred that has infected their historical relations and to support a respectful conversation. They have much to tell one another about their respective struggles with modernity, and plenty of struggle yet to come in which they need one another's support.

Specifically, on the theological level, a mutually critical dialogue on matters of ecclesiology and biblical faith is needed (it has begun) to sharpen up differences as well as to uncover commonalities. A broad discussion of the relation between faith, religious practice, politics, and culture over the next decade might uncover and underscore their complaints about the corrosive effects of modern intellectual and popular culture on religious life. They might even in common make a decisive difference in the impact modernization is having on the southern hemisphere. While neither Catholics nor evangelicals easily enter into ecumenical explorations of this sort (and "hardbitten" fundamentalists never do), that they do so is imperative for the health of both communities and the health of the public arena in general. I am not optimistic about the chance for a quick end to mutual distrust and dislike, for tribalism is a permanent feature of human life, and its ambiguities will remain. Nor am I sanguine that any of the large doctrinal differences can be resolved, but pessimism is no reason to stand still. Surely there is hope to be derived from the startling history of the past twenty-five years, years in which new conversations have begun on every hillock of the ideologically frozen terrain.

The looming problem that impedes the relationship between the two is that neither will recognize the other as fully Christian, and the grounds for that refusal is the tribal self-definition of each as the norm of Christianity. By each community's criteria of authenticity the other is not a Christian community, the other is a stranger. To comment on the Roman Catholic side of this impasse, I would say that, if there is such a thing as an empirically grounded ecclesiological judgment, it is this: Catholicism is not for all Christians. Catholicism no longer proclaims as part of its public doctrine that it is the only Church to which one may belong (the "may" needs exegesis, it must be said) but it is far from admitting that the Catholic Church does not and even cannot accommodate the spiritual needs and theological insights of every Christian and ought no longer to pretend to do so.

To my knowledge it has never publicly admitted that mainline Protestant Churches represent permanent and valid organizations of the Christian community; nor can it, or so it seems, admit that fundamentalism represents an entirely valid witness to Jesus. However, the fundamentalists are another tribe, there, real, living, active, preaching, teaching, baptizing, with a distinctive spirituality which is not compatible with Roman Catholicism but which is Christian nonetheless. The ecclesial and ecclesiological virtues and vices of each must be a subject of critical dialogue, but the differences should no longer propel each side to the judgment that the other is another religion, or perhaps no religion at all.

Bishops and theologians have as much to learn as their flocks do. I will give some examples of what I mean. First, if stopping the leakage is a primary concern, then another strategy is needed than polemic. I would start by taking it for granted that fundamentalism is a viable form of Christian life. That is, I would treat it as another Church rather than as blue bottle flies, with at least the respect a Catholic would give a Hindu and, as a consequence, assume that Catholics become fundamentalists for good reason, as many Catholics today would understand why a Catholic might become a Lutheran or some other variety of domesticated Protestant. Hundreds of Catholic priests, married and with families, have left the Catholic Church and have had their orders accepted by the Episcopal and Anglican Churches and there has been only the quietest and most ecumenically sensitive response to that phenomenon on the Catholic side. The reasons why "hundreds of thousands" of Catholics have joined evangelical and fundamentalist Churches may be at least as respectable and serious as those of the priests, and may deserve respect and self-criticism.

Second, I would pay very close attention to fundamentalist criticism of Catholic belief and practice, with the possibility that some if not most of it is worth attention. As most of our authors indicate, even if they would certainly not agree with my statement of the case, Catholics are not biblical or Bible people. They are not, they have not been, and, in my view, it is extremely unlikely that they ever will be.[142] Every one of our commentators would agree that they are a sacramental people, but is sacramentalism any less in need of criticism than prophetism or biblicism? To make it clearer, sacramentalism is one way of Christianity, while biblicism is another. The twain surely condition one another, but they are irreducibly different forms or modes of Christianity, and perhaps, it may be said, different Christianities. It is time that Catholic leaders wake to the possibility of varieties of irreducibly different Christianities.

Moreover, as fundamentalists charge, the Church is in fact controlled by a hierarchy and is in no way democratic or congregational. Is this fact theologically beyond criticism and question? Again, Catholics are no longer much concerned with the *Parousia*. Should they be? Furthermore, though their theologians constantly remind themselves and the laity of their "rich heritage in spirituality," perhaps they are an impoverished people spiritually. Finally, they are a people with many shepherds in whose voices it is often difficult to discern the voice of the True Shepherd—many an ex-Catholic convert to a fundamentalist Church would tell us that he or she never "heard the Gospel" in a Catholic Church. These are the common charges laid at our door, charges which sting and which need more than mere homiletic address by theologians in the closing paragraphs of their essays.

One absolutely crucial step in the direction of a more balanced assessment of fundamentalism's virtue and Catholic vulnerability would be for Catholic theologians to drop the reductionist psychologizing. This maneuver is part of the contemporary disposal of the stranger. By taking the discussion off the field of theology and forcing it onto the field of psychology, by setting the psychological discussion in such way that we speak of "them," we have insured our alienation from "them," we have guaranteed the outcome of the discussion is an end to discussion, and, worst of all, we have paid no

---

[142]Every Sunday morning, as I walk Isis, I watch the hundreds of Southern Baptists filing into or out of Tower Grove Baptist Church, each clutching a bible. I go to St. Margaret of Scotland, and there is no bible to behold, only a lectionary. Thus it always shall be.

attention to ourselves and our own psyche.

On this psychological reduction let me make some final observations. If we are to have resort to psychology, it should be universal in application, not one side to the dispute but both. It should be a genuine psychology of religion. We should call in the experts and drop the amateur practice. We should recognize that the practice of psychology is not the practice of theology, and the expert practice of one does not provide expertise in the practice of the other.

Third, I suggest that Catholic theologians and bishops do their homework on fundamentalist history, theology and life, and stop talking about it till they have. The way forward between the two communities is not silence any more than it is polemics; it requires mutually respectful theological and religious criticism based on each taking the other fully seriously as a Christian community. The way forward for theologian's respectful scholarship and pastoral concern should be dictated by love for the one who does not love us.

Fourth, when Catholicism faces contemporary Christian fundamentalism it finds more than a bit of its own reaction to features of modern world.[143] Both Catholics and fundamentalists have in common what George Kennan recently admitted about himself: that he has remained a "guest of one's time and not a member of its household." The Roman Catholic Church has passed through the same struggle with modern culture, and its struggle peaked when fundamentalism originated. Because of its doctrinal and organizational differences from Protestantism, the Roman Catholic Church solved its difficulties with theological modernism differently and more effectively. In the nineteenth and the twentieth centuries, the popes denounced political democracy, freedom of religion, and the separation of Church and state—as well as economic exploitation of workers by capitalists and the destruction of the family. They regarded Catholics who showed any interest in a constructive engagement with modern culture and politics with grave suspicion, and theologians who attempted to adopt and adapt modern methods of historical study were

---

[143]It does so also when it faces New Age, as David Toolan has recently made out in *Facing West from California's Shores: A Jesuit's Journey into New Age Consciousness* (New York: Crossroad, 1987). Unlike New Agers, however, Catholics and fundamentalists realize that sin is a permanent state and not solved in the least by nude dancing in the moonlight and shucking guilt by union with nature.

excommunicated or cowed into silence. The name for this Roman Catholic version of fundamentalism is integralism, and it is the dominant form of the Roman Catholic reaction to modernity from the French Revolution to the Second Vatican Council.[144]

Nor have the Roman Catholic *aggiornamento* and its constructive engagement with modern culture and politics at all removed the Catholic suspicion of Western secularism and its systematized appetites for natural wealth and markets. Surely this vigorous, though unfortunately sometimes vicious, response to the modern organization of life delivers a platform for conversation and common action. If negative characterizing could be replaced by exploration of common interest in mitigating the effects of "progress," then surely we will learn and our world will change.

There are further questions to be addressed. First, Bloom and Raschke may be correct: *the* American religion (Bloom) or *the* modern alternative religion (Raschke),[145] is gnostic, and fundamentalism is a form of gnosticism (the old Catholic charge against Luther). Consequently, from the perspective of this essay, Catholics are meeting an old enemy and quite familiar stranger. For Catholics, once strangers themselves in America and now, for good or ill, no longer the stranger, to meet the old stranger is a paradox indeed. And Catholicism's problem in American culture may only be signaled and not at all exhausted by its current encounter with fundamentalism. It may be hitting up against a much broader phenomenon and entering a far more problematic situation. The old Gnosticism was taken to be a strike at

[144]See Joseph A. Komonchak, "Modernity and the Construction of Roman Catholicism," in *Modernism as a Social Construct*, eds. George Gilmore, Hans Rollman and Gary Lease, 11-41 (Spring Hill, AL: Spring Hill College, 1991), and Daly, *Transcendence and Immanence*. Integralism is still favored in its pure form by Archbishop Lefebvre's Traditionalist movement, whose nineteenth century orthodoxy is now found to be heterodox—a fate frequently shared by conservatives who learn too slowly. See Hitchcock and Dinges, "Roman Catholic Traditionalism" 66-101.

[145]On the interpretation of modern religion as gnosticism, see Harold Bloom, *The American Religion: The Emergence of the Post-Christian Nation* (New York: Simon and Schuster, 1991), and Raschke, *The Interruption of Eternity*. Robert S. Ellwood, Jr., has been a leader in the exploration of America's "alternative tradition." See his *Alternative Altars: Unconventional and Eastern Spirituality in America* (Chicago: U of Chicago P, 1979), and also Robert Ellwood and Harold B. Partin, *Religious and Spiritual Groups in Modern America*, 2nd ed. (Englewood Cliffs, NJ: Prentice, 1988).

the heart of Catholicism and not merely a problem of "leakage." Could it be that Catholicism, in its edginess regarding fundamentalism, is face to face with another moment of transformation, a *krisis*, brought on by its contact with an alternative understanding of its message, which understanding is *the* American religion, so that Catholicism will once again find itself a stranger in a strange land?

Second, is fundamentalism the old Protestant anti-Catholicism? And is Catholic anti-fundamentalism the old Roman Catholic anti-Protestantism?

Third, why are Catholic theologians uninterested in fundamentalism? Why are there no studies in Catholic academic journals? Why, to this moment, is there no serious study of fundamentalism by a Catholic theologian?

Fourth, what is it about fundamentalism that bores and bothers Catholic theologians? The obvious *bother* are conversions, the vulnerable condition of the Catholic Church, fundamentalist anti-Catholicism, and the Roman Catholic right wing's continuing opposition to liberal hegemony in the American Church. Are there *reasons*?

Fifth, will the statistics hold—that large numbers drift out and most come back? If so, we have a bit of perspective on the question in the long run. But suppose they do not, and larger and larger numbers find themselves illuminated by the "alternative vision"?

Finally, the words concluding John A. Saliba's fine essay on new religious movements well express the need for a redirection of attention on the part of Catholic theologians:

> Rather than being a fearful threat to Christianity or a challenge to religious warfare, the new religious and spiritual movements provide an excellent opportunity for the Christian Church to further understand her mission, to adapt and react more meaningfully to the changing needs of our age, and to reform herself in the spirit of the gospel.[146]

Three ponderous obstacles to mutual understanding emerge from any serious review of the current status of relations between Catholicism and fundamentalism: the inherited anti-Catholicism of fundamentalists, well matched by the liveliness of inherited anti-Protestantism of

---

[146]Saliba 485. See his more recent and equally fine essay "Dialogue with the New Religious Movements," *Journal of Ecumenical Studies* 30 (1993) 51-80.

Catholics; and the lack of intellectual interest in fundamentalism on the part of Catholic theologians. We are all in need of conversion; whether we are ripe for it remains to be seen. Reason for hope exists in this literature as well.

At the outset of this essay, the stranger was said to be a focus of attention for the tribe, which takes the stranger to be at once a threat and a promise, both fascinating and fearful. The potency of the stranger matches the potency of the tribe, for its response to the stranger is ambiguous. The Christian tribe is especially torn, for it can never have self-protection and survival as its fundamental value, and so it must take even the threat and its own fear as a moment to be transcended in acceptance and even love, or so we are taught. The Catholic response to fundamentalism must run along these lines. We must find the grace of God at work in fundamentalists, for them and for ourselves. In the dynamic of the tribe and the stranger, the stranger speaks, willy-nilly, with the voice of God.

CONTRIBUTORS

A ll the contributors to this volume are faculty members of the Department of Theological Studies at Saint Louis University in St. Louis, Missouri.

BERNHARD A. ASEN is an associate professor and co-editor of *Theology Digest*. He received his Ph.D. from Saint Louis University, and he specializes in Old Testament prophets and Jewish apocalyptic literature. He has published essays on the prophets, most recently, "No, Yes, and Perhaps in Amos and the Yahwist," *Vetus Testamentum* 43 (433-41).

FREDERICK G. McLEOD, S.J., is an associate professor. His D.O.E.S. degree is from the Oriental Institute in Rome, and he specializes in spiritual theology and the history of ancient Syriac Christianity. His publications include a critical edition of the Syriac text and an English translation of "Narsai's Metrical Homilies," published in the series *Patrologia Orientalis*, volume 50, fascicule 1, no. 182 (Turnhout, Belgium: Brepols, 1979) 1-193.

RONALD E. MODRAS is a professor. He received his D.Theol. from the University of Tübingen in Germany, and he specializes in modern European and ecumenical theology. He is a recipient of the Micah Award of the St. Louis American Jewish Committee (1988) and a fellow of the Annenberg Research Institute. His publications include *Paul Tillich's Theology of the Church: A Catholic Appraisal* (Detroit: Wayne State UP, 1976); and *Human Sexuality: New Directions in American Catholic Thought*, with A. Kosnik *et al.* (New York: Paulist, 1979); and *The Catholic Church and Antisemitism, Poland 1933-1939* (Reading, UK: Harwood, 1994).

FRANCIS W. NICHOLS is an associate professor. His D. ès Th. is from the University of Strasbourg in France, and he specializes in modern European Roman Catholic theology, particularly seventeenth and nineteenth century France, as well as the history of the theology of marriage.

KENNETH L. PARKER is an assistant professor and director of undergraduate studies. He received his Ph.D. from Cambridge University and did post-doctroal studies at the University of Fribourg in Switzerland. He specializes in early modern English theology and, recently, in John Henry Newman. His publications include *The English Sabbath: A Study of Doctrine and Discipline from the Reformation to the Civil War* (Cambridge: Cambridge UP, 1988); and "Newman's Individualistic Use of the Caroline Divines in the *Via Media*" in *Discourse and Context: An Interdisciplinary Study of John Henry Newman*, ed. Gerard Magill (Carbondale: Southern Illinois UP, 1993).

JOAN A. RANGE, A.S.C., is an associate professor. Her Ph.D. is from Fordham University, and she specializes in late medieval and Catholic Reformation church history and law. Her publications include "Women, Law-Making and the Code of Canon Law," in *Proceedings of the Fifth International Congress on Canon Law* (Ottawa: U of St. Paul P, 1986) 1:105-14; and "The IP (Impostor Phenomenon) and Women in Theology," in *Women in Higher Education: Changes and Challenges*, ed. Lynne B. Welch (New York: Praeger, 1990) 46-56.

WILLIAM M. SHEA is a professor and chair of the Department of Theological Studies. He received his Ph.D. from Columbia University, and he specializes in nineteenth and twentieth century religion and American culture. He is a former president of the College Theology Society and fellow of the Woodrow Wilson Center at the Smithsonian. His publications include *Naturalism and the Supernatural* (Macon, GA: Mercer UP, 1984); and *The Struggle Over the Past: Religious Fundamentalism in the Modern World* (Lanham, MD: University P of America, 1992), which he edited.

KENNETH B. STEINHAUSER is an associate professor and director of graduate studies. His D.Theol. is from the University of Freiburg in Germany, and he specializes in patristics and early church history, particularly St. Augustine and his contemporaries. He also works in the area of manuscript studies. His publications include *The Apocalypse Commentary of Tyconius: A History of Its Reception and Influence* (Frankfurt: Peter Lang, 1987).

RICHARD VALANTASIS is an assistant professor. He received his Th.D. from Harvard University, and he specializes in the New Testament and the history of Christian origins. His research and publications presently center on the history and theories of asceticism and monastic spirituality. His publications include *Spiritual Guides of the Third Century* (Minneapolis: Fortress, 1991); and *Asceticism* (New York: Oxford UP, 1995), edited with Vincent Wimbush.

INDEX

Abrabanel, Isaac, 127
Abraham, 2, 20, 33, 48, 57, 105
Adam, Alfred, 88-89
Alamo, Tony, 259
Alexius: *See* Edessa, holy man of
Alfaric, Prosper, 89
Alter Christus, 41-43
Ambosiaster, 86
Ambrose, Saint, 86
Anderson, James, 206
Amelotte, Denis, 140
Amiaud, Arthur, 56
Anti-Semitism, 5, 203-04, 212. *See also* Jews
Arnauld, Antoine, 122-24, 132, 136, 145-47
Arnold, Patrick, 244-45, 248, 251
Asceticism: and Basil of Caesarea, 71-80; contemporary implications, 79-80; and culture, 73; historical implications, 77-79; personal implications, 75-76; philosophical, 77-78; practice of, 67-68, 70; social implications, 73-75; and strangeness, 64-65; Syriac, 39, 42-43, 45; theory of, 68-69. *See also* Legend of the holy man of Edessa
Augustine, Saint, 125, 154, 205-06, 219; and Jews, 205-06, 219; and marriage, 111;

and Paul, 85-91; and scripture, 146, 149, 154-56; two cities of, 88-93
Auvray, Paul, 143, 145, 151

Barkley, Roy, 233-35
Baronius, Cesare, 123
Barr, James, 229
Barruel, Augustin, 208, 210, 215
Basil of Caesarea, 71-80
Basnage, Jacques, 134-35
Batterel, Louis, 141
Bayle, Pierre, 159, 163-64
Beaude, Pierre-Marie, 161
Becanus, Martin, 123
Bellarmine, Robert, 123
Belloc, Hillaire, 259
Benedict XIV, 207
Bergant, Dianne, 253-54,
Bernus, Auguste, 136, 141, 160
Bertholet, Alfred, 19
Bérulle, Pierre de, 140
Beza, Theodore, 123
Bignon, Jean-Paul, 151
Bird, Phyllis, 94
Bloom, Harold, 284
Bochard, Samuel, 159
Boettner, Lorraine, 259
Bolland, Jean, 164
Bonsirven, Joseph, 215
Bossuet, Jacques Bénigne, 116, 120, 124, 136, 141, 145, 160, 162, 165, 167; attacks on Richard Simon, 133-34, 147-59. *See also* Simon, Richard

South Florida Studies in the History of Judaism

South Florida Academic Commentary Series

The Talmud of Babylonia, An Academic Commentary

South Florida-Rochester-Saint Louis Studies on Religion and the Social Order

South Florida International Studies in Formative Christianity and Judaism

DATE DUE

MAR 2 4 2000			
			Printed in USA